The Judas Game
The betrayal of New Zealand rugby
JOSEPH ROMANOS

Published by Darius Press
PO Box 3368
Wellington
New Zealand

First published 2002

ISBN 0–9582409–0–6

Designed and typeset by Egan-Reid Ltd
Printed in New Zealand by Publishing Press

CONTENTS

ACKNOWLEDGEMENTS

There are many people I would like to thank for helping me research and write this book. My father, Richie, a senior rugby player in his day, suggested the concept, voicing concerns that I found echoed by many others about the state of our national game.

Three journalists offered particular assistance, Lindsay Knight, Keith Quinn and Phil Murray. I have known Lindsay since 1975 when I was a journalism student at Wellington Polytechnic and he was *The Dominion*'s sports editor. By 1976 I was a cadet sports reporter on Wellington's *Evening Post* and he was the paper's sports sub-editor. He offered valuable advice back then about what stories to write and how to write them, and he has continued to give me help whenever I have asked for it. Lindsay has been a campaigning journalist on the way New Zealand rugby is run, and his stories on this subject have featured over many years in *The Dominion*. It is to Lindsay's credit that he has never been content merely to toe the party line. I thank Lindsay for his assistance in writing this book, and for his collection of newspaper clippings on the subject.

Keith Quinn, with whom I have collaborated in three rugby books, and Phil Murray, my long-time friend, read parts of the manuscript and offered timely suggestions and criticisms.

Many rugby people — coaches, All Blacks, officials, club players, parents, teachers — spoke to me with feeling and honesty about a subject that is obviously dear to them. My thanks to Don Adamson, Fred Allen,

Brent Anderson, Brian Cederwall, David Cooper, Mike Fairmaid, Daniel Faleolo, Andy Haden, John Hart, Norm Hewitt, Bruce Holloway, David Howman, Martin Isberg, Ken Laban, Keith Laws, Chris Laidlaw, Andy Leslie, Pat Martin, Brian McGuinness, John Mills, Roger Moses, the late Arthur Reeve, Bob Scott, Dave Syms, Dion Waller, Bryan Williams and Bryce Woodward.

In addition, I have used parts of interviews I have done previously with Grant Fox, Walter Hadlee, Robert Louis-Dreyfus, Colin Meads, David Moffett, Wayne Smith and Wilson Whineray.

Other people provided me with information for this book, including current All Blacks, team management and national and provincial rugby administrators. They asked that they not be named, and I have respected those requests.

There has been some excellent writing on some of the subjects covered in this book, and I have drawn on this at times. In particular, I would mention the superb series on club rugby written by Brent Edwards and Alistair McMurran for the *Otago Daily Times* in 2001; *New Zealand Rugby World* editor John Matheson's story in his magazine's October, 2001 issue entitled 'So What's The White Answer?'; Pat Martin's fine piece on Wellington club rugby, entitled 'On The Ball', written in July 1999; Chris Laidlaw's 'For Love and Money', published in the December 1999 issue of *New Zealand Books*; and Alistair Bone's article in the *Listener* of 26 January 2002, entitled 'The Beautiful Game'.

Several books were particularly useful in my research, notably *Cradle of Rugby* by Arthur Reeve, *NPC The Heart of Rugby* by Lindsay Knight, *The Encyclopedia of World Rugby* by Keith Quinn, *Grant Batty* by Bob Howitt, *Outrageous Rugby Moments* by Keith Quinn, *Legends of the All Blacks* by Keith Quinn, *The Encyclopedia of New Zealand Rugby* by Rod Chester, Ron Palenski and Neville McMillan, and various editions of the *Rugby Almanack*, edited by Clive Akers and Geoff Miller.

I made extensive use of newspaper files in researching this book. The newspapers that I found I was using most often were the *Sunday Star-Times*, the *National Business Review*, *The Dominion*, the *New Zealand Herald*, the *Evening Post*, the *Otago Daily Times* and the *Sydney Morning Herald*.

My thanks to Michael Laws, whose company, Darius Press, published this book. In addition, Michael provided me with sound advice on the format it should take and pointed me in the direction of some people who could contribute usefully. Linda Burgess was a diligent and meticulous editor. Some of the photographs have come from my own collection, and

many others from Andrew Cornaga and his Photosport agency.
Note: the official name of the body that runs New Zealand rugby is the New Zealand Rugby Football Union. For the purposes of brevity, I have omitted the word Football when referring to the national and various provincial unions.

INTRODUCTION

Rugby union might be New Zealand's national game, but it is a game in crisis. I say that, not as a result of the chaos surrounding the shakers and movers of the New Zealand Rugby Union in 2002, but after a thorough examination of the game at all levels in this country. The sudden resignations in July, 2002, of David Rutherford, Rugby Union Chief Executive, and Murray McCaw, Chairman of the board, and the departure soon after of other board members, indicated clearly that there were major administration problems at the top level. Unfortunately the picture is no brighter in junior, club and provincial rugby. The appointment of new people at the top of the New Zealand Rugby Union will be meaningless unless they act urgently in assessing and overhauling the way the game is administered at every level.

There is every chance that within 30 years rugby will not be New Zealand's national sport. In fact, by then we may not have a national game as such. Football (or soccer as we call it in this country), golf and the various strands of multisport are increasing rapidly in popularity. Cricket continues to attract widespread interest, and young New Zealanders are becoming ever more attracted to such adventure sports as mountain biking and kayaking. The days when rugby was the sport of choice for nearly every young lad in the country have ended.

At first glance, it seems preposterous to say rugby is under threat. It draws the largest audiences (live and on TV) of any sport. It has a huge player base, is steeped in tradition, attracts blanket media coverage and excellent income from sponsorship, television revenue and spectator attendance. And we're good at it. So good that New Zealand rugby acts as a feeder system (for players and coaches) for many competitions around the world, from Japan to France, Italy to Scotland. Our national sports team, the All Blacks, is more famous internationally than the country it comes from, surely the only case in the world where this is so. We won the Tri-Nations in 2002 and were able to look forward with increasing confidence to the 2003 World Cup.

Yet while researching this book and examining rugby at every level, I have heard almost nationwide disenchantment with many aspects of the game.

There is talk about the decline in the number of college boys playing rugby. Rugby lovers lament the death of so many rugby clubs, the downgrading of the Ranfurly Shield, the end of live free-to-air television coverage of top rugby, the financial plight of various provinces, the decline in playing numbers and standards. When rugby still seems so strong, why do so many predict its demise?

I believe the reason for rugby's imminent eclipse is simple: money. Since rugby went professional — in a shamateur way in the 1980s, and in the above-board professional era that began in 1995 — New Zealand rugby has lost its international edge. The rest of the world has caught us up because the game has not been run as well as it should have been in New Zealand — just witness the ineptitude of the New Zealand union in 2001–02 and the fallout that resulted. Rugby in this country has lost that indefinable something that made it so special.

If we think rugby in New Zealand is invincible, we don't have to look any further than Wales to see what can happen in less than a generation. For a century, rugby has been the national game in Wales. Youngsters have been brought up to rejoice in the great deeds of Ted Morgan and Haydn Tanner, Cliff Morgan and Gareth Edwards. Boyos in the Valleys dreamed of wearing the red jerseys of Wales, especially against the All Blacks. Welsh folk were fiercely proud of their national rugby team. They would tell you that Bob Deans did not score at Cardiff Arms Park against Wales in 1905, and would talk about the great Swansea and Cardiff and Llanelli club sides that beat the All Blacks over the years. But it's nearly all gone now. Welsh rugby is a joke at international level. If Wales even qualifies for a World Cup, its followers are in raptures. The Welsh union imports foreign coaches like Graham Henry and Steve Hansen to run its test side. The game in Wales, which relied so heavily on tradition, has not responded well to the challenges of professionalism and at all levels, from junior to international, is in desperate straits.

The change from amateur to professional rugby was not well handled by rugby administrators in Wales, as it hasn't been here. It's not as if there wasn't plenty of warning. For the 15 years before the game went professional, top New Zealand players had been placing increasing pressure on the game's officials to do something, at first for reimbursement for expenses incurred and for loss of earnings, then for payment for actually playing the game. Players began to resent ever more deeply the fact that sportsmen in other codes could make massive amounts of money for being the best in the world at what they did, while they remained unpaid, despite being so good that they drew millions of spectators during a season.

For many years world rugby officials buried their heads in the sand and clung to the amateur ethos that had abounded a century earlier. Then, in 1995, when rugby league was opening its fat cheque books to rugby union players, the game rushed into the professional era with ridiculous haste. There would have been no need to hurry if officials had shown vision. They didn't and what eventuated was rival bidders trying to secure the players' signatures on professional contracts.

It was an ugly time. Loyalty to rugby went out the window as the hunt for the dollar became all-important. At the end of it — of the accusations, pleading, threats — top rugby players were guaranteed hundreds of thousands of dollars a year. But it wasn't a pleasant time. Andy Haden, who was an All Black over a span of 15 years, and had remained in close touch with the game through his company, Sporting Contacts, told me: "I found it all pretty distasteful, and for a few years I lost quite a bit of interest in rugby. I kept my distance, didn't like what I was seeing."

This sounds odd, coming from someone like Haden, who was constantly pushing the boundaries when he was a player. But he explained: "I'm not averse to change. In fact, I encourage it, always have. The trick is, though, that the change has to be good for the game. Not everything that happened was good for the game."

Quite simply, professionalism means one thing — the only god worshipped is money.

When you read about all the players — international, provincial and club — that New Zealand loses each year to overseas interests, think of money. When you read about clubs failing because of falling numbers and income, think of money. When you think of All Blacks not playing club rugby and being reluctant to play even National Provincial

Championship games, think of money. When you think of many ordinary punters not being able to watch our national game live on television for free, think of money. When you think of families no longer being able to afford to attend test matches, think of money. When you think of why New Zealand lost the right to co-host the 2003 World Cup, think of money.

Former All Black captain and coach Fred Allen sums it up well: "Everybody in top rugby is money-hungry these days. The players are money-hungry; the New Zealand union is money-hungry. There's greed everywhere. The All Blacks aren't a sports team; they are a commodity that everyone is using in some way or other to get rich. It's all back to front now. The starting point isn't rugby, it's money."

In March, 2002 in Auckland a panel comprising a group of former outstanding All Blacks, such as Bryan Williams and Wilson Whineray, met to discuss the plight of modern rugby. "We all believed," says Williams, "that the amateur ethos was great for the game and that money had ruined rugby as we knew it. There are different motivations now. It's all money. When they talk about the World Cup, they talk about clean stadiums, not rugby."

As John Hart says: "We are struggling to get to grips with the balance between the professional and amateur side of rugby. The game's not in a healthy state here at the moment. We have to ensure that the money coming from the top end of the game doesn't just go to the top end. Where clubs, schools and minor provinces survived with sponsorship in the past, they are now having big difficulties because so much of the available sponsorship funds are going to the major areas and the big franchises. There is certainly a risk that the game is being taken away from the public, that administrators have lost some contact with the needs of the game."

Money is a fact of modern sport. But it is the reason the game has been stolen from the hands of ordinary New Zealanders. It has always been said that the clubs owned New Zealand rugby. The New Zealand union existed to serve the provincial unions, which administered the clubs, which were there because of grassroots interest in rugby. In that way, the ordinary punter owned New Zealand rugby. It is telling that these days when I speak to leading rugby administrators, they scoff at this sort of talk. Modern New Zealand rugby, they say, is owned by television. Without television's millions of dollars, there would be no professional rugby, and without professional rugby, the game here would wither and die.

In April, 2002, Sky Television announced the commencement of a channel dedicated solely to rugby. It sounds great, but when you look at it a bit more deeply, it's another example of our national game being taken away from the people. Sky spent a vast amount of money — more than $7 million according to some reports — to set up the channel. To recoup those expenses, and to capitalise on New Zealanders' infatuation with rugby, it placed rugby among its digital offerings. Just like with the Sundance Channel, Sky subscribers could watch the rugby channel only by paying an extra fee. So they pay once, to become part of the Sky stable, then again to get the rugby channel.

New Zealand rugby bosses would be wise to heed what happened in Britain when rugby went from free-to-air BBC to pay-for-view BSkyB Television with the advent of professionalism. Even stars like Jonny Wilkinson are now largely unknown sports figures. One recent survey revealed that viewers would recognise Annie Underwood, mother of former England players Rory and Tony, before they would recognise the record-breaking Wilkinson.

"Maybe if the games were on the BBC, he would have a higher profile because more people would see him," said Wilkinson's manager, Tim Buttimore, when informed that he was managing a virtually anonymous sports superstar. The research company, TW Research, said other leading England players, such as Lawrence Dallaglio and Martin Johnson, had little public recognition. It was felt that by taking rugby to BSkyB, the television viewer audience had been cut by nine-tenths.

In chasing television dollars, the New Zealand Rugby Union should note these statistics. Is it losing a core part of its public by going the pay-for-view way? This situation will only get worse. Where will Sky eventually place its best rugby? If it has two or three Super 12 or NPC matches, where do you think the pick of them will be placed? On the rugby channel, where they will make Sky the greatest amount of money. That's fine for those so passionate about their rugby, and wealthy enough, to be willing to fork out twice to watch a game. But at the same time, the sport loses another significant chunk of the New Zealand public.

Fred Allen: "Putting the rugby on Sky is a sore point for me. Rugby's our national game and we have to pay to watch the big games live. I sit here and ask myself what I went to war for — democracy and freedom of speech. Well, that's gone. Now if you want something, it isn't your right. You have to pay for it."

Bryan Williams feels New Zealand rugby is at risk and change is needed. "We'll always have rugby players, but unless we can regenerate interest in rugby at secondary school level — that's a key area — we will lose forever our pre-eminent position among the world's rugby nations. Other countries have their numbers of schoolboy rugby players increasing. How are we going to match them if our junior rugby base is decreasing?"

Over the past few years, there have been attempts to more accurately detail exact playing numbers in various sports. The figures are alarming for rugby. In early 2001, the Hillary Commission revealed that 114,000 young New Zealanders were playing soccer regularly, compared to 99,500 who played rugby. Rugby's overall playing numbers, from five-year-olds to veterans, were put at 131,000. This was sobering stuff for rugby officials, but worse was to follow. The next year, after its own research, the Rugby Union stated that there were 119,000 players in the country, and that of them 83,000 were juniors.

Amazingly, and this is part of the problem, rather than admit things were looking grim, the Rugby Union, at its 2002 annual meeting, trumpeted how numbers were increasing. You can do a lot with statistics, if you twist and turn them, then hold them up to the mirror, but you won't get far if you won't accept what's plainly evident. That's the situation the New Zealand union is in at the moment: still claiming black is white.

Other sports are simply appearing more attractive to participants of all ages. Among adults, golf, touch football, tennis, bowls, indoor bowls, netball, basketball and skiing are the top eight participant sports (depending on the age of the adults — touch football is No 1 among 18–24-year-olds, indoor bowls among adults 55 and over), with rugby far off the pace. I am talking here of competitive sport, so discount joggers and lane swimmers who are not interested in competition but are seeking active recreation. It is clear that the once-dominant sport of rugby has come back to the pack. Of course, there is a huge rugby following among people who are neither players nor affiliated members of clubs, but it should be worrying to national rugby administrators that they no longer have the dominant position among participants.

Many rugby clubs, urban and rural, have collapsed, or are on the point of collapse. Clubrooms, which on winter Saturday nights used to vibrate with laughter and beer, rugby talk and beer, speeches and beer, are vanishing. Changing attitudes to drink-driving, weekend shopping, the appeal of restaurants and cafes and declining memberships are all reasons.

When this is put to rugby officials, they are quick to blame these changes in society. Yet many other sports continue to thrive. Soccer, for instance, has been bedevilled by poor administration for the past 25 or more years. It has tinkered with its trailblazing national league, altering the format, the timing (to summer for a while!) and even regionalising it. There have been pathetic, petty rows between the game's leading figures, coaches and officials. The Kingz club, in its short lifespan, has had to endure results that have ranged from mediocre to disastrous, financial problems, rows among officials and coaches, and continued uncertainty over its future.

In spite of all this, soccer continues to grow. In 2001, there were 113,800 children under 17 who played soccer. Bill MacGowan, Soccer New Zealand's Chief Executive, told the *Listener* in January, 2002: "The feeling I've got is that we have been ahead of rugby for some time. There has been a trend, in the last five to 10 years, of young people moving away from rugby into soccer." He points to a report from soccer federation managers that showed a 20-30 per cent increase in junior numbers in 2001.

Soccer has a lot going for it. It is a genuine world sport, arguably the biggest of all. Probably athletics is the most global of all sports, for people run and walk in every country. But on an organised and international level, soccer is a massive sport, heading off even other such virtually global sports as basketball, volleyball, swimming, golf and tennis. Soccer's four-yearly World Cup is the major sports event in the world.

The soccer industry is immense, not just in Britain, where New Zealanders tend to focus, but in Germany, Spain, Italy — indeed, all of Europe. And in South America, too, which in Argentina, Brazil, Colombia, Paraguay, Uruguay, Ecuador, Chile and Peru has eight of the world's top 40 or so soccer nations. The sport is snowballing in North and Central America, Africa and Asia. There was coverage recently of the first soccer international between Tibet and Greenland. The match was played in Denmark and emphasised to me the global nature of soccer.

It is only natural to suspect that sooner rather than later, soccer could become the dominant sport in Oceania. Australia these days is a bona fide world soccer power. It produces a string of magnificent players who are plying their wares overseas, mainly in Europe. Though the sport in Australia is riddled with financial problems and unimpressive administration, it has continued to grow, despite the dominance in various states of Australian Rules, rugby league and rugby union.

The same thing must surely happen in New Zealand, where the sport has several advantages. Most young boys start their winter sports careers playing soccer. In the past, many transferred to rugby about the time they started college. Now, though, it is not unfashionable to be a soccer player and college soccer has strengthened markedly. In the early 1970s, my college, St Pat's Town in Wellington, fielded 19 or 20 rugby teams and four or five soccer teams. All the boys in the First XV were heroes. No-one knew or cared who was playing soccer for the school. Now there is genuine prestige in being in a college's top soccer team.

Soccer has benefitted through Sky TV. Even in non-World Cup years, the station shows up to 150 hours of soccer in some months. In the past we were fed British soccer and that was it. Now we can see packages of Spanish, Italian, German, South American soccer; we can see the Australian Soccer League matches; there is a vast amount of British soccer and we see the various European competitions, such as the Champions League and UEFA Cups. Just as basketball has captured the imagination because of the visibility these days of the American NBA, so soccer has become more popular as it has become more visible.

The entry of the Kingz into the Australian Soccer League has helped, even though the team has not managed to make the competition play-offs and is permanently under threat of expulsion from the competition. Amazingly, the Kingz retain a strong following, despite woeful results. And their fans come from not just the rather raucous patrons of the Bloc 5 at the North Harbour Stadium, but all around the country. Soccer followers and more general sports followers tune in to hear Andrew Dewhurst's radio broadcast, or Gordon Irving's television call of the Kingz' latest match. The Kingz have given soccer a national identity in New Zealand. Each week it is our Kingz taking on another Australian team. New Zealand youngsters can see now that if they play and improve, a career in a professional soccer team is certainly attainable. The under-17 World Youth Cup, held here in 1999, opened New Zealand youngsters' eyes to the way they could play soccer and to the opportunities that would arise if they could.

Another big plus for soccer is that it is a simple game, easy to coach and understand. Rugby, with its ever-increasing web of rules, is extremely complicated. Few people are game enough to attempt to referee it and many who have played to quite a high level are hesitant about trying to coach now. As there can be no junior teams without coaches, soccer again appeals ahead of rugby.

Youngsters' attitudes to sport have changed. With so many new sports, from touch football to triathlons, mountain biking to hang gliding, dragon boat racing to wind surfing, rugby has lost that massively dominant pull. Now it is okay to play whatever sport you want. Boys aren't so easily shepherded into rugby by their parents, not when their mates are playing soccer or skateboarding. And parents and teachers, with an eye to safety, often encourage young boys and girls to opt for soccer (or hockey or netball) as their winter team sport. They like the fact that there isn't the same level of physical contact, and the same risk of injury.

Apart from the attraction of soccer, there has been a marked change in those who participate in rugby. There is no doubt that rugby has "browned" in recent years. I will examine this issue in depth later, but it is enough to say at this point that in Auckland and Wellington especially, there has been a staggering increase in the number of Maori and Polynesian boys playing rugby, and that has persuaded large numbers of white boys to look at other sports, especially soccer, as a more attractive option. Maori and Polynesian boys mature physically very early and they dominate teams in which they are involved. Many smaller white boys get sick of having the daylights knocked out of them by boys who have such physical advantages.

Youngsters these days play and follow the sport that most appeals to them. It is a more cynical age we live in. The era in which young boys idolised players from the past as well as the present is over. Young sportsmen no longer appear to care about the Deans incident of 1905, or George Nepia, Maurice Brownlie or Ron Jarden, or the flour bomb test, or the Cavaliers. That stuff, to quote youngsters today, belongs in the Woodstock years. It's old. Who cares about it? If a boy in his late teens decides to play rugby seriously these days, he'll have at least one eye on the money he can make from the game if he succeeds, rather than simply playing because he wants to be part of a tradition.

Ian Robson, when he was running the Auckland Warriors, as they were then known, once said: "Pretty soon, youngsters will not know what came first, the All Blacks or the Warriors." He was right. Anyone under the age of 25 has hazy recollections at best of when New Zealand won the first rugby World Cup. Youngsters today, who get so much of their knowledge from television and the Internet, don't generally care to wade through yellowing and dusty autobiographies and almanacks for their fill of rugby history.

Who is to blame for what has happened, and is happening, to rugby? Who has stolen the game away from the people? That's what this book aims to investigate.

part ONE

HIGH-FINANCE

chapter ONE

THE **MONEY** GAME

HOW MONEY HAS CHANGED RUGBY

There was a time when Christchurch's main rugby ground was Lancaster Park, when the national rugby team was the All Blacks, when the top teams in the country played for the National Provincial Championship first division title. Now it's Jade Stadium, they're the adidas All Blacks and it's the Air New Zealand NPC.

Every aspect of rugby that can be sold has been. Even the cheerleaders are sponsored. It would be simplistic to think of top rugby as merely a sport, played by men who are good at it. It's a commodity, to be milked financially at every turn. The All Blacks aren't a team any more; they're a brand. The game at representative level has passed from the players and spectators into the hands of the marketers, who label it with tags such as Crusaders, Lions, the Bull Ring.

Look at a top rugby game now. The field has huge advertising signs painted over it, advertising hoardings encircle the pitch. New Zealand rugby's major sponsors, adidas, Philips, Air New Zealand, Telecom and Steinlager, feature prominently. The All Blacks' jerseys have adidas logos on them. The referees, too, are sponsored. The ball is not being used because it is durable or cheap, or was on special at a sports shop nearby. Gilbert, or whatever ball is being used, will have paid the New Zealand Rugby Union many thousands of dollars for the privilege of having its ball used.

Companies throw their goods at the players, hoping to gain some commercial spin-off. So the All Blacks wear sunglasses, shoes, jackets and trousers given to them by various companies. They swing golf clubs they have been supplied with. They watch televisions and listen to radios, stereos and CD players they have been given. They all drive Ford cars. They travel where possible on Air New Zealand. We're told the National Bank is the All Blacks' bank of choice. Their favourite soft drink is Coca-Cola. And they eat Weet-Bix for breakfast.

These companies, spending hundreds of millions of dollars on rugby, want their pound of flesh. Of course they do — it's business. That's why they get apoplectic when players wear boots with the wrong logo on it. Why pay all that money and see an All Black advertising the brand of a rival?

In 1995, Jock Hobbs was in France doing some television commentary work for TVNZ. He was also representing Mizuno, the official sponsors at that time of the All Blacks. Hobbs was shocked to watch three players, Jeff Wilson, Josh Kronfeld and Ian Jones, run on to the field for a test match wearing non-Mizuno boots, and there was some strong talking afterwards.

Recently, one All Black was going to speak at a rugby academy. His agent asked for a new top and trousers for the player. Why? Well, his agent explained, when the player finished an All Black tour, his clothes were destroyed. Otherwise he found he was running into trouble wearing the wrong company's clothes.

It seems amazing to those who aren't involved in this area that the New Zealand Rugby Union would need to employ staff specifically to ensure these sorts of problems are avoided, but that is a fact of modern rugby. Players are like moving billboards, on and off the field. Their clothes, their car, their equipment, all require constant monitoring. This task falls to the New Zealand Rugby Union's commercial department, which also ensures that before any major rugby match, the ground looks as it should — with appropriate signs in appropriate places.

adidas, of course, is the biggest sponsor of the All Blacks. It took over from Canterbury in 1999, in a $US100 million five-year deal that had adidas chiefs describing the All Blacks on the same terms as the Brazilian soccer team. The All Blacks have so much adidas gear shovelled at them that they wear it, store it, sell it, give it away and still can't get through it all.

Former All Black Chris Laidlaw dealt with this subject well when he contributed an article, "For Love *and* Money", to the December, 1999 issue of *New Zealand Books*. "The All Blacks are no longer a team," he wrote. "They are a brand that is proving irresistibly attractive to international sponsors who can see the marketing value in the colour black. The players who, barely a decade ago, enjoyed none of the trappings of full-on professionalism, are surrounded by an ever-growing phalanx of coaches, managers, media advisors, counsellors, psychologists, motivational experts, doctors of varying specialty and, of course, accountants. They are contractually bound to do this or not say that. They are on an endless conveyer belt from place to place, signing merchandise, posing for photographs, making television commercials and acting out the part as 'brand ambassadors' for Philips, adidas or the ubiquitous purveyors of alcohol."

WHAT PROFESSIONAL PLAYERS EARN

These days the All Blacks, all on annual salaries of at least $200,000, are wealthy young men. They live in style. They generally own plush houses in fashionable suburbs. They travel business class (and get to keep their air points — Eric Rush once joked that he had enough air points to get to Mars and back). During the 1999 World Cup, they had a mid-tournament break on the Riviera, all expenses paid. Top players — and many more who consider they should be, soon could be, or would like to be — have agents.

The minimum All Black salary is $85,000 (quite apart from Super 12 and NPC earnings), but this really is a bare minimum and All Blacks quickly progress beyond that figure. High profile, established players earn more than $300,000 a year and the stars get about another $100,000 on top of that. Jonah Lomu, the world's most famous player, has his own category and earns more than any other All Black. It has been reported that Lomu earns up to $3.5 million annually when his commercial deals are added to his pay for playing.

WHAT LEADING PLAYERS ARE PAID

— For representing the All Blacks (paid by New Zealand Rugby Union)

Star	$400,000–plus
Established	$300,000–plus
Current	$200,000–$300,000
Former	$100,000–$200,000

— Super 12 (paid by New Zealand Rugby Union)

Minimum salary: $65,000, including $15,000 for NPC matches. Most players' Super 12 contracts are far in advance of this figure.

— NPC

First Division: Super 12 and test players get what they can negotiate for their NPC appearances. Besides the $15,000 from the NZRFU, their provincial union will pay them as well. These payments can be as high as $100,000 for the most valuable players. For non-Super 12 players: $5000–$30,000.

Second Division: $5000.

Third Division: $1000.

— New Zealand Sevens representatives (paid by New Zealand Rugby Union)

$20,000 retainer, plus $1800 per tournament (the world sevens circuit has about 11 tournaments)

— New Zealand Colt:	daily allowances
— New Zealand Under-19:	daily allowances
— New Zealand Secondary School:	daily allowances
— New Zealand Academy members:	daily allowances

In 1995, when rugby went professional and two groups were vying for the players' signatures, there were some huge contracts offered. The Rugby Union justified these because it was desperate to hold on to its players, or else it would not have been able to offer a quality product to News Corp and would possibly have lost its massive 10-year television deal.

In the intervening years, what has been surprising is that in New Zealand players have generally been able to continue to command very high prices. There has been a slight downturn in the amount being offered, but only at a base contract level. Established All Blacks are still able to demand, and get, massive amounts.

One of the pay negotiators explained to me: "It's a game of bluff, but it's a game the Rugby Union can't afford to lose. The Rugby Union offers a lesser amount and the player, or his agent, says that if that's the most money on offer, he'll look overseas. The Rugby Union has to then decide whether to increase the offer or let that player head overseas. If too many good players go overseas, the game here would be shattered. So usually the players win."

Interestingly, this negotiator told me he felt that generally the Rugby Union caved in too quickly. "In the seven years since rugby went professional, only one player who would still have commanded a place in the All Blacks, Josh Kronfeld, has taken up an overseas contract. Perhaps that's an indication that the Rugby Union could have adopted a tougher line." Since he said that, All Black vice-captain Daryl Gibson has signed for Bristol and former All Black Bruce Reihana for Northampton.

It's often said that Jonah Lomu is able to ask for so much more than any other All Black because he is in so much demand commercially. The negotiator I spoke to disputed this. "They could definitely have called Jonah's bluff. It's true there is a big demand for Jonah's signature, but that's because he is an All Black. The moment he signed to play overseas, he would be a former All Black, and his price would fall dramatically. It's a simple fact: former All Blacks are not worth as much. I'm sure that's one factor that Jonah and his advisers have had to consider."

It should not be overlooked that these days leading players are international mercenaries, seeking to sell their wares (their playing skills) to the highest bidder. Most would like to remain in New Zealand, but will go off-shore if that's where the big money is being offered.

The way the professional players' contracts are structured draws all sorts of complaints. Andy Haden believes the security of the contracts is one reason why the All Blacks have not performed very impressively in tight matches over the past few years. "The decision-making at crucial times is very, very important," says Haden. "When teams I was in got to those vital stages of a game, we had terrible fear of losing because we stood to lose our reputations and our chances of selection. Now players are paid in case they do a good job, not because they have done one. They virtually know three or four years out what their salary is — they are basically being paid for staying alive after that. The contracts should be restructured so they are much more performance-based."

With top players now professional, and money such an integral part of the equation, it seems rugby has lost a little of its magic. The question is asked: can you have genius without the joy of playing the game for love?

With pay packets that would make most Chief Executives smile, many All Blacks have had to become financially savvy.

Haden was the first All Black to really cash in blatantly on his reputation as a player. He set up Sporting Contacts in 1984 and has been a major player in the agent/promotions/marketing side of sport ever since. Haden was ahead of his time, but these days most All Blacks are well aware of the need to invest their earnings wisely. Zinzan Brooke was one of the first high-profile players to become a business high-flier. Brooke began buying properties around Auckland, then raising a mortgage off one to buy the next until pretty soon people stopped counting how many he had. Brooke became known to some of his mates as the Bob Jones of rugby.

Most established leading players have set up their own companies, and some have more than one, besides being shareholders in others. Many of the top players own a substantial amount of property. For instance, Anton Oliver is the director of three companies, each of which owns a Viaduct Harbour apartment on Auckland's waterfront. Other players have delved into the hospitality business. Jeff Wilson and Tony Brown are part-owners of Dunedin café and bar Ombrellos, and Taine Randell owns a food bar in Dunedin among his businesses.

National Business Review estimated Jonah Lomu's total worth to be $6 million. Recent estimates put it at $10 million. Lomu, or rather his financial advisers, have cashed in big on his worldwide reputation, through endorsements and appearance fees, and have invested the big winger's income widely.

CORPORATE ALL BLACKS

Here are some current or recent leading New Zealand players, and, according to the New Zealand Companies Register, the companies in which they have an interest, either as directors or shareholders:

Christian Cullen	CC Promotions Ltd
	Christian Cullen Promotions Ltd
	Cullen and Monnery Associates Ltd
	Tilley Promotions Ltd
Jeff Wilson	Clifftop Holdings
	Ombrellos Restaurant
Jonah Lomu	JL 11 Ltd
	Stylez Ltd
	Godzilla Ltd
	Imbodan Ltd
Tana Umaga	U-Ah Holdings
	Cabrison Ltd
Pita Alatini	Amandla Ltd

Nathan Mauger	Waka Madate Ltd
Aaron Mauger	Alino's Ltd
	Maugini Ltd
Tony Brown	Ombrellos Restaurant Ltd
Justin Marshall	Bocchus Investments Ltd
Byron Kelleher	Rugby Pro Tours NZ Ltd
Ron Cribb	Ron Cribb Promotions Ltd
Taine Randell	Cut Company Ltd
	Royston Holdings Ltd
	CPI Dunedin Ltd
	Royston Holdings No 2 Ltd
	Sandbar (Napier) Ltd
	D R Properties Ltd
Troy Flavell	Flavz Ltd
	Flavz Property Investments Ltd
Norm Maxwell	Skintax Ltd
Greg Somerville	Somerville Enterprises Ltd
Kees Meeuws	Meeuws Holdings Ltd
	Meeuws Ventures Ltd
Greg Feek	Penrith Enterprises Ltd
	M J Feek Ltd
Anton Oliver	3B East Ltd
	AOAB Apartments Ltd
	2D West Ltd

As a matter of interest, the New Zealand Companies Register notes many well-known former New Zealand players or coaches are also directors of more than one company. John Hart is involved with nine, Wilson Whineray eight, Haden six, John Kirwan four, Zinzan Brooke, Brian Lochore and Sean Fitzpatrick two each.

In 2000, *New Zealand Rugby World* issued a rugby rich list which, while obviously nonsensical in the sense that no-one except the people themselves know how much they are worth, was interesting because it hinted at just how well New Zealand rugby players can do financially these days.

The magazine's top 10 were Kevin Roberts 1, Andy Haden 2, Jonah Lomu 3, Bernie McCahill 4, Brian Lochore 5, Zinzan Brooke 6, Sean Fitzpatrick 7, Inga Tuigamala 8, Graham Henry 9, Wilson Whineray 10.

I liked Whineray's comments on the list: "I'm a bit surprised in the sense that I didn't think I was interesting to anyone. I only earned 10 bob a day when I played. It's an interesting list, but a bit of a nonsense, really, because the guys are just guessing at best."

What is interesting when looking at such a list is that most rugby people make the bulk of their money after they retire. Roberts, a Rugby Union board director for some years, headed Lion Breweries and then Saatchi. Haden has become a celebrity manager. McCahill and Brooke have invested very heavily in property. Whineray has been a successful businessman, notably as boss of forestry giant Carter Holt Harvey.

The lesson to be taken from such a list is that while All Blacks today can earn good money, it's what they do with that money and what skills they develop for life after rugby that are more important. As Grant Fox said: "Wearing the black jersey opens doors for players, but you have to be pretty sharp to carry on once you get inside."

SEE YOU IN THE CORPORATE BOX

It would be wrong to focus on players alone when discussing the money side of the game. Rugby now is a major industry that provides employment for thousands of people in all sorts of areas — from players, administrators, referees and coaches, to caterers, marketers, journalists and groundsmen, to secretarial staff, web site designers, sponsor representatives, lawyers, technicians, public relations experts.

The rugby world is about money these days. Just have a look at the major rugby grounds in New Zealand. They're now oozing with corporate boxes. Income is being maximised.

The addition of all these corporate boxes has greatly changed the nature of rugby crowds. Decades ago, rugby fans queued for hours and then were willing to stand in the cold, the wet and the wind, to watch their favourite teams play. They were squashed in uncomfortably, but put up with the discomfort because they were hardy souls who loved their rugby.

Now at every big match — international, Super 12 and NPC — thousands of corporate clients are in attendance. Generally, these people are not rugby fanatics, but are important business people who have been offered a day at the rugby as a treat by a company — be it Telecom, adidas, Lion Breweries, IBM, Carter Holt, Fletchers or some other high-flier. There they are up in their plush boxes enjoying wine and/or champagne, eating delicate finger food or full meals and enjoying their day at the rugby. Good on them. All I know is those people are a long way removed from the many thousands who used to be willing to queue up in the cold and the wet to get tickets to watch their favourite rugby team.

The capacity of most of the big stadiums has shrunk considerably over the years — you can cram in far more people on terraces than you can seat in a stand. In 1956, when New Zealand wrapped up the series against the Springboks, there were reported to be 61,240 people present (plus those who entered without paying) at Eden Park. The ground's permanent seating capacity now is 46,000. (Some stadiums can add temporary seating for a sellout match.) Just under 58,000 people were at Lancaster Park, Christchurch, to watch the All Blacks and the British Lions do battle in 1971. Now Jade Stadium, as it's called, accommodates just 36,500. Athletic Park in Wellington held as many as 59,700 (for the 1959 New Zealand v British Lions match). Its replacement, the WestpacTrust Stadium, has a permanent capacity of a mere 34,500. The capacity of Carisbrook, Dunedin, has decreased by 4000 since the day in 1959 when nearly 44,000 fans squashed in to watch the first All Blacks-Lions test. Carisbrook's capacity fluctuates a little because it has retained some of its terracing that seems to find favour with the student population in Dunedin.

THE SIGNS OF THE TIMES

MAIN RUGBY GROUNDS OF NEW ZEALAND'S 27 PROVINCIAL UNIONS

PROVINCE	NAME 20 YEARS AGO	CURRENT NAME
Auckland	Eden Park, Auckland	Eden Park
Bay of Plenty	Rotorua International Stadium	Rotorua International Stadium
Buller	Victoria Square, Buller	Victoria Square
Canterbury	Lancaster Park,	Jade Stadium Christchurch
Counties-Manukau	Pukekohe Stadium	Lion Red Stadium, Pukekohe (changing to Pacific Arena, Manukau in 2003)
East Coast	Whakarua Park,	Whakarua Park Ruatoria
Hawke's Bay	McLean Park, Napier	McLean Park
Horowhenua-Kapiti	Levin Domain	Levin Domain

King Country	Taumarunui Domain	Owen Delany Park, Taupo
Manawatu	Showgrounds Oval, Palmerston Nth	Arena Manawatu
Marlborough	Lansdowne Park, Blenheim	Lansdowne Park
Mid Canterbury	Ashburton Showgrounds	Ashburton Showgrounds
Nelson Bays	Trafalgar Park, Nelson	Trafalgar Park
Northland	Okara Park, Whangarei	ITM Stadium (previously Lowe Walker, Stadium, Whangarei)
North Harbour	—	Albany Stadium
North Otago	Centennial Park, Oamaru	Centennial Park
Otago	Carisbrook, Dunedin	Carisbrook
Poverty Bay	Rugby Park, Gisborne	Rugby Park
South Canterbury	Fraser Park, Timaru	Alpine Energy Stadium
Southland	Rugby Park, Invercargill	Rugby Park Stadium (Homestead Rugby Stadium until 2001)
Taranaki	Rugby Park, New Plymouth	Yarrow Stadium
Thames Valley	Paeroa Domain	Paeroa Domain
Waikato	Rugby Park, Hamilton	Waikato Stadium
Wairarapa-Bush	Memorial Park, Masterton	Memorial Park
Wanganui	Spriggens Park, Wanganui	WestpacTrust Stadium
Wellington	Athletic Park, Wellington	WestpacTrust Stadium
West Coast	Rugby Park, Greymouth	Rugby Park

Since 1982, Counties has become Counties-Manukau. North Auckland has become Northland, Horowhenua has become Horowhenua-Kapiti, and North Harbour has been formed.

Twenty years ago, no main grounds were named after sponsors; now eight are, with more to follow shortly.

It's not just the names of some of the major grounds that have changed. They look totally different inside. Two decades ago, all of them had extensive terracing. Now, except for Carisbrook, the main grounds are all-seaters. All four main centres boast stadiums that are crammed with corporate boxes (or suites, as the corporate jargon-masters like to call them). That's where the attendance money is really made.

CORPORATE SUITES

STADIUM	NUMBER OF CORPORATE BOXES/SUITES
Eden Park	80
Waikato Stadium, Hamilton	5
WestpacTrust, Stadium, Wellington	64
Jade Stadium	63
Carisbrook	42

Prices for corporate boxes vary, according to their position in the stadium, the city in which the stadium is located, and supply and demand.

— Boxes at Eden Park cost from $75,000 to $200,000 to buy, plus an annual fee of $50,000.

— At Christchurch's Jade Stadium they cost between $45,000 and $56,250 per year for a five-year term.

— At the WestpacTrust Stadium in Wellington the annual fee ranges from $48,000 to $57,000. Initially there was also a fee of between $180,000 and $240,000, but my understanding is that recently this fee has been waived.

— At Carisbrook, one of the 24 suites on the Terrace side of the ground costs $25,000 plus a share of the overheads (about $2500 per year). This rental gives the purchaser 20 tickets and the right to buy 10 more. Suites in the main stand range from $17,600 a year to just under $30,000. The four suites at the Railway Stand end, range from $10,500 to $30,200,

New Zealanders had tremendous pride in the All Blacks. Seeing them, supporting them, was everything. Test matches — all big matches — were played on Saturday afternoons. Now there are Sunday tests and night tests. The fabric of society has changed with the virtual loss of the weekend. Rugby scheduling has changed with it.

Those who couldn't get to the game would tune in to the wireless and listen to Winston McCarthy's exciting commentaries. Even into the 1970s, hundreds of thousands of New Zealanders would turn on television and listen to Keith Quinn's television commentary of the test, if the match was being played away from where they lived. Virtually anyone who wanted to attend a test could afford to do so. There was less to spend money on and attending big rugby matches was a priority.

By the 1980s, nearly all big games were pre-sold, so the days of people heading for the park for a long all-night vigil had disappeared. Still, if you wanted to go, you could generally get a ticket. Parents still took their kids. Otherwise entire families gathered around the TV to listen to Quinny.

Fast-forward to the situation today. It is now not easy to get a ticket. The best way is to get one through a corporate channel, for big businesses each seem to have dozens to hand out. You can often buy a ticket through your local rugby club. But if you don't belong to a club, if you are simply a rugby fan, ticket-accessing is a difficult task.

In the classic case of market forces ruling, ticket prices have rocketed, not so much for the minor tests, against the likes of Tonga and Fiji, but for the big games. For mum and dad to take their three kids to a test against the Wallabies can now cost more than $500, and that doesn't include parking, or any food and drink costs. Some of New Zealand's major stadiums don't have children's prices in many parts of the grounds. If parents want to buy tickets in good seats and want their children with them, then each member of the family must pay about $110. It's a huge financial commitment.

Because the main stadiums (except Carisbrook) are all-seating affairs these days, things are easier to organise and more comfortable, but it means a certain spirit of rugby has vanished. The massive banks, full of spectators who had stood for hours to watch the big game, were inhabited by working class people, who revelled in each other's company.

WHERE HAVE ALL THE PEOPLE GONE?

If rugby crowds at major matches have shrunk, and so many of those attending are now corporate types, there to be seen, to drink wine and eat nibbles, we might ask where all the dedicated rugby fans have gone.

Some will be at home, watching the game on Sky TV. Sky's ratings for the 2002 Super 12 gradually picked up during the competition, perhaps as summer gave way to winter and an evening in front of the TV became more attractive. The major Super 12 game of the weekend generally drew 250,000 Sky viewers and, for some of the big clashes, that figure reached 280,000. Games of less interest (involving the poorly-performing South African sides or where no New Zealand team was involved) generally drew viewing audiences of from 80,000 to 116,000. The final, as the country eagerly awaited a Crusaders win over the Brumbies, had 332,000 Sky viewers. During the test match portion of the 2002 season, the biggest match was the Australia-New Zealand test at Sydney, which drew 424,000 viewers, the highest figure I have seen listed for a Sky programme.

TV3 replayed the pick of the Super 12 games as a delayed telecast, and its viewing figures were surprisingly good, usually well over 200,000 and sometimes higher than for the live screening on Sky. The Super 12 final replay drew 476,000 viewers. Its replay of the big Australia-New Zealand test drew 521,300 viewers.

(Anyone doubting the attraction of sport, and rugby in particular, should have scanned the top 10 viewing lists during the Super 12. Sport often filled all 10 of Sky's most watched programme slots, and the replay generally featured well up the list of TV3's most watched programmes for the week.)

Thus, for an occasion like a Super 12 final, we can say up to 800,000 rugby fans watched a televised version. For the biggest test of the season, in prime-time, 965,000 viewers tuned in, to watch either live or delayed coverage.

But the TV3 figures tell us that well over half the rugby viewing audience isn't watching international or top provincial rugby live these days because they don't have Sky TV. That's one significant way the game has been taken away from so many New Zealanders who can't afford to pay to watch their national rugby team play tests matches live.

The decision in April, 2002 by Sky to launch a dedicated rugby channel, for which subscribers must pay a second fee, will only take the game further away from the average punter. The pick of the games will be found on the rugby channel, which means only those willing to make a substantial financial investment will still have access to all the televised rugby.

More alarming for rugby administrators is the fact that so many people — maybe 150,000 — who used to watch all the big footie on television now don't bother. In the days when Television New Zealand covered major matches live, viewing audiences sometimes reached 1.1 million. A lot of people these days see the result and a short highlights package on their evening news and that'll be enough for them.

As well as selling big rugby to pay-for-view television, national rugby administrators have been ever more inclined to schedule important matches for the evenings. This is at the request of television, which is concerned with maximising its audiences. In doing this, administrators have ignored the fact that everyone — coaches, spectators and players — would prefer games to be played in the afternoon, when the weather is warmer and the ball less slippery. The rugby is more attractive when played in the afternoon — twice as many tries are scored in afternoon games as in night games, which often become reduced to kicking duels. As with television, though, the wants of the rugby public, and the players, take a back seat to commercial interests.

The professional era has split the country into a nation of rugby haves and have-nots. Decisions are made now not to suit the rugby or even for the benefit of the game, but purely to increase income. Do the changes over the past few years signal the beginning of New Zealanders, or at least some of them, no longer identifying as closely with their All Blacks?

BETTING

The game has changed in other ways since the advent of professionalism. Betting on matches has become commonplace and accepted. Initially, when the TAB sought to introduce sports betting in 1996, some sports bodies, such as Netball New Zealand, refused to be involved. But the TAB pays each national sport a small percentage of its take from betting on that sport, which puts pressure on national associations to allow their sports to be included.

Betting on rugby is increasing all the time. There was a 31 per cent increase on Super 12 betting in 2002 over 2001. And it's not just betting on results, but on the spread, or who will score first points, or the halftime score. Punters devise particular bets — in 2002 one brave (and happy) punter gambled that the Brumbies would make the top four and put up $100,000 to back his belief.

The TAB's 2001 annual report broke down the percentages of sports betting for each sport. Rugby was way ahead:

LEADING SPORTS IN TAB BETTING TURNOVER FOR 2001

Rugby	38.5%
Rugby League	22.4%
Soccer	6.7%
Cricket	6.5%
Basketball	5.1%
Tennis	4.5%
Boxing	3.2%
Golf	3.1%
Baseball	2.2%
American football	2.0%

The David Tua-Lennox Lewis heavyweight boxing title fight in November, 2000 drew $2.6 million in bets at the TAB, but this was a freakish one-off situation. Until 2002, the major rugby matches were invariably the most appealing to punters. Tua-Lewis broke the TAB betting record of $1.1 million in bets, established in the 1996 Bledisloe Cup rugby match in Wellington. The 2000 NPC drew $8.2 million in bets, well up on the $5.5 million of the previous year. The trend is clear — sports betting is here to stay, and rugby usually dominates.

Sports betting at the TAB for the 2000–01 year was worth $69.1 million, and the TAB paid a total of $1.3 million back to the 25 national sports bodies on its register. Obviously rugby, with its market domination, got the biggest slice of that money.

The soccer World Cup in mid-2002 altered the figures for 2001–02. In that period the TAB took $108 million in sport, an increase of 55 per cent over the previous year. The World Cup was responsible for $22 million of that and meant that for the first year since sports betting was introduced, soccer headed off rugby.

The TAB is so much part of the landscape now that Grant Nisbett works for the TAB while he is also a Sky rugby commentator. He is often used by newspapers in a guest selector capacity and is introduced as a TAB man. Newspapers run stories about the odds on particular matches in the lead-up to a Super 12 or NPC weekend.

'GONE TO PLAY IN THE TEST MATCH'

It was obvious many years before 1995 that rugby would eventually be a professional game. Once the World Cup was such a resounding success in 1987, the change was inevitable. If rugby didn't start paying players, they would be snapped up by rugby league.

During that 1987 World Cup, teams (and their officials) visiting New Zealand had their eyes opened to what the professional rugby world would be like. All Black skipper Andy Dalton did some television advertisements for Yamaha farm bikes. Dalton was one of the most recognised people in New Zealand at the time, and the advertisements were a clear attempt to cash in on his profile. Visiting players watched the ads on television, knew that great bloke though Dalton was he wouldn't have been pushing Yamaha to further New Zealand's bonds with Japan, and decided they would also like a slice of the action. Visiting officials saw the ads and wondered what could be done to bring the damned colonials into line.

New Zealanders didn't seem to mind Dalton making a few dollars out of the so-called amateur game. It was only a few years earlier that both All Black skipper Graham Mourie and his deputy, Dalton, had had to decline trips overseas with the All Blacks because they had recently bought farms and couldn't afford the time away from home. New Zealanders knew Mourie, Dalton and many others like them had lost thousands of dollars representing their country and were happy if they could get a little of it back.

Unfortunately, the world's leading rugby administrators were not so enlightened and held on tightly to their beloved amateur ethos, with the result that instead of having a graceful and smooth transition to professional rugby, the whole thing happened in an unseemly, almost embarrassing fashion in 1995.

Professionalism was inevitable. Even in the seventies players began making noises about needing compensation for lost wages, wanting to keep their book royalties, and getting more tickets to test matches. Into the 1980s, the pace quickened further, with under-the-table payments from clubs, players openly doing advertisements and being involved in sponsorships. Finally, in 1995, it was like the race entering its final lap, with all the runners sprinting furiously for the line.

You would think someone like Andy Haden would have been delighted that the game finally went openly professional. After all, he had been one of the thorns in the side of amateur rugby, pushing for better deals for players and always aware of the commercial aspects of the game. But the way it went professional made him rather uncomfortable.

"It wasn't quite what I had in mind," says Haden. "I always imagined certain values would be retained — the soul of rugby, ethos, spirit. They are important. They seem to have vanished. I understood things would be different, but I didn't think the profession would be shonky. I just feel that the profession that I was part of creating turned ugly."

Haden says it was amazing that rugby administrators were caught napping in 1995. "They tried to say it happened overnight, but that was rubbish. There were so many warnings over such a long time that they should have known what was coming. What was required was a managed transition.

"Rugby officials did the players a terrible disservice for years. Rugby was a game of good honest endeavour. There were salt of the earth characters involved, yet the top echelon of players had to be dishonest, hide payments, tell lies. It was demeaning."

I know what Haden means. In 1990, the Wallabies, led by Nick Farr-Jones toured New Zealand and, in a sneak preview of what was to happen at the World Cup the following year, upset the home team in Wellington to end a record unbeaten All Black test sequence. They were a team with such great names as Farr-Jones, Campese, Lynagh, Poidevin, Kearns and Horan. Before the tour they had a large number of T-shirts made, at a cost of about $3 each, and at each stop along the way, would hawk off the T-shirts for $15. They proved big sellers, especially when the Wallaby stars were lined up outside grounds selling them. Those T-shirts, and the match tickets the Australians were able to acquire and then flog off, enabled each of the Wallabies to make about $650 in cash from the tour. Fancy some of the greatest sportsmen in the world being reduced to the role of street vendors so they could come out of a tour with a little petty cash.

This sort of thing had been going on for years. Not necessarily T-shirts, but players being paid to make appearances at shopping malls and corporate boxes. It was all very degrading. No wonder people like Haden looked around the stands, jam-packed with thousands of paying spectators, and wondered where all the money was going. They didn't want it all, they thought, but it would be nice to get a slice.

"When rugby finally went professional," said Haden, "I hoped things would be better, but it was awful. After 1995, I really didn't want to be around rugby for a while, though I must say I'm a bit more encouraged by what's happened recently. There are some good people coming through — guys like Sean Fitzpatrick, Kieran Crowley, Peter Sloane, Robbie Deans, John Mitchell . . . I like seeing them involved in various ways. I'm sure they will remember what the game should be about and go about regaining and retaining some integrity."

In 1971, Brian Lochore, who had retired from top rugby the year before, was asked by coach Ivan Vodanovich to make himself available for the All Blacks for the third test against the Lions, in Wellington. The famous No 8 had been induced to come out of retirement to represent injury-stricken Wairarapa-Bush against the tourists and had performed pretty well. Now Vodanovich found that his two leading locks, Peter Whiting and Colin Meads, were both in doubt because of injury. He might need a lock and a captain. Could Lochore pull on the jersey one more time?

"You don't say no to the All Blacks," says Lochore. "I wasn't looking to make a comeback or anything like that, but if Ivan felt they needed me for one game, then of course I'd be there." So Lochore departed his

Wairarapa farm on the Friday before the Saturday test. He left a note to his wife Pam on the kitchen table. It said: "Gone to play in the test match."

No match fees to be discussed. No agents to be consulted. No Rugby Union spin doctors to give the story a positive slant. Lochore's pedigree was well-known. If the All Black coach wanted him to play, and he said he would, then that was that. There was no need for Lochore to confirm his ability in a series of Super 12 matches. Everything has changed. That third test was played at Athletic Park. The ground doesn't exist now.

chapter TWO

THE **NEW ZEALAND** RUGBY UNION

THE WORLD CUP FIASCO

New Zealanders got an insight into the world of modern rugby during the fracas over the hosting of the 2003 World Cup that led to a retired High Court judge, Sir Thomas Eichelbaum, investigating the whole affair. His report resulted in the resignations of the New Zealand Rugby Union Chief Executive, David Rutherford and the board Chairman Murray McCaw, and the departure of other board members, including the ubiquitous Rob Fisher.

To hundreds of thousands — millions maybe — of New Zealanders, rugby is not only a great game but our national sport. But at the top levels, in the offices of the New Zealand Rugby Football Union, rugby is no longer a sport. It is a business, just as surely as Sky TV, or The Warehouse or Michael Hill Jeweller are businesses. New Zealand rugby entered the corporate world many years ago, but the line in the sand was drawn in 1995, when the game went professional on a global scale. Since then New Zealand rugby has been run by ever more corporate-minded people, administrators who seem to devote more attention and energy to branding and copyright, exclusive deals and contract negotiations, than to coaching and club and junior rugby.

The more trusting rugby followers might have thought naively that the World Cup was about playing a rugby tournament with the aim of discovering which team was the world champion. Of course, those who follow these things more closely know that for many people, the prime motivation for staging the tournament now is money, not rugby. If anyone didn't know it before the 2003 World Cup row, they do now.

Rugby fans might join supporters' tours and travel to the other side of the world to watch their heroes in action. Various national teams will train and build towards the World Cup. The media will preview the action.

But the World Cup is the sport's cash cow. Betting agencies like the TAB look to score big during a World Cup. All sorts of people associated with the World Cup in various ways — ranging from caterers to the media (especially television), advertisers to travel agents — look upon the tournament as a wonderful way of making money.

The trick is to make money out of rugby, but not to lose sight of the fact that it is still a sport. As former All Black star Bryan Williams says: "The issues over the World Cup prove that rugby isn't just a game of passion any more. It's an industry. People have to learn what makes rugby tick."

The IRB itself chases the money in a big way. When the inaugural World Cup was proposed back in the 1980s, there were far nobler motives. Such leading New Zealand and Australian administrators as Ces Blazey, Dick Littlejohn, Russ Thomas and Nicholas Shehadie thought a World Cup would be a great way of bringing together all the best rugby talent on the planet. They felt rugby was ready for a World Cup, following in the footsteps of sports like soccer and cricket. Against the wishes of many leading world rugby officials, and with only lukewarm support at best from the IRB, New Zealand and Australia went ahead and organised the first World Cup, in 1987.

There really was a tortured history to the staging of that first tournament. By 1984, 26 years after the IRB had passed a resolution specifically forbidding member nations getting together for such an event, both Australia and New Zealand had presented proposals for a World Cup. The IRB approved a feasibility study that was accepted at the IRB's Paris meeting in 1985. That left just two years of frantic activity before the first Cup. Organisers would have preferred 1986, but that was too soon; 1988 was an Olympic Games year, so it was 1987, almost by default. It takes officials the best part of five years now to plan a World Cup, so the efforts of those Cup pioneers back in the 1980s were quite incredible.

The first World Cup wasn't perfect, but in hindsight it was pretty good. It was ludicrous to have Englishman John Kendall-Carpenter as Chairman of the organising committee when he lived 20,000km away from the action. (In fact, Kendall-Carpenter did a good job in awkward circumstances, but the decision to have an Englishman chairing the organising committee was surely no more than tipping the hat to the old order of doing things, a nod to the time when much of rugby's administrative power was based in the northern hemisphere.) And teams did not gain entry by qualifying, but at the invitation of the IRB, which caused some furrowed eyebrows in certain sections of the world. South Africa was excluded for political reasons and the 16 teams invited were: New Zealand, Australia, France, England, Wales, Scotland, Ireland,

Argentina, Canada, United States, Japan, Fiji, Tonga, Zimbabwe, Italy and Romania. The unluckiest to miss out were probably Spain and Western Samoa.

Australia helped to host the event, staging at Sydney and Brisbane all the matches from the pool that contained England, Australia, United States and Japan. The Australians, as the junior partner in hosting the 1987 World Cup, did well out of the arrangement, getting the Australia-Ireland quarter-final, plus both semi-finals. Matches in Australia were played only at Sydney's Concord Oval and Brisbane's Ballymore. In New Zealand, matches were played at 11 centres. This was a lot more evenhanded than the original arrangement offered to New Zealand to sub-host the 2003 World Cup, but they were simpler times back then.

New Zealand's 1987 side, selected by Brian Lochore, John Hart and Alex Wyllie, and brought together skilfully by coach Lochore, played brilliantly to win the event in a canter. Scotland, Wales and France (29-9 in the final) were put to the sword in the post-section matches and even the injury to captain Andy Dalton, which resulted in David Kirk leading the team on the field, did not seem to affect morale or standard.

The tournament organisation was far from faultless. Some of the arrangements were ludicrous — sometimes games were played on the same grounds on consecutive days, meaning there were poor crowds on the "second" days. There were also a few problems with the marketing of the tournament, and a bit of a fuss now and then over what signs should be placed where. Back in 1987, the New Zealand union was naïve, with no idea how to cope with a major rugby event. A media sub-committee, chaired by John Dowling, found it very difficult to persuade local unions to move season ticket-holders so that visiting overseas media could sit in seats with a good view. Only a whirlwind nationwide tour by deputy Chairman Eddie Tonks and Graham Mourie (working then for West Nally, the promoters of the World Cup), during which unions were told emphatically where to place the media, sorted out things. Keith Quinn, the news media representative on the tour that Tonks and Mourie undertook, is emphatic that the pair of them never received the credit owed for helping save a situation that could have blown up into a public relations nightmare.

These glitches aside, the World Cup ran well in 1987. There was a good spirit among competing teams. The event was new and there was a freshness about the tournament, with the emphasis very much on the results on the field. Happily the tournament also returned income of

$9 million, quite apart from ticket sales. Unfortunately, life was never to be so straightforward again.

The IRB quickly grasped what a money-spinner had been provided for it. By 1991, the World Cup, hosted in Britain and France, was regarded as a big earner and duly returned non-ticket income of $57 million. That figure rose to $93 million for the 1995 World Cup in South Africa and a massive $210 million for the 1999 World Cup in Britain.

By 1999, there were all sorts of problems with the draw (brought about by the baffling decision to split the tournament into five groups, which meant things became very messy when it came to working out some of the qualifiers), and with scheduling and ticket allocation. But the IRB was apparently able to shrug off these glitches, content that it had reaped a financial bonanza.

The broadcasting rights skyrocketed. The 1987 tournament was televised in 17 countries to what rugby chiefs claimed was a viewing audience of 300 million. (I'm very sceptical of the viewing audience figures for all these events, be they the soccer World Cup, athletics world champs or Olympics. It should be termed a potential viewing audience.) By 1999, these figures had shot up and the World Cup that year was screened in 214 countries with a viewing audience claimed to be 3 billion (which probably assumes that hundreds of millions of poverty-stricken Indian and Chinese villagers were camped in front of their TV screens throughout the tournament). It is envisaged that by 2007, there could be as many viewers watching the tournament as watched the 1998 soccer World Cup. We can see how crucial the broadcasting income for the World Cup is — for the 1999 event, the broadcasting rights brought in $132 million, compared to the $51 million sponsorship added to the cash pile.

When the 2003 World Cup loomed, the IRB and the Rugby World Cup Ltd body that was set up seemed to devote more time to corporate contracts than to worrying about which countries might best promote or support the game. Concepts such as "clean" (no existing advertising or sponsorship) stadiums were all-important, as they are with all major sports events, from the Olympics to the soccer World Cup. The international heavyweights that decided where the World Cup would be held also wanted clean areas within a 500m circumference of each stadium. Further, they wanted to take control of all the corporate boxes. Then there was the matter of catering, another potential gold mine.

Host countries were told, somewhat belatedly according to New Zealand officials, that they would need to pick up the entire travel costs for every competing team, the full expenses of all the tournament freeloaders — IRB officials and guests (including Olympic officials), plus the costs of special invitees from a large and seemingly ever-expanding number of countries. This added dramatically to the cost of staging the event.

The New Zealand union was very slow in grasping these concepts and their commercial implications and lost ground to the clued-up Australian rugby hierarchy, led by John O'Neill. It was revealing that whereas in the end Australia had upwards of 50 staff working on planning for the World Cup, New Zealand never had more than four and often just one or two. The New Zealand union was "honest, but naïve" according to Sydney-based New Zealand rugby writer Spiro Zavos, and while that's a fair assessment, I would add the words "arrogant" and "incompetent". Let's face it: the IRB gave the Cup to New Zealand to sub-host and New Zealand gave it back because it didn't grasp the commercial realities of the situation.

It didn't matter a fig that New Zealand had been largely instrumental in there being a World Cup in the first place. It didn't matter that New Zealand had a wonderful tradition in rugby, having produced champion teams decade after decade and having the most famous national team in the rugby world. It didn't matter that New Zealand crowds in such centres as Napier and Invercargill, Timaru and New Plymouth so loved rugby that they would turn out in big numbers to watch less fashionable national teams like Italy and Japan.

Forget all that. Money is what rules rugby these days, and it was money that dictated what decisions Rugby World Cup Ltd and the International Rugby Board made. When Australia sought to have sole hosting rights, one of its major points of leverage was that by having much bigger stadiums and being able to charge more per ticket, it would be able to greatly increase tournament revenue. That concept was too enticing for the IRB to turn down. New Zealand's view of things was amazingly simplistic, and took little account of business reality.

By the time it dawned on the New Zealand union that the World Cup would be decided not by sentimentality, but by harsh commercial reality, it was left playing catch-up. It did manage finally to put itself in a position to offer clean stadiums, but it was all too late. Australia had already locked up the deal.

Ultimately, the brouhaha over the World Cup has done New Zealand rugby a favour, because it rid us of two lacklustre figures who had been charged with leading the game in this country, Rutherford and McCaw.

The Eichelbaum Report reached 18 key conclusions. Among them:

- The initial bid for the World Cup, submitted by Australia and New Zealand in 1997, was disadvantageous to New Zealand as arrangements were open-ended and left the New Zealand union in a vulnerable position.
- The New Zealand union waited until the bid reached a crisis situation before seeking Government funding.
- It was known from October, 2001, that New Zealand's sub-host status was at risk.
- The crisis arose because New Zealand could not deliver clean boxes, yet the New Zealand union initially took no steps to obtain access to the boxes, believing Vernon Pugh would agree to a "pragmatic solution".
- The union's board was not informed of Pugh's advice to McCaw that clean boxes were a fundamental condition to getting hosting rights.
- The New Zealand union's approach towards sub-hosting the cup was cautious and gave the appearance of not being fully committed.
- The World Cup board and the Australian union lost confidence in the New Zealand Rugby Union.
- The personal attacks on Pugh by McCaw and Rutherford were bad tactics.

To be honest, there wasn't much in Eichelbaum's report that was revealing. The amazing aspect was that Rutherford and McCaw had not resigned earlier. Why did it need Sir Thomas to put in writing what everyone knew before Rutherford and McCaw fell on their swords? Even then, McCaw clung to power as long as he could. He initially resigned only as board Chairman, before realising his position as a board member was untenable. He never really seemed to get it, saying, even as he departed, that he had come out of the whole thing with his integrity intact.

More questions: how could Rob Fisher, who was so involved in the whole messy affair, possibly think he was the right man to take over as board Chairman? He'd already had the position once and stepped down under pressure. Now, as a Rugby World Cup board member and a deputy-chairman of the International Rugby Board at the time New Zealand lost its World Cup sub-hosting rights, he was implicated in the fiasco. It seems incredible that as intelligent a person as Fisher could think he was suddenly the right man to chair the board. He was soon disabused of that idea, despite saying that Vernon Pugh was pleased he was back as Chairman of the New Zealand Rugby Union board.

And why did other long-serving board members, who'd also been party to the shambles, not quit immediately? It was clear they had not done their jobs properly. Why did it require a meeting of all 27 provincial chairmen, and a subsequent call for a special meeting before the board members took the hint and quit? As Andy Haden said: "It looks as if the board members decided to live on their feet rather than die on their knees."

The over-riding impression is that all these people, from Rutherford and McCaw down, were clinging to power for power's sake (and perhaps for the glory and money that went with it). It's certainly difficult to believe that the good of New Zealand rugby was foremost in their minds.

A SPORT OR A BUSINESS?

Until the 1970s, a secretary, Jack Jeffs, and his assistant basically ran the Rugby Union. Even into the early 1980s, genial Barry Usmar was the hands-on official, with Sylvie Gentry as his PA. There might be one or two other subsidiary staff floating round (including a gear officer), but not many. Ces Blazey, the Chairman of the Rugby Union, would attend to his paperwork and spent an inordinate amount of time on union business, on a voluntary, unpaid basis. There was a 19-strong union council of mixed ability. A few other well-known figures, such as Ivan Vodanovich and Bob Stuart, would often be found at Rugby Union headquarters, at the Huddart Parker building, attending to various matters, such as organising coaching clinics or tidying up International Rugby Board business. There was no doubt in those days that when you entered the Rugby Union offices, you were entering a sports environment. People were there because they wanted to serve the sport they loved. Now, the over-riding feeling on walking into the Rugby Union offices is that people are doing a job simply for the money. The feeling of goodwill towards rugby has vanished.

The fuss over the World Cup is further evidence of the way rugby has gone. In New Zealand, the Rugby Union is not so much a sports body as a corporate giant. The Chief Executive, be he David Moffett, Rutherford or Steve Tew (promoted immediately to replace Rutherford as temporary Chief Executive), is not a sports official but a businessman. The All Blacks are not a sports team, but a brand. The players are international mercenaries, people who chase the market place.

As former All Black halfback and current Auckland Rugby Board member Lin Colling told *The Dominion* newspaper: "Since rugby has gone professional, we have had this corporate culture involved in administration. Maybe this [World Cup fiasco] is a consequence of the outside influences." There is the question of competence, as well. If the people making the important decisions for the New Zealand union were all extremely competent, perhaps the complaints about the corporate influences would not be as vehement.

Former All Black captain Andy Leslie is one of many who feel rugby people have stopped running their own game. "We had the Boston Report in 1994–95," says Leslie. "There was a big emphasis placed on business people being brought in to administration to add their expertise. Then the various provincial unions adopted the thrust of the Boston Report. Now it has got to the stage where many of the provincial unions are being run by business people who don't have any special feeling for, or knowledge of, rugby. In a way, the game has been taken away from rugby people."

Staff members told me, when complaining about the performance of their then boss, David Rutherford, that if it weren't for the fact that they could not earn such big money elsewhere, virtually all the senior management at the union would have left. It was only money holding them, not passion for rugby or desire to serve the Rugby Union. Experienced rugby journalist Lindsay Knight touched on this subject in a column in the October, 2001 issue of *New Zealand Rugby World* magazine, writing: "Almost 12 months ago, frustrated and irritated by the increasingly bureaucratic methods of the NZRFU staff and the inaccessibility to most in the hierarchy, I compared them unfavourably with the administrative giants of the past, the likes of Cuth Hogg, Tom Morrison, Jack Sullivan, Tom Pearce, Charlie Saxton, Ces Blazey, Russ Thomas and others.

"The point was made then that while these gentlemen may have made mistakes and there were occasions when some of their positions and decisions could be argued, the one thing which could never be in dispute was their passion for rugby and their knowledge of the game in just about every aspect."

There used to be a small, tight unit, geared almost totally towards running the game. It certainly wasn't perfect. It seemed extremely difficult to get information out of the union. Chairman Jack Sullivan was correctly tagged "No comment Jack". His successor, Ces Blazey, ran union business and meetings in a tight, clinical fashion. So, a few years later, did Richie Guy, who had a particularly no-nonsense attitude towards chairing meetings. There wasn't a lot of flair shown by the union, but by the same token there was a lot of efficiency. Of course, these were the days of amateur rugby, and the union did not have to cater to the same level to sponsors, including television companies, and hadn't signed contracts totalling a billion dollars or more. But still the union oversaw school and provincial rugby, set the international calendar and generally performed quite well.

By the late 1970s, though, the players were beginning to get increasingly tetchy about such issues as the provision of free tickets, compensation for money lost while representing the All Blacks and other money-related matters. Andy Haden was a constant thorn in the union's side, niggling and needling.

In turn, the union moved only slowly, making decisions that were generally conservative. Into the 1980s, it was still banning stars like Graham Mourie and Stu Wilson because they'd been paid for writing books. The Rugby Union pointed out it was merely following the dictate of the International Rugby Board. New Zealand fans shook their heads and wished for a more far-sighted national rugby body, one that didn't so quickly fall into line with the wishes of a world body that so often made irrelevant, behind-the-times decisions. As Mourie said, when explaining why he was coaching in Taranaki during his "banned" period: "It's a long way from Twickenham to Opunake."

When we look back now, we can see that New Zealand rugby officials didn't do enough to ensure their game kept its hold at college level, or to increase the standard and number of coaches, or to compensate top players for the increasing demands on their time. The union could have more actively promoted rugby, but, having inherited a position where rugby was all-dominant, they were not alert enough to the way things were changing.

I recall writing stories in the 1980s complaining about how journalists had yet again been excluded from council meetings, about the union secrecy, about how out of touch union officials were with the grassroots of the game. But when I think back to those times, and then compare them to the situation now, I know when it felt more like a sports body was running the sport.

WHEN ENOUGH IS ENOUGH

The exact current staffing level of the New Zealand Rugby Football Union has been a matter of dispute, probably because it is so fluid (though the graph is upward). *The Dominion* newspaper ran an excellent story on this issue in September, 2001 (written jointly by Glen Scanlon and Lindsay Knight) and stated that there was a staff of 73, including those housed at head office, plus All Black coaches or referees or staff at Palmerston North's Rugby Institute. In total, the newspaper stated, the union was employing more than 475 people, including the All Blacks and other contracted players. The Rugby Union took exception to the figures (and to the tenor of the article, which was that the union was over-staffed), but they proved to be almost spot on.

In its next annual report, in April, 2002, the union itself, while noting that "there are lot of myths about the numbers the NZRFU employs", put staff levels at head office alone at 62.5. They were employed in this manner:

All Blacks and other national teams	4
All Black coaches and management	8
Rugby	20.5
Commercial	10.5
Communications	6.5
Finance	5.5
Support service	4
Legal	2
CEO	1.5 (!)

The report noted: "In addition, the New Zealand union funded, via provincial unions, five franchise professional development officers and 12 provincial referee education officers. That was on top of the 400 full and part-time referees, players, coaches and team management contracted by the NZRFU."

Rutherford, who was always particularly sensitive to questions about staffing, seemed aggrieved when asked by *The Dominion* if the Rugby Union was over-staffed. "That sort of thing is quite fanciful, frankly," he replied. "People who were around back then told me that sometimes the phone did not ring till April. The scale of business now is different. People don't really understand the work that goes into organisation, competition management, games, air travel, referees, the judiciary . . . those things are full on."

The point is that when you walk into the Rugby Union headquarters now, you feel like you are entering the headquarters of Telecom or Fletcher's, or some other corporate high-flier. David Moffett, the Australian who preceded David Rutherford as union Chief Executive, used to say that rugby was too much a business to be called a sport, and too much a sport to be called a business. Looking at things from the outside, I'm in no doubt it's the business side of things, rather than the sport, in the ascendancy these days.

It does not appear to be a particularly well-run business, as we saw all too clearly during the fiasco over the hosting of the World Cup. The union falls between two stools, neither running as slick a business operation as many companies, nor, considering the funds available to it, running the sport as well as it should be. The union seems as if it is financially greedy and operationally poor.

It is intriguing that for many of its appointments, the union has employed Sheffield to advertise various positions. Sheffield receives applications, runs psychometric tests and interviews and culls the applicants down to a manageable number of about three or four for the Chief Executive and other union representatives to meet and interview. While no doubt Sheffield and firms like them have their uses, I have often wondered if they fully grasp that they are looking for people to staff a sports organisation, as well as to run a business. Ironically, when Rutherford was hired, the Rugby Union was delighted because it was getting a person with a passion for the game. What wasn't checked closely enough was whether he brought the right business acumen to the job.

Rutherford's statement, repeated many times in his first few months in the Chief Executive's chair, that winning for the All Blacks was the 15th and last priority, the least important thing about being an All Black, probably foreshadowed his demise. Rutherford came to this conclusion, he said, after speaking to many former All Blacks, who mentioned team spirit, integrity, pride and other factors. But someone running the New Zealand Rugby Union should have grasped immediately that for the All Blacks, the sport's shop window, winning was absolutely critical. If the All Blacks lose, everything — sponsorships, television contracts, advertising, playing numbers — is jeopardised. Rutherford eventually came around to this line of thinking, but it was a concept he should have grasped from his first day on the job.

And there was more bad news for the traditionalists. Concerned that

Above: *About here it started to go all wrong. Outgoing chairman Richie Guy hands over the NZRFU reins to Auckland lawyer Rob Fisher. CEO David Moffett (middle) already seems distracted.*

Below: *Feeding the chooks. CEO Moffett and Saatchi supremo Kevin Roberts opine on matters rugby before an enthralled media. The corporate era holds court.*

Above: *And then it got worse. Rob Fisher hands over the NZRFU reins to new chairman Murray McCaw. Incredibly Fisher stayed on at the IRB with Tim Gresson.*

Below: *Yeah, but corporate rugby wasn't all bad. Coach John Hart and captain Sean Fitzpatrick celebrate another All Blacks series success.*

Above: *Sponsors' ecstasy. Marika Vunibaka scores for the Crusaders but so too do Ford, Caltex and Telecom.*

Below: *Just in case you didn't know that the Super12 was a corporate beast. Ford, Telecom, the ASB Bank and Carnegie affix their stars to the Blues.*

Above: *Save us Jock! The headlines trumpet the 2002 grassroots revolution. But has a saviour really been found?*

the ever-increasing staff numbers could not all be housed in their two floors of the Huddart Parker building, the Rugby Union moved its headquarters 1000 metres north to opposite the WestpacTrust Stadium — to the former offices of TelstraSaturn TV. I loved the fact that the Rugby Union had occupied the Huddart Parker since 1921 — that famous meetings had been held there — from protests about the selection of the 1924 Invincibles, to Ces Blazey in 1981 discussing the latest developments on the Springbok tour of New Zealand. I loved it that right across the courtyard of Post Office Square, where the Huddart Parker building is located, is a tobacconist that still bears the name of Clarrie Gibbons. But then I wonder how many of the current staff at the union even know who Clarrie Gibbons was. Forty years ago, he was one of the big figures in New Zealand rugby, four times a selector or coach of successful Ranfurly Shield challengers, Otago once and Wellington three times. He later became Chairman of the Wellington union, and president of the New Zealand union. When the union moved head-quarters, another link with its history was lost.

ENTER THE SPIN DOCTORS

You always know a sports body has got away from core business when it starts employing spin-doctors. Just as politicians seem to devote as much time to putting a positive spin on various mistakes and miscalculations as on formulating constructive policy, so it seems to be these days with the Rugby Union. All sorts of press releases emanate from Rugby Union headquarters. Some are mundane, offering unsolicited and generally unwanted previews or reviews of rounds of the Super 12 or NPC, or informing the media when the All Blacks will be available for interviews, or which hotels they'll be staying at and when.

But there are also a lot of damage-control media releases. Through late 2001 and into 2002, we had various explanations and clarifications for the mess the union got itself into over the decision to advertise again the position of All Black coach, the row with Australia over the decision to veto any move to change the Super 12 to a Super 14, and for the union's long-running contretemps with the Australian union and with Rugby World Cup Ltd (especially Chairman Vernon Pugh) over the World Cup fiasco.

When the New Zealand union bosses travelled to Dublin in April 2002 for the International Rugby Board meeting that would decide where the 2003 World Cup would be held, quite a sizeable contingent travelled, including the Chief Executive, the board Chairman and the two IRB members from New Zealand. Another taken to Dublin was the union's chief communications man Peter Parussini. Perhaps the union figured there was bad news on the horizon and some massaging of the media would be required. If so, then Parussini did his job, for selected members of the rugby media were phoned and offered "exclusive" titbits and behind-the-scenes accounts of what had gone on in Dublin. Naturally all those accounts favoured the New Zealand union, even though the union left Dublin having been accused by the IRB of "wholly inappropriate behaviour" and having lost its right to be a World Cup sub-host.

In the end, no amount of spin doctoring could save the Rugby Union bosses from their own ineptitude and within four months they were gone.

If there was ever any doubt that the New Zealand union had entered the spin-doctor game, it was erased in September 2001, when a Rugby Union circular to provincial unions found its way into the media. The circular spoke about a "crisis response team" that was to be set up to deal with controversies such as the appointment of the All Black coach (this was at the time when the union was involved in the sacking of Wayne Smith and his replacement by John Mitchell, a process that lacked both logic and transparency).

Under the heading of Crisis Management, the union noted that "despite the best planning, events often do not run smoothly" and that "failures in systems and processes can result in misinformation or a lack of information being communicated through the news media". The document outlined how the Rugby Union should restrict what the public knows by controlling the documents released to the media. As one newspaper noted, the Rugby Union document read more like a Secret Service report than a rugby circular. Potential problems listed in the report were:

- Failed drugs test.
- Stadium incident.
- Player death on field.
- Player off-field problem.
- Problem involving sponsor's product.
- Act of God, for example foot and mouth outbreak.
- Fans fighting.
- Unexpected loss of key provider, for example airline.

The paper said the Rugby Union's media manager would have the information for most inquiries, but events of a more significant nature, where the safety of people or the operation of the event was threatened, would need a more considered response. For these more serious issues, it was recommended that a Crisis Response Team be established.

Recommended steps were:

- Establish a holding position for the media, to try to control unfounded speculation and inaccurate reporting.
- Appoint a media spokesperson on the issue, to ensure consistent messages were communicated through the crisis.
- Have the Rugby Union's main phone line staffed to handle public inquiries.
- Have regular media updates even when there was not much progress on the issue. This would limit speculation and inaccurate reporting.

It was important, the paper noted, for creating perceptions after the event that the organisers were thorough in their handling of the crisis and as helpful as possible.

How ironic then that when a few months later the Rugby Union found itself in a serious situation over the 2003 World Cup, it went to ground. After some insulting comments about IRB and World Cup Ltd Chairman Vernon Pugh, both David Rutherford and Murray McCaw became extremely wary of making any public comments at all in the lead-up to the critical meeting in Dublin. Board member (and IRB deputy Chairman and World Cup director) Rob Fisher was even more tight-lipped. Parussini had little to say on the record on the issue.

There was another example of spin doctoring during and after the Rugby Union's annual meeting in April 2002. The annual meeting used to be the time when provincial delegates, having sounded out their clubs, could question New Zealand's national administrators about the way the game was being run. There used to be robust discussion as questions from the floor were aimed at the union Chairman and his councillors. This was how it should have been.

These days, though, the annual meeting is more like an American political convention, with everything well choreographed and everyone at pains to ensure there is nothing contentious or controversial raised in front of the media. When reporters ask why various issues were not aired at the meeting, they are told they have been dealt with at special meetings of CEOs, or in workshops. The whole event seems totally stage-managed. Shouldn't an incorporated society, which is what the Rugby Union is, be more open in its dealings?

At the 2002 annual meeting, delegates and the media were given a press release, prepared by union staffer Matt McIlraith for Chairman McCaw, which painted a ridiculously glowing picture of the state of rugby in New Zealand. *The Dominion* newspaper headed a report of the meeting: "Rugby's tone of optimism just doesn't ring true."

At a time when junior and club rugby — the backbone of the game in this country — are really struggling, it was misleading not to say so. McCaw spoke of the increase in playing numbers to 119,000 (including 6500 female players). There may have been an increase on the previous year, though the history of the Rugby Union's record-keeping has been so erratic no-one could be sure, including the NZRFU. But the general trend in playing numbers in New Zealand rugby is steeply and undeniably downwards. To paint any other picture was silly. A more realistic comparison of rugby's numbers would have been to compare them to 10, 20 or 30 years ago.

This spin-doctoring was evident in other claims. For instance, McCaw said attendances for Super 12 matches in 2001 were 551,000, "the third highest in the six years of the competition", and "an increase of 6 per cent on the previous year". I am sceptical about these figures, as the union has been trying for several seasons to get accurate attendance figures and has never succeeded. It cannot get the stated attendance to even closely reflect the income from tickets. As for the 2001 figures, these were surely distorted by the fact that Christchurch's Jade Stadium underwent massive renovations that year; work that temporarily halved, then increased, the ground's spectator capacity. Was this taken into account when the figures were released?

McCaw's glossy view of things was the sort of review one would expect from the Chairman of a company like Air New Zealand or Television New Zealand, with the rosiest possible slant put on every aspect of performance, and never mind the real picture.

The spin-doctoring goes on all the time. When the All Blacks' first test squad for 2002 was released, in a press statement from the All Blacks' Communications Officer, this was the second paragraph: "Of the 26 players who attended the training camp at Whangamata, Canterbury fullback Leon MacDonald, his provincial colleague and front rower Greg Somerville and the province's No 8 Scott Robertson are being allowed to miss the first international of the winter." Being allowed? Did they beg not to be picked for the All Blacks? All Black coach John Mitchell was dropping three of his first-choice players because the opposition, Italy, was only second-rate, but no-one quite wanted to say that.

THE BOARD

While there has been justifiable criticism of Rugby Union staff, the first area that should be examined is the board. Until 1995, a 19-man council served the union, but after the Boston Report, which led to the revamping of New Zealand rugby's set-up, a streamlined board was put in place. This was done, apparently, to give the union a better combination of rugby knowledge and business expertise.

The architects of the Boston Report planned for the nine-member board to comprise just one representative from each of the three (Northern, Central and Southern) zones, to try to take much of the parochialism out of the New Zealand Rugby Union. But this idea was just too revolutionary. In the end, it was agreed the board would comprise two representatives from each zone, plus a Maori representative and two independent members.

So it was that on 18 December 1995, at a meeting held at Wellington's Park Royal Hotel, across the road from Rugby Union headquarters, the New Zealand union's administration was drastically altered. About 80 of the eligible 104 votes supported the change and union president Rodney Dawe announced the decision, saying: "Gentlemen, the motion is passed." Interestingly, one of the strongest advocates of the change was former All Black captain and sitting council member Jock Hobbs, who said rugby more than ever needed bold leadership. "Accepting this motion is the right and proper thing to do," he said.

Within a few months, a startlingly poor decision was made when Hobbs was overlooked for a position on the board. Hobbs — the man who had negotiated for weeks with the country's leading players, trying to stop them from signing with the breakaway World Rugby Corporation.

There have been many exaggerations of who played what role in the Rugby Wars of 1995. I believe that ultimately WRC failed because of a top-level meeting in Europe between Rupert Murdoch and Kerry Packer, or if not them, then some of their leading henchmen. It was decided at that meeting how various segments of the market might be divided between these huge media organisations. Asian horse racing and other subjects were discussed, and so was rugby. After that meeting, WRC negotiators were told to back off, and that was what allowed the New Zealand union to contract its players. Hobbs (and Brian Lochore, who worked with him) did not know about these high-level talks. He worked hard, pleading, reasoning, almost begging top players to stay under the New Zealand union's umbrella. As far as New Zealand was concerned, he succeeded. He had some initial success with provincial unions, and then scored a big break-through when Josh Kronfeld and Jeff Wilson walked away from WRC contracts and elected to stay with the New Zealand union (for a price reputed to almost exactly equal what WRC would have paid them). It didn't take long after that before the other players followed them.

So Hobbs emerged a hero, the saviour of New Zealand rugby, some said. He did not ask for, and was not paid, a cent for all this work. Within months he had been overlooked for a position on the board. Thus New Zealand rugby lost not only a former captain, but also a lawyer and a person who had been intimately involved in the goings-on of the union through 1995. By any stretch of the imagination, it was a monumentally bad decision. Were the people who voted for the board members back then putting the good of New Zealand rugby first, or were they operating in self-interest? Keith Quinn, in *Outrageous Rugby Moments*, wrote: "It was a decision that was as callous as it was ungrateful."

Hobbs should have been one of the leaders of New Zealand rugby since 1995. Instead he was marginalised. He still attended some rep matches, but as much to assist his company Strategic Limited, as for any particular passion for the game. Otherwise his links with rugby just about ended with watching his teenaged son play school games. In the early 1990s, he was a coach and an administrator and was putting a lot back into the game he graced as an energetic loose forward through the 1980s. Apparently he didn't have what was required around the New Zealand board table, baffling as that may be. Ironically, it was to Hobbs that many in rugby turned in August 2002 when the World Cup shambles resulted in wholesale resignations. "Hobbs asked to save New Zealand rugby again" was how one newspaper described the situation. It would have been a lot better if he hadn't been booted out in the first place.

There can be no quibbling with the decision to replace the old council with a board. Times were changing in rugby and with the game having gone professional, different strengths were going to be required in those running the game. For instance, dealing with players' contracts called for a level of expertise not previously needed in New Zealand rugby. Clearly, too, there was a need for a greater awareness of exploiting commercial opportunities.

It's not much use installing a board if you don't elect the best possible people. Like any board, the New Zealand Rugby Union has had some impressive people and some less impressive. Ironically, one board member who was the subject of much vilification was Kevin Roberts, who headed Lion Breweries before he became the Saatchi boss. Roberts was accused of grandstanding, loving the limelight, seeking reflected glory, failing to see there was more to New Zealand rugby than just the All Blacks and so on. From my limited dealings with Roberts, I'd say all those charges had some truth. However, he was used to mixing in big business circles, and had a vast amount of commercial expertise, good international contacts and vision. It was Roberts who was partly responsible for securing the massive adidas sponsorship of the All Blacks, a deal which has been the New Zealand Rugby Union's lifeblood over the past few years.

When the New Zealand union's previous All Black sponsorship with Canterbury was nearing its expiry date, it sought potential bidders for a new contract. There was a flurry of initial interest, but eventually only Canterbury and Nike were left chasing the deal. Then, out of the blue, the New Zealand union received a call from Europe: adidas was interested, after all. Roberts and then Chief Executive David Moffett hopped on a plane to Europe and met the adidas bosses. The result was a five-year deal that is worth $US10 million a year to the union, plus that much again each year in adidas' back-up advertising.

Roberts didn't last long on the board, and his departure certainly didn't seem to help matters. Some board members through 2001–02, like Fonterra's Craig Norgate and Carter Holt Harvey Chief Executive Chris Liddell, are astute businessmen but that didn't make them good rugby administrators. Fisher was largely sidelined on the board after yielding to pressure and standing down after the 1999 World Cup disaster, when New Zealand capitulated in the semi-final to France. After that, he looked increasingly out of step with McCaw and Rutherford.

There was a decreasing amount of rugby expertise on the board. Former All Black prop Richie Guy was booted out in April 2001, after serving the union for 17 years. He was a rugby man, pragmatic and full of commonsense; just what the board needs. When Guy left, it meant there wasn't an All Black left on the board. When new directors were appointed, we often heard that they had an "interest" in rugby, but this could apply to millions of New Zealanders. They brought no special passion for rugby, or any particular knowledge of the game, to the task.

Fred Allen laments what is happening. "The New Zealand Rugby Union people don't seem to realise what they're doing to the game, how they're losing the goodwill of the ordinary people. There are too many people who are NZRFU board directors who know little about rugby. In the past you might have argued with councillors like Norm McKenzie, and they might not have been great fellows, but at least they had played the game and were passionate about it. This new lot don't talk about camaraderie and comradeship. They talk about contracts and money."

Former All Black Murray Mexted, who these days watches things from the Sky Television commentary box, is one who has expressed concern about the lack of rugby knowledge on the board. He told the *Evening Post* during the 2002 season that the crucial balance between grass roots traditions and modern business practices would be hard to achieve unless there was balance at the top. Mexted believed the board didn't have enough "rugby people", and that businessmen dominated it. "I would be the last person to challenge their business acumen, but there needs to be a balance. I'm not saying they don't understand rugby issues; they probably do. But there needs to be people who were lucky enough to be exposed to how the whole thing works and what's important."

Over the past few years, it's been the board that has devised strategy for the Rugby Union. This is bizarre. The union employs a senior management team, who, overseen by the Chief Executive, are in charge of various departments: Commercial, Rugby, All Blacks and other national teams, Finance, Legal, Support Services and Communications. Amazingly it hasn't been this group that formulated strategy. This job fell to Chief Executive Rutherford and selected board members. This is one of the systems the new Chief Executive must surely change.

You would assume that the senior union staff, who think about rugby throughout their working days, would be responsible for putting together the policy, which would then go to the board for consideration and endorsement. Instead Rutherford, plus some board members, who, let's face it, have other things to do in their working lives besides think about rugby, took on this responsibility. This method of doing things caused problems and frustrations for senior union staff, who felt decisions were being made by people not closely in touch with the day-to-day activities of the union and not always aware of the implications of the plans they made.

Perhaps the union figured it had to get some value from its directors, who annually share more than $200,000 in fees. This payment of directors is, again, a major departure from the union's council days, when people like Bob Stuart, Pat Gill, Merlin Shannon, David Galvin, Ivan Vodanovich and Graham Atkin served without pay, but expected to get invited to official functions and be given free tickets for important matches by way of thanks.

It was interesting that at the union's 2002 annual meeting, the then board Chairman, McCaw, had his fee increased to $50,000. It's hard to see what grounds there were for an increase, as it had hardly been a stellar time for the Rugby Union, quite apart from the World Cup debacle. In his presentation to the annual meeting, Chief Executive Rutherford rated the Rugby Union's performances for the previous year 67 out of 100 for meeting its targets in game development, competitions, rep team, governance and financial.

While discussing the annual report, it should not go without comment that possible areas of conflict between directors and the Rugby Union were mentioned in the notes to the financial accounts. Decades ago, the finger used to be pointed at the firm of Morrison and Vodanovich, the men's clothing shop situated in Featherston St, Wellington, because they had the rights to ticket sales for major matches at Athletic Park. There would be queues of people outside the shop, which in the end can't have been bad for business for these two long-serving national rugby administrators.

But that was chicken feed compared to what was revealed in the notes to the annual report. There we learnt that during the 2001 year:

- Rob Fisher was a partner of the law firm Simpson Grierson. The NZRFU and its subsidiaries received services from Simpson Grierson, based on normal commercial terms, and in 2001 these totalled $703,820.
- Murray McCaw was the Chief Executive Officer of Infinity Solutions Limited and a non-executive director of Infinity Solutions Ltd. The NZRFU and its subsidiaries received services from Infinity Solutions Ltd on normal commercial terms, and in 2001 these totalled $514,240.

Rob Fisher and Murray McCaw remained directors of the union until forced out by the Eichelbaum report. The notes did not say if this work was tendered, as required by the policies of the Rugby Union. It would be disappointing if it was not.

Compaq Computer Systems was previously a large sponsor of the New Zealand Rugby Union and now is not. Compaq, both a sponsor and a supplier, was replaced by the board Chairman's company, not as a sponsor, but as a supplier only on "normal commercial terms". Did the board do all it could to keep the relationship with Compaq? Was what happened best for the Rugby Union in the long term?

It's been eight years now since the Boston Report was prepared and seven since the subsequent administrative structure revamp was adopted.

At the time there was a recommendation that the situation would be reviewed regularly, at least every two years. To my knowledge, just one review has taken place, in 2000, when the Boston Consulting Group had a look at how things were progressing in the professional era. Any recommendations they made, though, were largely overtaken by the report prepared shortly after by Accenture for Sanzar. Both reports contained some good material but, for the ordinary punter, things rolled along virtually unchanged. Yet the Rugby Union remains an incorporated society, not a private business company, and still operates on behalf of affiliated clubs and provincial unions.

THEY WORK HARD, BUT DOES IT WORK?

The professionalisation of the game has certainly raised a number of issues that the New Zealand union would never have had to consider previously — transfer fees, post-rugby programmes for players, contracts for players, referees and coaches, and tax issues. But quite apart from that, one of the biggest problems facing the Rugby Union has been its leadership. Behind his back, staff were fiercely critical of Rutherford, describing him as a ditherer, a good enough bloke but a person who could not make a decision and stick with it. Rutherford was short on charisma and brought little stature to his job.

From the 1960s to the '80s, leading rugby officials like Tom Morrison, Jack Sullivan, Tom Pearce, Ces Blazey, Ron Don, Russ Thomas and JJ Stewart had a certain presence. They were well-known public figures who reflected rugby's standing in the community. Until they gained a level of notoriety because of their botch-up over the hosting of the World Cup, Rutherford and union board Chairman Murray McCaw could have walked down Lambton Quay or Queen Street and hardly been recognised.

Rutherford did make some good decisions. It was obvious that New Zealand rugby had lost a very large number of television viewers with the decision to give the live rights to major matches to pay-for-view Sky. Right from when he took over from David Moffett as Chief Executive, Rutherford grasped the importance of exposing rugby through television and during his time in charge the New Zealand union paid for some lower grade rugby to be shown on TV3 and organised for a few college matches to be shown on TVNZ. This cannot but help expose rugby to an audience that does not subscribe to Sky TV and must therefore benefit rugby.

The challenge for the new Chief Executive is to run the Rugby Union more tightly and efficiently. Tew, if given the job permanently, would be more visible than Rutherford because he enjoys being interviewed and often seeks out the media. He is well-spoken and has a certain presence. He ran Canterbury rugby well and there are hopes that he might be the person to galvanise things at the New Zealand union. Here's hoping.

So what sort of work *is* being done by the New Zealand union? It was revealing to read these comments in Rutherford's report to the 2002 annual meeting: "There was plenty of confusion about who should do what. As most of the money in New Zealand rugby was earned at national level, there has been a tendency to create positions at the national level to do things that we have now clearly agreed are provincial responsibilities.

"The other tendency was to do things like have the national union appoint coaches of the Super 12 teams or interfere with the marketing decisions of the Super 12 franchises. This trend has been reversed and wherever possible resources, processes and accountabilities have been put in place at the local level."

It was interesting to learn that Rutherford was aware of this problem. It has certainly looked as if the New Zealand union didn't want to let provinces run their own business, as they have done successfully for decades. A good example has been the staging of test matches. Provincial unions used to run without too much bother tests in their own area. Now the NZRFU sends in its own staffers to test venues. They are easily picked out in their suitably-emblazoned black jackets. From my observation, this causes resentment on the part of provincial administrators.

There is a vast amount of wasted effort in the union offices. In the communications area, with which I am most familiar, press releases in the form of email and fax pour from the union. Most are binned or deleted without even being read. During some seasons, several pages are issued each week on club competitions and each week, too, there is provided a comprehensive preview of the NPC. The NPC information merely duplicates what the news media is already doing for itself, and seems to me to be an example of people trying to look busy, rather than working constructively.

For a company with an annual turnover of about $80 million (expected to top $100 million within two or three years), the size of the staff is average to small. New Zealand Rugby Union officials point out, by way of comparison, that the Scotland Rugby Union employs 90 staff and the Australian union's staff is much bigger than New Zealand's.

However, comparing the NZRFU staff numbers to Scotland's is somewhat disingenuous. The Scotland union owns Murrayfield and that requires significant staffing. Incidentally, Ireland owns Lansdowne Road and the England union owns Twickenham. The NZRFU owns no grounds at all.

Further, unions like Scotland and Australia don't have a provincial union system like ours. Hundreds of people are employed in New Zealand by provincial unions and their job is to attend to rugby at grassroots level.

People in the Rugby Union no doubt work very hard. They claim they are working 50 hours a week and more, and perhaps some are. But to what effect? Staff members have told me that under Rutherford they operated in a very counter-productive fashion, having meetings, making half-decisions, reviewing those decisions, having more meetings, making new decisions. They hope things will improve under the new Chief Executive.

Many of these staff are highly competent people, frustrated at not being able to do a better job. Peter Ciurlionis, a former policeman who later worked as an Income Support Service manager, led the Rugby Union's Finance team efficiently for some years. Ciurlionis, who had a staff of five, left the union in November 2001 and was finally replaced, after a long delay, by Therese Walsh.

Former journalist and media consultant Peter Parussini leads the Communications group that over the past few years has included people like James Funnell and journalists Anna Kominik, Dave Worsley and Matt McIlraith. Stephen Cottrell, the former Otago player, heads the Legal section.

One of the key union staffers is Trevor McKewen, who is the general manager of Commercial, a department that has a staff of 11. McKewen has a colourful background that involves time as a newspaper sports editor, as one of the Super League officials and as the Chief Executive of the Warriors rugby league club. Tew was, until his elevation in July 2002, the general manager Rugby. Other staff includes an IT manager and an outfitting officer.

Beyond head office are the 30-plus staff coaches, plus many part-timers and casuals, including such well-known figures as Murray Mexted, Richard Loe, Dave Loveridge and Earle Kirton.

DO MANY HANDS MAKE LIGHT WORK?

The expansion in staff numbers over the past decade is well illustrated by the number of staff the union now sends on tour with the All Blacks.

In 1967 Charlie Saxton managed and Fred Allen coached 30 All Blacks through a 17-match tour of Canada, Britain and France. Their backup was provided by a secretary appointed by the Home Unions, and a baggage man. A local liaison officer travelled with the team. At the end of 2001, John Mitchell took the All Blacks on a five-match tour of Ireland, Scotland and Argentina. Not only did his team contain 30 players (excluding Jason Spice, who travelled to Argentina as a replacement), but the New Zealand team management comprised manager Andrew Martin, coach Mitchell, coaching co-ordinator Robbie Deans, assistant manager Gilbert Enoka, doctor John Mayhew, fitness trainer Mike Anthony, technical adviser Nico Le Roux, physiotherapist Paul Annear, media liaison officer James Funnell, sponsor's rep Paul Scoringe, forward coach Richard Loe and throwing coach Ross Nesdale. Don't smile: the list could easily have been longer. Only 30 players were selected, down from the 36 originally mooted. Kicking coach Daryl Halligan did not make the trip in the end. And, for this tour, it was decided to dispense with the services of a biomechanist and a masseur, while because of the takeover at the top, the co-selectors (in this case Peter Thorburn, Tony Gilbert and Wayne Smith) did not travel.

This is the professional era. One spin-off seems to be the attitude of why use two people when you can use four? Why use four when you can use eight? And yet what possible value could a kicking coach add when the tour management already included Deans, one of the finest kickers in New Zealand rugby history, and the team's best kicker was Andrew Mehrtens, arguably the world's best goal-kicker? Whatever happened to a team pooling its resources?

"The funny thing about it," says Fred Allen "is you wonder if anyone is actually coaching them. I always wanted to be the coach, the boss, the one guy in charge. It must be bloody distracting now with all sorts of team personnel running round in circles, trying to look busy, and I wonder if they are getting good, simple advice. I went to a Carbine Club luncheon at Eden Park a while back and I was in the toilets when I ran into Carlos Spencer. Now he has some great rugby skills, but never uses half of them. I said to him, 'You don't know me. I'm just some old bugger. But there are two or three things I'd like to suggest.' At this stage you think, 'He's young and getting paid a fortune. Is his head too big to listen to advice?' I asked him how old he was and he said 25 or 26, I can't remember. I told him he had four or five years of his best rugby in front of him and it was time he started playing to his potential. So I talked to him about how to work the blind, the double tap through, things like that.

I said he usually went too far probing and looking, all the sort of stuff one first-five can tell another.

"He went out and played a blinder against Wellington on the Saturday. Maybe it had nothing to do with me. But I do know he was listening and it seemed he was having some ideas put to him he hadn't thought of before. You wonder what all the head-shrinkers and the rest of them are there for. It's bloody ridiculous."

POOR ADMINISTRATION

In researching this book, I was far from impressed with some areas of the Rugby Union. It is amazing that for all its income since 1995, the union has only in the past year or so actually seriously endeavoured to find out how many registered players it has in New Zealand. Until 2002 it had not made any real attempts to find out why so many junior players were leaving the game. These are the sorts of basic issues that you'd think the union would have investigated thoroughly, but that has not happened.

Another area in which the union has seemed both indecisive and ineffective has been over the exodus of good players leaving New Zealand. Not just former test, or current representative players, but good, solid club-level players. They're heading away in droves to Japan, Britain, Spain, Italy, France and other parts, and their absence is proving devastating to New Zealand rugby. It is greatly hurting the standard of club rugby and draining the country of potential coaches, referees and administrators.

The Rugby Union responds disappointingly to crises like these and can appear petty, truculent and arrogant when crossed. In 1998 it received the news that Auckland coach Graham Henry intended to leave New Zealand to coach the Welsh test side. The union did not react well. They had Henry on contract but Wales bought it out. The union then introduced a rule — often called the Henry Rule — that people who have coached national teams overseas were ineligible to ever coach the All Blacks. Not surprisingly, the union's reaction was seen for what it was — churlish and vindictive — and the Henry Rule has now been altered. John Mitchell, former assistant England coach, was eligible to coach the All Blacks in 2001.

The New Zealand Rugby Union used to hold what was termed a "wool sale" in Wellington at the end of the season. That's when the rep calendar for the following year would be sorted out. There were all sorts of tradeoffs, favours, compromises and concessions. It was quite comical to follow the bartering but, at the end of it, officials went away having done the best by their province.

If we look at the NPC draw now, we find that it is a shambles, especially in the second and third divisions, where teams can be scheduled to play away from home for a month or more on end. Instead of spreading matches around different venues, lower division teams are meeting in the same towns each year. To my mind, the NPC draws have got worse since about 1995, when farmers Merlin Shannon from Manawatu and David Galvin from Wairarapa-Bush, both union councillors, stopped doing them. These days the draws are done in-house — I understand they are the responsibility of Neil Sorensen — and criticism seems to be ignored.

Terry McLean, the doyen of New Zealand rugby journalists, was presented with the Steinlager Salver at the 2001 Rugby Awards ceremony at Auckland's Sheraton Hotel. McLean struck a chord when he chided the union in his speech. In the context of the occasion, his criticism of various aspects of union administration might not have seemed particularly appropriate, but there was a clear impression that evening that many people at the function agreed with him. It wasn't the happiest of occasions for the union. Invitations stated that it was black tie, which most took to mean a formal, sit-down dinner was being held. Instead it was no more than a cocktail evening and not a memorable one at that. Food was sparse, many elderly guests and their wives stood for hours, and the TV link with Britain for Todd Blackadder and Brendan Laney broke down. Many of the sponsors there were not impressed.

The union, in its drive to promote top-level rugby and so reap financial rewards through sponsorships and advertising, seems far less concerned with the grassroots level of the game. We could excuse the union in 1995 for throwing money at the All Blacks to get them to sign. At that time there was a rival bidder seeking the players' signatures and the union was desperate to hold on to its players. At a critical point of the negotiations, when the New Zealand union had Sean Fitzpatrick back in the fold and was just about to hold a triumphant press conference announcing that fact, Fitzpatrick hit them with another demand — he wanted a further $50,000 because he was the All Black captain, and, presumably, needed compensation for the onerous extra duties the job entailed. Rugby Union boss Richie Guy hesitated only a few seconds. He knew Fitzpatrick had him over a barrel. The media was waiting and the Rugby Union could not afford *not* to produce Fitzpatrick. In the time it took to click his fingers, Fitzpatrick had earned an extra $50,000 a year. They were mad times.

In 1995 players were getting a minimum — and I stress minimum — of $150,000 to commit to Super 12 and the NPC. That figure these days, now that the Rugby Union is negotiating more from a position of strength, and the threat from rugby league having dissipated, has shrunk to $65,000. Surely the New Zealand union should ensure when re-negotiating contracts, that players are compelled to give something back to the game, by making a stipulated number of appearances at schools and clubs.

CORPORATISATION RUN AMOK

Concern about the corporatisation of rugby can be seen everywhere. Lin Colling has several times called for New Zealand rugby to return to some of its old values by re-emphasising the importance of club and provincial competitions and steering away from the corporate culture and mentality that he believes is having a suffocating effect on the game.

"Rugby's basic problem," says Colling, "is that it is now being run by non-rugby people. Rugby has lost control of its own destiny now that the people making the decisions are guided by marketeers and what is best for television and sponsorships."

Even the *New Zealand Rugby Almanack*, which normally concerns itself more with the facts and statistics of the game, was roused to make some strong comments in the 2002 edition. Clive Akers and Geoff Miller dwelt at length on the subject in their editorial, noting: "While professional is the noun, commercial is the adjective that best describes the top end of the current rugby industry. If nothing more or new is created in the commercial world, it is then very much a case of the rich getting richer and the poor getting poorer . . . and being rich to start with is a decided advantage . . ."

Or, as John Hart says, "The rich are getting richer, the strong are getting stronger, and the rest are being left to fend for themselves too much."

The *Rugby Almanack* spoke of the spat during 2001 between the Rugby Union and former sponsor Canterbury International over the use of the Invincibles jersey: "That was a long way from the man in the street. The image of this spat was that of big brother coming down heavily — a stance not guaranteed to win popularity, no matter how sound it is commercially. The current image of the NZRFU is not unlike the image of a government department head office."

The editorial for 2002 ran to nearly three pages and more than half of it was devoted to the commercial aspects of the game. It's an indication of where rugby has gone.

The battle with Canterbury International is a good illustration of the naivety and ineffectiveness of the Rugby Union. Basically, the Rugby Union was seeking to preserve its ownership of the All Blacks. The union knows its most powerful marketing tool is the All Blacks and is desperate not to allow other commercial interests to cash in. But in 2001 it lost its case when Canterbury International decided to manufacture and sell Invincibles jerseys, Invincibles being the name given to Cliff Porter's unbeaten 1924–25 All Black team.

In 1996 former All Black Gary Cunningham had asked the union if he could use the Invincibles trademark for some private ventures, which the union understood would be relatively small in scope. The union, while not breathlessly happy about this, raised no objection, perhaps because Cunningham was a former All Black. Three years later Cunningham sold the Invincibles trademark rights to Canterbury.

Already the New Zealand union has squandered any chance of being able to retain exclusively and market the Silver Fern that its teams wear. In 1924 the Government asked the Rugby Union if it wished to have exclusive rights to the Silver Fern but the union, whose Chairman at the time was Stan Dean, declined the offer, a decision which today's union employees must rue. In the 1980s, when Andy Haden was doing some work for the union, it was decided to design a new Silver Fern with a view to getting some sort of exclusive rights to it. But at the same time, the union raised no objections when other sports bodies such as New Zealand Cricket and Soccer, fielded their national teams with silver ferns of very similar design.

In making his ruling in the 2001 NZRFU v Canterbury International case, Justice Doogue said that in his judgment the All Blacks were a part of New Zealand history and the New Zealand Rugby Football Union didn't have exclusive rights to All Black imagery. In commercial terms, it was a chilling statement for the union to hear. But maybe Justice Doogue grasped better than the union the fact that rugby, and the All Blacks, belong to all New Zealanders.

It would behove the union to heed that message, and use it as the basis of its decision-making, because it seems to have forgotten or overlooked the fact in recent years.

part TWO

RUGBY AT THE TOP LEVEL

chapterTHREE

THE **INTERNATIONAL** GAME

THE ALL BLACKS AS PROFESSIONALS

Sean Fitzpatrick is my personal touchstone when I seek to compare the All Blacks of before and now. I interviewed Fitzpatrick in 1989, when he had been an All Black for three years. He was a carpenter by trade and we spoke at a house he was working on near Newmarket. He put down his tools for half an hour and gradually, as we spoke, the sweat on his brow disappeared and his shirt, which had been wringing wet, began to dry. He was amiable, knew what he wanted to say and what he didn't, and gave me a good interview.

Now fast-forward a decade to early 1999. Keith Quinn was doing some television interviews for the outstanding series "Legends of the All Blacks". It was the day an interview with Fitzpatrick had been arranged. It wasn't easy securing the interview, not because Fitzpatrick was unwilling, but because, even though he had retired from playing, he was still heavily in demand. He was a busy man. Anyway, it was arranged he would meet Quinn and they would drive back to Fitzpatrick's beautiful house in Remuera, to do the filming. As they drove up his driveway, Fitzpatrick looked across at the house next door where some carpenters were hard at work, sweating profusely on a scorchingly hot day. Fitzpatrick allowed himself a slight smile and said, "There but for the grace of God . . ."

Fitzpatrick was good to the All Blacks. He gave them 12 years of yeoman service and became a legendary rugby player. But they were good to him, too. In that time he progressed from being a carpenter to an extremely well-paid professional sportsman. Even when Fitzpatrick retired (after a record 92 tests — 51 as captain), his earning power barely diminished, for he was employed by the Rugby Union in a variety of capacities. In addition he was offered more lucrative speaking engagements than he was able to accept and a number of other commercial opportunities.

Over the years, Fitzpatrick didn't really change much. He probably mellowed a little off the park, and his gamesmanship on the field became a little more refined, but he remained a good bloke.

If Fitzpatrick's personality didn't change during his career, the image of the All Blacks in that time certainly did. In the mid-1980s, All Blacks were not professionals. They were carpenters, schoolteachers, salesmen, farmers. They held down jobs and juggled their training and playing commitments as best they could. They played a lot of club rugby and could be seen regularly at their local clubrooms.

By the late 1990s, the All Blacks were extremely wealthy young men earning upwards of $250,000 a year. Most had formed companies and invested their earnings in property or businesses. Any club affiliation was nominal. They were fulltime rugby players, with plenty of time for training, travelling and playing. Their lifestyles were far removed from those of ordinary New Zealanders.

Until the 1980s, rugby players wanted to be All Blacks for one reason: the honour. They did not become rich through wearing the famed black jersey, but they would run barefoot over broken glass to earn the privilege of being an All Black. No-one questioned their motives. Imagine suggesting that Kevin Skinner or Graham Mourie wanted to be All Blacks for any reason other than the honour of representing their country in our national game.

By the late 1990s, that was no longer the case. Josh Kronfeld is as good an example as any. In 1995 it was Kronfeld, just turned 24 and with only a handful of test matches under his belt, who, with Otago teammate Jeff Wilson, eventually turned his back on the World Rugby Corporation contract and decided to stick with the New Zealand Rugby Union. Kronfeld liked being an All Black and wanted a lot more of it (not that his decision hurt him financially).

His attitude was different from that of some of the seasoned pros in that 1995 All Black squad — men like Richard Loe, Mike Brewer and Fitzpatrick — who appeared more than ready to throw in their lot with the rebel WRC when it seemed that was where the most money was to be made, even if it meant closing their All Black careers.

By the end of 2000, the wheel had turned the full circle. Kronfeld had now played 54 tests and was 29 years of age. He was still widely regarded as the best flanker in New Zealand and could have easily continued his All Black career.

But now it was not so important for Kronfeld to represent the All Blacks. Now he wanted to make as much money as possible while his body held together. So he signed a substantial deal with the Leicester Tigers in England and retired from test rugby.

With the advent of professional rugby, being an All Black is no longer the be-all and end-all, even for a player as committed as Kronfeld. He is an example of the way rugby has gone. Ian Jones, Alama Ieremia, Todd Blackadder, Lee Stensness, Daryl Gibson, Bruce Reihana, Mark Mayerhofler and many dozens more former All Blacks have headed overseas to cash in on their ability and reputation, rather than stay in New Zealand and fight to try to regain their test spots.

That's what the professional era has done for the All Black image. It means that the ordinary All Black fan has a cloud of doubt in his mind. Is this player or that player giving his all to the team because he is so proud to be an All Black, or is his first concern the money?

Former All Black fullback Bob Scott summed it up like this: "I played because I wanted to perform and to entertain people and enjoy myself, and to help my team. Now it's all about the big money. I cried one time when we lost. I sat in the dressing room in South Africa and cried. That's how much it meant to me. Now the players run round after a game and shake each other's hands and smile. Why should they worry? They have another game next week, and another one the week after. From my perspective, the money thing has done a lot to change attitudes of players."

Fred Allen says: "You'd never get them to admit it, but the All Blacks are out there playing for money now. That's my opinion, honestly. They say they are playing for pride, but I don't see the same tremendous feeling that former All Blacks had when they pulled on the black jersey. The passion is missing. It's definitely the money. Who'd have believed it?

"I turned down an offer of £4500 to play league for Wigan. I was on tour with the Kiwis at the time. It was the end of the war. I didn't have any money and the offer was mighty tempting. It was a helluva lot of money for those days. But I wanted to be an All Black, and I wanted to do my best for New Zealand rugby. That was my motivation and it never changed. I was offered 150,000 grand to coach the Cavaliers in South Africa, but I turned that down too, because I thought the Cavaliers tour was not a good thing for rugby. You really cared about the game. I don't believe that's the case now."

All Black midfielder Pita Alatini, talking to Brent Edwards in the *Otago Daily Times* in 2001, said: "Money can never buy the All Black jersey. When you wear it, it's like a flashback to all the players you've seen wear the black jersey when you were a kid." Alatini was 25 years of age and had played 10 tests when he made those comments. It will be interesting to watch Alatini's career choices in three years' time.

From my observation, All Blacks stay in New Zealand for the lifestyle and the jersey. When they want a change of lifestyle, or the thrill of wearing the jersey dulls a bit, they look overseas for richer financial pastures.

John Hart defends the All Blacks stoutly on this issue. "I hear the comment all the time that the players are only there for the money. It's just not a fact. From what I saw in my time as All Black coach, the money was never the driving force for them. It was sometimes a distraction, though, and they would become greedy. But 99 per cent of them wanted to be All Blacks regardless of the money. Things were a bit different in 1995, when they had two parties vying for their signatures. At that point, the highest bidder was the key, though even then, nearly all of them would have preferred to stay as All Blacks. It's just that they were able to go after the money as well at that point."

However, Hart said, it was noticeable that older players started to think increasingly about the money. "I had some players, very high-profile and with outstanding records, who hung on when I was advising them to retire. They wanted that one last big contract."

THEY'RE NOT NORMAL BLOKES ANY MORE

The All Blacks used to not only represent New Zealand; they used to be ordinary New Zealanders. Not any more. All Blacks now belong to an exclusive rich people's club. In two years they make what most New Zealanders will spend more than 10 years or more trying to earn.

The *New Zealand Herald* touched on this subject on 25 August 2001 in an insightful editorial entitled "All Blacks need the common touch".

It began: "Time was when we felt very close to the All Blacks. But that was when the country's finest players downed milking cups, hammer and even the occasional office notebook to don the black jersey. That was when Colin Meads went into town every Friday to get in the weekly supplies, just like farmers in every corner of the land. Then, the All Blacks were part of the community, and totally accessible. They enjoyed an elevated status, but not an elevated income. Rugby earned them a pittance, even as their efforts enriched the New Zealand Rugby Football Union. No more. Today's All Blacks are wealthy professionals . . .

"It is instructive that the zeal of both the Rugby Union and adidas [the major All Black sponsor] has attracted popular scorn. Many clearly feel the national game is being commercialised to an unacceptable degree, and that All Black images are not solely the preserve of the Rugby Union, so integral are they to our heritage. That heritage involves, first and foremost, a sense of community. Even in a professional era, this must not be betrayed. Regard for players begins to diminish quickly if they are seen as petulant, self-absorbed or wealth-obsessed . . .

"American baseball provides a cautionary tale of where it can all lead. Many fans are totally disenchanted with the mercenary attitude of some of the players. The sense of community upon which even professional sport relies has been shattered. No longer do the people of Boston or Baltimore feel a sense of ownership of their teams. The lesson for rugby is that the All Blacks must not be allowed to become removed. They will never again be like Colin Meads striding the main street of Te Kuiti but, equally, they must not be inaccessible. The balancing act is difficult, but it is not impossible to achieve."

There is little doubt that when the game went professional, some of the romanticism attached to the black jersey went with it. When the All Blacks were amateurs and had jobs like everyone else, they were still the guys down the road who just happened to be extra good at rugby. Once upon a time we'd all get up in the middle of the night to watch the mixture of farmers, teachers and students take on Wales at Cardiff Arms Park or South Africa at Ellis Park. To an extent we identified with them. It's harder now they have flash sports cars, earn hundreds of thousands of dollars a year, have their own companies and probably own several properties spread around the country.

"SHOW ME THE MONEY"

At the end of 2001, more than 90 per cent of New Zealand's top players signed the first collective contract with the New Zealand union. It means the players are now employed by a company, set up by the union, called New Zealand Rugby Promotions. They are protected by standard core conditions, including minimum salaries, but retain the right to negotiate individually.

The minimum pay rates set are $65,000 for Super 12 players (including $15,000 for playing in the NPC) and a further $85,000 for those who reach All Black standard. To repeat: these are bare minimum payments. Most regular All Blacks are receiving $300,000 a season for playing (excluding any endorsements, advertising or individual sponsor deals), some substantially more than that. For instance, All Blacks also negotiate with their provincial unions before they play NPC. So a player like Andrew Mehrtens might receive the standard $15,000 from the New Zealand union for playing in the NPC, but he might well be receiving a further $100,000 from the Canterbury union for those matches. There are cases of players who are no more than fringe All Blacks being offered close to $100,000 to move provinces.

Other contract details agreed to were that professional players would get four weeks' continuous annual leave and one-off payouts of up to $150,000 if under 30 years of age and forced to retire early on medical grounds. For those 30 and over, the payout would be $100,000.

This is a far cry from the way All Blacks were treated in the 1970s. Dynamic winger Grant Batty told some frightening stories of miserly and unfair administration back in the 1970s in his book (imaginatively entitled *Grant Batty*). Writing in 1977, Batty said: "Probably the major dissatisfaction All Blacks have is the matter of expenses. They don't ask for payment or bonuses, simply reimbursement of out-of-pocket expenses genuinely incurred while representing their country, including loss of wages. Their expenses are invariably cut by the NZRFU by anything up to 30 or 40 per cent. It's ridiculous that a player like Bryan Williams should have his expenses in Christchurch for the second test in 1977 cut from $25 to $19 when you consider the takings for the game were some $200,000 and that Beegee must have attracted tens of thousands of paying spectators through his career."

Batty also reprinted a rather churlish letter from New Zealand team manager Ron Don, complaining about expenses he had incurred at Christchurch before that second test of the 1977 series against the Lions. Batty withdrew from the All Black team just before the match because of a knee injury that eventually forced him to retire from rep rugby. In his letter to Batty, Don complained sternly about toll calls and drinks costs incurred by Batty and the charge of an additional meal for a person described as "Batty's guest". He said he was surprised and disappointed at Batty's actions.

Batty felt Don's letter was grossly insulting. "It made me wonder about all I'd gone through, the training, the pain in South Africa, the knee operation in an effort to get fit for the test series against the Lions. This letter dismissed me as if I was an irresponsible schoolboy." Batty's guest was Reece Williams, the local liaison officer appointed by the Canterbury Rugby Union. The cost of the meal was $4. The drinks were shared by Andy Haden, Lawrie Knight and Batty and cost in total $6. It transpired no toll call was made by Batty.

Talk of toll calls brings to mind a story from the 1972–73 All Black tour of Britain and France. The players were away for four months and slogged their way through 32 matches. These were the strictly amateur days, when players were given 75p ($1.50) a day for expenses. Veterans from that tour talk about how each day they would have to choose between buying themselves a beer or a stamp. If they had a beer, they posted no letter home that day. The New Zealand union, in a display of largesse, decided to give all the players a Christmas present, and that it would be a three-minute toll call home to New Zealand. On Christmas Eve, the players, from captain Ian Kirkpatrick and vice-captain Sid Going down to international fledglings like lock Andy Haden, lined up by the hotel phone waiting their turn to make their call home. When I see the All Blacks on their team bus now, each with a mobile phone pressed to his ear, that story always comes to mind.

The level of luxury enjoyed by today's stars, with business class air travel, fine hotels, massive amounts of sponsors' products and big pay packets, is in stark contrast to the treatment meted out to New Zealand representatives of previous decades. Yet the All Black reputation, which is what today's sponsors and advertisers are paying for, was built by players like Batty and Williams. Do today's All Blacks realise they are earning what they are on the backs of these former stars? "If they do," one outstanding ex-All Black told me, "they do their best not to acknowledge it. I think it makes them slightly uncomfortable."

No-one doubted why Colin Meads played. He cherished that silver fern and his spot in the All Blacks. It took a near-fatal car accident to hasten his exit from test rugby at the age of 35. Otherwise he wasn't going anywhere. The question now is: would the All Blacks play for free? No-one is asking them to, of course. Rather, it's a question of motive. Are they playing to make money or to represent their country?

The mere suggestion of money being the prime motivation is scary.

The All Blacks deserve to be paid well. They are outstanding sportsmen. But does money now over-ride honour and pride? It's hard to be emphatic about this. It takes all sorts. Some players would play for nothing except pride. Others wouldn't cross the road now if they weren't paid to do so. It's the trend that's concerning. It seems it's getting to be more about money and less about honour.

Andy Haden's answer was similar to those of many I asked. "The only way to test it for sure," said Haden, "would be to select the team, then call all the players together and say there's to be no money for this game, then ask who is staying. You'd like to think it would be like our best days in the Davis Cup and that players would want to put their country first, but I have a feeling most of the players would bypass it now. My impression is that they are there primarily for the money. I remember the days when you'd follow a test on Saturday by playing for your club on Sunday. You'd maybe have a midweek rep game and then the next test the following Saturday. You played because you loved it. Other factors dominate now."

Norm Hewitt played 23 times for the All Blacks over a span of six years and says his motivation for wanting to represent New Zealand changed over that time. "For a start," he says, "I was desperate to be an All Black. You grow up and being an All Black is such an honour. You strive to win that black jersey. Then after you've been in the team a couple of years and seen the good and the bad of being an All Black, dealt with the administrators, been shafted over contracts and all that, you start thinking much more about the money. How much can you make by being an All Black?

"This lasted a few years for me. Then in my case I spent my last year or two genuinely trying to help others and really cherishing my time in the All Blacks. I remember offering to give Anton Oliver, who was the promising young hooker back then, some tips and he looked at me and asked me why I would possibly want to help him, a rival for the hooker's position."

But, says Hewitt, there are many examples of players seeing the All Black jersey as simply a bigger pay cheque. "I was a little shocked one day when Robin Brooke told me that he was pleased he'd been made All Black vice-captain because it meant an increase in his pay. He was injured at the time and couldn't get on the field, but he didn't care. He was more interested in the fact that he was going to be paid more money."

The money for top players is considerable and should not be over-looked. As one All Black told me: "When it comes to the first of the month and you see another $25,000 go into your account, that's a big reason to want to stay in top rugby."

Teenage boys with athletic talent are now shunning academic careers in the hope that they'll make a success of rugby and win Super 12 and All Black contracts. They are making financial decisions in their mid-teens to go for the big money and play rugby. That sort of thinking eats away at the special magic of New Zealand rugby.

Ricki Ellison, the New Zealander who cracked it big in American gridiron, offered the All Blacks some sensible advice when he addressed them in early 1996. Ellison won four SuperBowl titles with the San Francisco 49ers, and had an annual salary of more than $1 million during most of his 10-year career. Speaking to the All Blacks at a specially-organised seminar in Auckland, Ellison passed on two particularly relevant pieces of wisdom. He warned All Blacks, who were then new to the professional ranks, to be very wary of agents and "other commercial predators" and, even more importantly, to be sure they knew why they were playing professional sport.

He said the principal motivation should not be to see how much they could earn, but to strive for levels of excellence: "Don't get too carried away with the professional aspects of the game, or you will be side-tracked. You must play for each other, not for your coaches, the media or the money."

THE WORLD CUP CYCLE

Two factors have dramatically changed the face of international rugby over the past 15 years — the introduction of the World Cup and the advent of professionalism. In a sense, the two are inextricably linked.

The World Cup has radically altered the rugby landscape. Now rugby runs in four-year cycles. Players and coaches are chosen with the next World Cup in mind. As an example, did Wayne Smith drop Todd Blackadder from the All Black captaincy at the start of the 2001 season because Blackadder had suddenly become a worse player than he was the year before, or because he doubted Blackadder would still be an effective international player by the time the next World Cup rolled around, $2\frac{1}{2}$ years later?

Was Smith himself dumped as All Black coach later in 2001 because he wasn't up to it, or because New Zealand Rugby Union officials felt that the two years before the next World Cup was the minimum time a replacement (who turned out to be John Mitchell) would require to prepare for the tournament? If there hadn't been a World Cup looming, would Smith have been sent packing?

It's the same in any country. Players and coaches and teams are judged by their World Cup results. Bob Dwyer and Rod Macqueen are therefore regarded in Australia as great rugby coaches, having both delivered World Cup triumphs. Conversely, Graham Henry and Clive Woodward failed to deliver in 1999 for Wales and England respectively, which puts a cloud over their coaching records.

Alex Wyllie is statistically the most successful All Black coach since Fred Allen stepped down in 1969 (the jury is still out on John Mitchell), and is challenged only by Jack Gleeson. Wyllie's teams won 86 per cent of tests they played, which is way above Brian Lochore (78 per cent), John Hart (75 per cent), Wayne Smith (71 per cent) and Laurie Mains (68 per cent). Yet Wyllie is not judged by history to have been a resounding success. Why? He led the All Blacks through 38 matches without defeat from 1988–90. We wouldn't mind a winning sequence like that now. Wyllie's problem: the All Blacks were bundled out in the 1991 World Cup semi-finals. True they lost to eventual champions Australia, and true they easily won the third place play-off against Scotland. But third place by the defending champions wasn't good enough to satisfy a rugby-mad public. Because of that World Cup defeat, history regards Wyllie as having been no more than a reasonable All Black coach, and certainly not the hugely successful coach he was.

John Hart produced All Black teams that performed brilliantly in his first two seasons in the job, 1996 and 1997. His team became the first from New Zealand to win a series in South Africa, thus ending a jinx of nearly 70 years. After two years, Hart's All Blacks had won the Tri-Nations trophy twice, had the Bledisloe Cup in safekeeping, and had lost just once in 23 tests. Yet Hart's reign ended in controversy and he was widely condemned because his All Black team capitulated at the 1999 World Cup, squandering a 24-10 lead in the semi-final against France. Hart's All Blacks lost five matches in succession in 1998, a horror run, yet that would have been overlooked if he'd been able to deliver the 1999 World Cup.

Laurie Mains had a grim time of it in his first three years as All Black coach. In 1992, he dropped a test to a World XV that had been hastily thrown together, and lost the Bledisloe Cup series in Australia. The following year, Mains' All Blacks lost to England at Twickenham. In 1994 they lost both tests at home to France and to Australia in Sydney. There were some bright spots, including victory at home over South Africa (two wins and a draw), but generally his team's record was spotty and he looked to be struggling. He very nearly lost his job at the end of the 1994 season. But in 1995, with brilliant young players like Andrew Mehrtens, Jonah Lomu and Josh Kronfeld having come on board, Mains' team suddenly revived. The All Blacks were the best team at the 1995 World Cup and if they had won a tight final over South Africa — don't forget, they lost only in extra time and then only because of two drop goals, one that missed and one that went over — he would have been saluted as an all-conquering coach.

Brian Lochore's place in the All Black coaching pantheon is secure. BJ, as the country knows him, delivered the World Cup to New Zealand in 1987 when his side, boasting such brilliant young talent as Michael Jones, John Kirwan, Sean Fitzpatrick and John Gallagher, and a core of hardened and well-performed players, waltzed away with the World Cup. Never mind that Lochore's All Blacks had almost lost a test to Argentina in 1985, had been outplayed in the Bledisloe Cup series of 1986 and had only split a two-test series in France that year. By winning the World Cup, Lochore cemented his reputation as a coach.

Such is the importance in the public mind of the World Cup. Because of that, coaches tend to indulge in four-year plans. Administrators, in consultation with those coaches, try (not always successfully) to plan schedules that will bring the national team to a peak every fourth year.

So that's one change from what is affectionately termed "the good old days". Until the advent of the World Cup, international rugby generally comprised a few traditional tournaments, such as the Five Nations, a few one-off matches and, most important of all, long tours, during which the visiting team played a test series of three, four or five matches, plus any number of provincial games.

WHERE DID ALL THE TOURS GO?

Those tours were the lifeblood of international rugby. To New Zealanders, they not only meant that every few years the Lions or Springboks would play a major series, but they meant that international stars would be seen in such centres as Blenheim, Greymouth, Timaru and Whangarei; Napier, New Plymouth and Taumarunui; Masterton, Invercargill and Ashburton.

Those matches were good battles, too. Before the Super 12 ensured that the talent pool of New Zealand rugby was confined largely to five or six cities, every provincial team worth its salt felt able to take on a touring side and, with a combination of parochial support, determination, fire and skill, either beat or push them. There were some shock results.

In 1949, the West Coast beat Australia 17-15 at Greymouth. The same Wallaby team won both tests against New Zealand that year. In 1958, North Auckland, marshalled superbly by Ted Griffin, upset Australia 9-8 at Whangarei, following on from victories over the tourists by Hawke's Bay, Southland and Manawatu. In 1961, South Canterbury outplayed the French side 17-14 in a match that became famous for the walking stick attack of grandmother Pam Marsden on Michel Crauste, after she became disgusted with Crauste's rough play. North Otago fans had their great day in 1962 when their team beat Australia 14-13 at Oamaru. Those Australians provided joy throughout New Zealand — Thames Valley beat them 16-14, and Southland and Canterbury beat them as well.

In the pre-professional days every New Zealand provincial side was formidable. Otago, Canterbury, Auckland, Wellington and Waikato were big Saturday games for touring sides, but there weren't any easy fixtures and Hawke's Bay and Southland were always particularly tough. In 1964, Australia lost 16-10 to Mid-Canterbury at Ashburton; Wanganui-King Country beat the 1966 Lions; Marlborough beat the 1968 French; the 1972 Australians (the Woeful Wallabies as they were dubbed) lost to Otago, West Coast-Buller, Waikato and Hawke's Bay and drew with Bay of Plenty. Wellington, Canterbury and Taranaki beat England in 1973.

Besides the provincial games, other combinations such as the New Zealand Universities and the New Zealand Maori would take on the tourists. The tours went on for perhaps 24 or 25 matches and were massively beneficial to New Zealand rugby. The tourists became extremely well-known to the New Zealand public and rugby was greatly enhanced nationwide. Occasionally a truly great side would tour the country and grab the imagination.

Perhaps the most significant of all tours was that of the 1956 Springboks, when national fervour reached almost wartime proportions. There was great rejoicing when the All Blacks beat Danie Craven's South Africans 11-6 at Eden Park to sew up the series 3-1. Don Clarke, Peter Jones, Kevin Skinner, Ron Jarden and other All Blacks cemented their reputations during that series. Craven addressed the Eden Park crowd and there was prolonged cheering when he said, "It's all yours, New Zealand." Shortly afterwards, Jones amused those same spectators, and a nationwide radio audience, by telling them he was "absolutely buggered".

That was the year that an advertisement was placed in a Christchurch newspaper before the third test: "Refined gentleman wishes to meet cultured widow, view matrimony. Must have independent means and two tickets to third test. Please send photographs of tickets."

The 1937 Springboks came and conquered, earning the reputation as the greatest team to leave New Zealand, a clever description that credited the South Africans for the improvement they made during the tour. Players like Gerry Brand, Louis Babrow, Danie Craven, Philip Nel, Tony Harris, Jan Lotz, the Louw brothers, Pierre de Villiers, Ferdie Bergh, Dai Williams and Freddy Turner were household names at the time and sparked respect, even fear, in the hearts of New Zealand rugby followers.

In 1971 John Dawes led a particularly colourful Lions team to a narrow series win over New Zealand — 2-1 with one drawn. Barry John came and showed New Zealanders what round-the-corner place-kicking was all about. Mike Gibson, Gareth Edwards, JPR Williams, Gerald Davies, David Duckham, Mervyn Davies, Ian McLauchlan, Fergus Slattery, Derek Quinnell, Willie-John McBride . . . these were great players and New Zealand saw a lot of them.

But those days are gone. The All Blacks used to make tremendously long overseas tours, and not just the epic pioneering journeys of the 1905 Originals and 1924 Invincibles, either. In the days before air travel, those early tours were whoppers. The 1888 Natives were away for 14 months. Dave Gallaher's Originals played 35 matches in five months in the United Kingdom, France, Canada and the United States, and you can add another three months for boat travel. Cliff Porter's Invincibles undertook a tour of similar scale — 32 matches in five months, plus the sea voyages. As late as 1972 Ian Kirkpatrick led the All Blacks on a seemingly never-ending journey through Canada, the United States, England, Wales, Ireland, Scotland and France, a tour that lasted 17 weeks and encompassed 32 matches. In 1976, Andy Leslie's All Blacks spent 12 weeks in South Africa, playing four tests and 24 matches overall.

To the average rugby fan, these were great times. There was time to get to know the opposition in lead-up games, to gauge how various New Zealand players were progressing as they vied for test spots, and to see how the coach was moulding the team. The tests, held every few weeks, were highpoints of the tour and were eagerly anticipated.

Now touring teams indulge in Entebbe missions, flying to another country, ripping through yet another series of tests as quickly as possible and returning home. Furthermore, the trend recently has been for All Black coaches to take two teams away, one to play the tests and the other the midweek matches. Sometimes the test players have not even bothered to watch the midweek games. What's happened? Why have the popular long tours been abandoned?

WHEN A TEST IS NOT A TEST

Though players and coaches will tell you differently, test results aren't as important now. The next World Cup is always just around the corner and the great increase in test matches has very much devalued their currency.

Not everyone feels there is too much test rugby. John Hart says that, ideally, the All Blacks would play from seven to ten tests a year. "The end-of-year tours are a killer. That's the big issue. Those tours are what cause burnout. I took a real stand on that issue and got two tours canned. But as for the rest of the year, well, I agree there is a danger of too much rugby. But that's professionalism. We need to service agencies like television and sponsors. You wouldn't want to ruin the product by over-exposing it, but I feel ten tests or less is not a problem. Of course, the timing of those tests is important. From a coach's point of view, playing a test every second week is fine, but not on consecutive weekends."

Hart feels that as rugby becomes ever more a world sport, the sooner the game develops a global season, like tennis, golf and some other major sports, the better.

It took the indomitable Colin Meads 15 seasons to reach his record of 55 tests. Modern players like Christian Cullen, Josh Kronfeld, Jonah Lomu, Justin Marshall and Jeff Wilson have passed their half-century of tests in less than half the time it took Meads. On the other hand, no player has beaten Meads' record of 133 matches for New Zealand, and only Sean Fitzpatrick has even approached the mark. That's because Meads made seven major (at least 10 games) tours during his career, stacking up piles of appearances for his country.

I believe test rugby is going the way of international one-day cricket. There are cricket enthusiasts — and I am one of them — who can recite the result of every Ashes series over the past century, and who know the result of every test series New Zealand played, certainly until about 1990, when the number of matches began to increase seemingly exponentially.

Try that with one-day matches. True cricket followers know the World Cup one-day winners since that tournament began in 1975. But who won the World Series tournament in Australia in 1986? Who won the Sharjah tri-nations tournament in 1992? For that matter, who won the one-day series between New Zealand and Sri Lanka in 1991? When Allan Border (twice), Mark Taylor and Steve Waugh led triumphant Australian teams through Ashes test series in England, what were the results of the one-day contests?

One-day cricket results are largely meaningless. They matter massively at the moment the games are played, but then they're gone, seldom to be thought of again. Unfortunately, it's getting to be like that with test rugby now. Who can remember that it was Samoa, Argentina and France who were beaten by the All Blacks in their first three tests in 2001? There is no way rugby followers in the 1950s would not have known who the All Blacks' tests opponents were a year or two previously.

Once, a test cap was really something. Now they are given away in absurd circumstances. Against Australia at Sydney in 2000, coach Wayne Smith replaced prop Carl Hoeft with Craig Dowd for the last 28 seconds of the match. There was no tactical reason for the change. All it achieved was to give good old Dowdy another test cap.

When we look at the New Zealand rugby record book, we find that Dowd is New Zealand's most capped prop, with 58 test appearances in that position (he had 60 test appearances in all). You have to wonder if this figure has any meaning. In his last test season, 2000, Dowd recorded six test caps, yet only once against Tonga, did he actually start a match. On the other five occasions, he was on the field for only a part, sometimes a small part, of the second half.

The big increase in test matches has rendered rugby records largely meaningless. Players from the professional era dominate the lists for appearances, tries and points-scoring (assisted by the fact that five points are now awarded for a try, instead of three, and then four). The use of tees and non-leather balls, and the high-quality drainage of fields make life vastly easier for modern kickers. Using the record books to try to compare players of different generations requires a lot of ingenuity. For instance, to evaluate the All Blacks' most prolific try-scorers, rather than merely look at the lists of most tries, a slightly more accurate gauge is to work out the ratio of tries scored per match.

TRY-SCORING RATIOS

Compare these two tables, updated to the end of the 2002 Tri-Series:
TOP 10 ALL BLACK TRY-SCORERS IN TEST MATCHES:
Tries

46	Christian Cullen
45	Jeff Wilson
35	John Kirwan
35	Jonah Lomu
23	Tana Umaga

22	Justin Marshall
20	Frank Bunce
19	Stu Wilson
19	Terry Wright
17	Zinzan Brooke

TOP 10 ALL BLACKS BY RATIO OF TRIES/TEST MATCH (MINIMUM 10 TRIES)

Ratio	
.90	Frank Mitchinson
.82	Christian Cullen
.73	Jeff Wilson
.72	Doug Howlett
.72	Marc Ellis
.72	John Gallagher
.63	Terry Wright
.58	Jonah Lomu
.55	Stu Wilson
.55	John Kirwan

In terms of try-scoring ratios, Zinzan Brooke's is 19, whereas Ian Kirkpatrick's is 41, yet at first glance, Brooke looks the more prolific try-scorer. Even this ratio list is not entirely fair, as it does not take account of the number of "try-glut" tests the All Blacks play these days. For instance, Ellis scored six tries in one match against Japan in 1995, while Jeff Wilson scored five against Fiji in 1997 and four against Samoa in 1999. Heavy try-scorers of the past, such as Grant Batty and Ron Jarden, never had that sort of advantage.

For the kickers, too, records are almost meaningless. It is unarguable that modern kickers, with their round-the-corner style, are much more accurate than the toe-kickers of decades past. But they also get far more kicks at goal. Simon Culhane kicked 20 conversions in one match against Japan in 1995. The number of penalty goal attempts per match has trebled.

You almost feel like there should be records for "real" tests and records for "second-rate" tests. It's not such a bad idea. After all, New Zealand coaches have begun to rank their test matches in terms of importance. Australia and South Africa are worthy test opponents and we always field our top combinations against them. But when early-season tests against the likes of Samoa, Argentina and Tonga are played, coaches will experiment. On 16 June 2001, New Zealand met Samoa at the North Harbour Stadium in Albany. While the All Blacks were running on to the field, the world's most famous and feared footballer, Jonah Lomu, was turning out for lowly Wellington club side Wainuiomata at Tawa's Lyndhurst Park.

Andrew Mehrtens, who has been New Zealand's No 1 first five-eighth since 1995, is almost always selected for the major tests of the season. But check back and see how often he has missed the softer tests against the likes of Samoa, Tonga and Argentina early in the domestic season.

This sort of thing makes a mockery of test rugby. How can Lomu's replacement, there only because the opposition is not rated as threatening by the All Black coach, be deserving of a test cap? How can the match therefore be rated as the pinnacle of rugby, as tests should be? If coaches don't feel they need to field their best team, that undermines test rugby's standing.

HOW TO ANNOY A FORMER ALL BLACK

Former All Blacks, who strove so hard and cherished every test cap, generally look with distaste upon today's devaluing of test rugby.

"When I was growing up," says Andy Leslie, "I could tell you the names of every All Black in a touring team. Every All Black team that went overseas was a big deal. Now, it is hard to remember who were in the teams from just a couple of years ago. There are so many matches played that the teams get blurred in your mind."

Commentator Keith Quinn feels that while a test might mean as much on the day of the game, in terms of recollection many of them quickly become hazy in the memory. "They tend to be rat-a-tat-a-tat. Even someone like myself, who is very keen on the statistics side and who tries to keep up with the players and records, struggles. I find myself thinking, 'Did that happen in the Tri-Nations? What game was it? What year?'"

Andy Haden: "I hate what's happening, and so do all my mates I played with. We used to play against the likes of Romania and Fiji and Argentina, but they weren't official test matches. We'd talk to their players and their administrators and hear how difficult it was for them to push ahead with rugby in their countries, where it was such a minor sport. I used to feel sorry for someone like Hugo Porta, who was a truly brilliant first-five but, because he came from Argentina, was confined to minnow status in world rugby.

"So we had a lot of sympathy for their predicament and were very happy to play them. When the All Blacks visited their countries, it gave rugby there a big boost and we liked that. But there is no way we would have regarded matches against those sorts of teams as tests.

"These days they are accorded test status, but it's as plain as could be that they're not genuine tests. Any time a coach deliberately selects a sub-standard team, you have to question the status of the match. I'd be a lot happier if when New Zealand met Argentina or Tonga, for instance, the team was billed as a New Zealand XV, and not given official test status. The New Zealand coach could use the game to field an experimental team. That way the integrity of test matches would be maintained, and the All Black coach could rotate his players. At the moment, the All Blacks line up to play the Bismarck Archipelago or Rotnest Island and it's called a test. There is a need for clear judgment before they roll out the full 21-gun salute. There are second-class tests now. But should there be any such thing? We should say that we aren't fielding our best team because we don't think it merits international status."

Bob Scott on the same issue: "There's so much test rugby now, and so much that is meaningless, that the edge has been taken off. Even test rugby is becoming mundane. The Bledisloe Cup, the Tri-Nations — after a few weeks who cares if we win them or not? People have a take it or leave it attitude towards test rugby now. Imagine saying that in days gone by."

Haden's suggestion has merit, because New Zealand XV matches would still provide good quality rugby to satisfy the demands of television.

Coaches will talk of rotating, of avoiding burnout and other fancy phases. Non-stop loose forward Kel Tremain made five major tours and played his heart out mid-week and on Saturdays. He cherished every match he played for New Zealand. Colin Meads used to get right grouchy when told he was missing a game, even a midweek fixture. "I never wanted any bugger taking my place for any game," he said. "It made me uncomfortable sitting in the stand watching. What if he played so well that he took my place?" Fred Allen felt the same: "I used to want to play in every game and I'd get bloody shitty on tour if I had to miss a game, especially when I was away with the Kiwis."

How can dropping Lomu from the All Blacks be said to avoid burnout when he plays the same day for another team?

Rotating players is a sore point among most former All Blacks, who strove so hard for every test appearance. We should exclude World Cups from this discussion because that is a tournament and different rules apply. But for one-off tests, or series, the practice of rotating players causes consternation. It is a by-product of the professional era, where the introduction of the Super 12 means players are now being asked to play up to 20 test matches, or their equivalent, in six months. John Hart tended to start with his best teams, but Wayne Smith really embraced the concept of rotating his teams, made all the more farcical by him not admitting he was not playing his top lineup. He was, he would claim, "playing the best players for this circumstance", which was a cute way of saying it didn't suit him to put some of his best players on the park.

John Mitchell, during his first tour as All Black coach, went back to the tradition of picking the best team available, and, further, not giving away test caps by making meaningless substitutions a minute or two before the end of the match.

But it didn't take long for Mitchell to adopt the practice of awarding test caps to players who didn't merit them. When the first All Black squad of 2002 was named, for the test against Italy, Leon MacDonald, Greg Somerville, Scott Robertson and Tana Umaga were not chosen. Mitchell said all four players could have been selected if necessary. Minor injury concerns of Umaga and Robertson were mentioned. "We are by no means underestimating Italy," said Mitchell. "No All Black side will ever take any opponent for granted, but we have balanced our immediate needs alongside the bigger picture." Players not deserving of selection in the test side at that moment were being selected because Mitchell was using the opportunity of an international against a minnow like Italy to experiment. And yet the match was billed as a full-blown test match.

If New Zealand are playing so many tests that the All Black coach doesn't feel he can field his best players, then it is blindingly obvious there are too many tests being played. There's only one reason for that. Money. The New Zealand Rugby Union has commitments to television and must provide seven tests a year, five at home. That explains why each season the All Blacks begin with three second-rate tests, followed by four Tri-Nations matches, two at home and two overseas. It's television, and the money it pays, that is running the show.

Except for World Cups, test rugby doesn't really matter much these days, sacrilegious as that sounds. In 1999, New Zealand won the Tri-Nations Trophy, bettering Australia and South Africa in that annual competition. At the end of that year, following a fourth place at the World Cup, how many New Zealand rugby supporters gave a toss about the Tri-Nations silverware nestled snugly in the New Zealand Rugby Union's trophy cabinet in Wellington?

South Africa and Australia, New Zealand's two greatest test opponents of modern times (since the demise of Wales), are terribly over-exposed now. Not only are there two Tri-Nations internationals against each country every year, but the Super 12 competition means the mystique of players from those two countries has long since disappeared. Whereas once a victory over South Africa was cause for national celebration, now it causes little more than a smile of satisfaction. Unless the victory was to take place at a World Cup (and after four such tournaments, New Zealand had beaten neither country in a World Cup), even victories over our major rivals are regarded as somewhat routine.

There are other signs that test rugby has ceased to be especially meaningful. Over the past few years England, Scotland and France have sent such sub-strength teams to New Zealand that they have been derided as a joke. Top players have either refused to tour, been refused leave to tour by their clubs, or not been selected to rest them for other "more important" fixtures. Since when did test matches against the All Blacks rate as unimportant?

Administrators are doing an impressive job of killing interest in test rugby. It seems futile to have a tour if the coach and players don't want to go and if results really don't matter. Why have a Tri-Nations series every year, when there would be more needle and greater public interest if the series was held only every second year? Why not go back to the long tours of yesteryear, when touring teams touched every area of the country?

Again, the answer is simple: money.

HE WHO PAYS THE PIPER...

In 1995, New Zealand, Australia and South Africa signed a 10-year $US550 million deal with Rupert Murdoch's News Corporation group, guaranteeing there would be Super 12 and Tri-Nations competitions available for his company to broadcast for the next 10 years. New Zealand committed to playing seven test matches a year, five at home. That's why there is no chance of the over-exposed Tri-Nations competition being pared back for now. It can't happen, because the three national rugby unions are committed to the annual series of tests. It's also why the Super 12, which so many rugby followers in New Zealand say is hurting domestic rugby, is here to stay.

Because of the deal that was signed in 1995, there is no room on New Zealand's international calendar to host a long winter tour by, say, the Lions. There is room during the international segment of the season for a couple of test matches, perhaps against a Pacific Island team, or Argentina or an under-strength Home Nation side. Then it's into the Tri-Nations.

At the end of the year the All Blacks often go on tour, usually unwillingly. In 1995 they toured France. In 1997 they went to Britain and Ireland. In 1999 there was the World Cup in Britain. In 2000, Wayne Smith took them off to France and Italy. In 2001 John Mitchell had his first experience as All Black coach with tests in Ireland, Scotland and Argentina.

Why undertake these end-of-year tours when the players profess to be exhausted and in need of rest and recuperation? Money.

The New Zealand Rugby Union has a commodity, the All Blacks, which other countries are willing to pay for. New Zealand is bound to provide for television a certain number of test matches each year. To get teams like England and France to tour here (to meet those television requirements), New Zealand must undertake reciprocal tours, whether the players, coaches and officials want them or not.

Television revenue cannot be under-estimated. It accounts for just over half of the New Zealand union's income. If we compare this situation to English soccer, we see that television revenue provides glamour club Manchester United with only 20 per cent of its income. That, in a nutshell, is why the New Zealand union is flogging our top players. They are the union's most valuable commodities.

Successive All Black coaches have complained about too many demands being put on their players. Coaches like Hart, Smith and Mitchell understand only too well that in such a physical game as rugby, there is only so much a player can take. By the time the Super 12, international and NPC phases are over, players need a rest, not another overseas tour. It doesn't make sense to keep asking ever more of the players, except that the All Blacks can earn money for their employers.

This view is absurdly short-sighted and it's time the Rugby Union woke up to the fact. In 1975 an All Black played a five-month season and about 18 first class matches. Now the same player would have to turn out for close to 40 first class games and his season would last nine months. A typical season now comprises about 12 Super 12 games, 10 tests, 10 NPC games and four end-of-year tour matches and maybe the odd sundry outing such as for New Zealand Maori or non-championship rep fixtures. In 1975, top players used to enjoy club matches, Barbarians-type early-season games and lots of rep fixtures against lesser opposition. The level of intensity was a notch or two down from the big stuff. Not now.

Virtually every time a top player takes the field now, he will have to put his body on the line against international-calibre opposition. By comparison, England players are not permitted to play more than 32 matches in a season.

I realise that the New Zealand Rugby Union has to be commercially smart. To fund the professional game, it needs to maximise its income. In the years since the amateur era ended in 1995, the union's annual revenue has risen from $13.8 million to, in 2001, $80.2 million. Its expenditure has increased from $14.9 million to $76.8 million. The bills have to be paid somehow and the All Blacks are the great earner.

The Rugby Union must beware of cooking the goose that lays the golden eggs. If it hammers the All Blacks into the ground, they will start losing more, and therefore become less commercially appealing.

HOW MUCH IS TOO MUCH?

Compared to the All Blacks' workload, most other professional foot-ballers play surprisingly little.

I always feel English soccer players are forced to play an absurd number of games during their excruciatingly long season. Even when canny managers like Alex Ferguson make a point of resting their stars for lesser games, the big names like David Beckham can play 50, even 55, games a year, what with English league, European commitments and internationals. But with all due respect to the multi-talented Beckham, it is surely only fair to point out that 40 rugby matches will more than likely take a far greater toll on the body than 50 soccer games.

What about versions of football where there is more body contact? American pro footballers can play no more than 21 games a season and the maximum number a college footballer can play is 13. The American football season is a short one and allows players plenty of time for recuperation and rehabilitation, another important point of difference with rugby union.

The Australian rugby league season is more demanding, but even then it runs only from March to September, and is therefore a month or so shorter than our domestic rugby season. Top Australian rugby league players turn out a maximum of 28 times a season in the NRL competition, and that's if they go all the way through to the Grand Final. They have three state of Origin matches, and get a week's rest before each one. There may also be three or four test matches. In all, the league stars play up to 31 or 32 matches a year, about 20 per cent fewer than our rugby players. In addition, league players do relatively little travelling. Rugby players play two competitions in which teams from New Zealand, Australia and South Africa compete, and the end-of-year tour is in the northern hemisphere. That's a lot of energy-sapping travel each year. It's important to note that Australian rugby players are not committed to the same intense schedule. They have the Super 12 and the Tri-Series, but because Australia has no competition like our National Provincial Championship, the players' schedules are much lighter after August.

THE adidas DEAL

Rugby union in New Zealand is able to attract massive sponsorship (all up the All Blacks' adidas deal is worth $US100 million over five years) for one main reason: the reputation of the All Blacks. Sponsors and advertisers will go to great lengths to be associated with New Zealand rugby because of the profile and prestige attached. Most of that stems from the All Blacks' international reputation as a great rugby team.

adidas bought a vast amount of publicity when in July, 1999 it took over from Canterbury as the All Blacks' chief sponsor. Although the alterations to the All Black strip were minimal — a black collar, three white stripes around the top of the socks, and a different sponsor's logo — the change of sponsorship featured heavily on the television news and in all major newspapers, and not just on the sports pages, either. It just goes to show what big news the All Blacks are in New Zealand. The sponsorship change outdid Wimbledon, the British Open golf and cycling's Tour de France as a news item in New Zealand.

Old-time All Blacks seemed somewhat bemused by all the fuss. Fred Allen said: "I'm not too keen on the three stripes around the top of the socks, but I suppose they need something to hold them up."

Frenchman Robert Louis-Dreyfus, who became president of adidas in 1993, is a rugby man from way back, and played as a winger at school. He grew up in Lourdes, idolising the Prat brothers, Jean and Maurice. Jean was the first great French player, a John Eales-type forward who place-kicked and dropped goals, and an inspiring captain. Louis-Dreyfus also admired hard French forwards such as Michel Celaya, Michel Crauste, Walter Spanghero and Benoit Dauga, and brilliant backs like Jo Maso and Pierre Villepreux. But his reason for supporting the adidas rugby sponsorship had little to do with his own sports choices. It was pure business.

He described the deal with the All Blacks as the company's second largest, after one with the New York Yankees baseball team. The 1998 World Cup soccer champions France also wear the three stripes. "Rugby is not such a major sport in Europe," explained Louis-Dreyfus, "but many people know the All Blacks. After the Brazilian soccer team, the All Blacks are the most famous national team in the world. For us, the attraction is not a particular individual. People have mentioned Jonah Lomu, but the team is more important. A player can get injured, or retire, but a team will always be there."

What about the prestige of the All Blacks? Was adidas just as keen to take up the sponsorship after the All Blacks' nightmarish five-losses-in-a-row season in 1998? "Brazil didn't win the World Cup in 1998, but they were still Brazil," says Louis-Dreyfus. "The All Blacks are still the All Blacks, but if they had three or four seasons in a row like 1998, the situation would change."

HOW NEW ZEALAND RUGBY HAS LOST ITS ADVANTAGE

You would think that the Rugby Union, recognising just how valuable the All Blacks are, would do anything to protect its greatest asset. Instead, it places too many demands on its top players, meaning there are constant injury problems. These force coaches to name second-string combinations to try to rest key players, and they help persuade players like Kronfeld to turn their backs prematurely on New Zealand to head overseas for a more lucrative and softer rugby lifestyle.

A cursory examination of the financial statements of the Rugby Union in its annual report seems to reveal that everything is rosy. What other New Zealand sport wouldn't like an annual income of $80 million? But, I say again, this all stems from the All Blacks' reputation. The moment the All Blacks lose regularly, that special magic vanishes. It is starting to happen already.

Down the years great teams like the Originals, the Invincibles, the 1956 and 1967 All Blacks, Graham Mourie's Grand Slam team of 1978 . . . they established, strengthened and reaffirmed New Zealand rugby's great reputation. That reputation, build on the image of the indomitable Meads, the fearless Batty, the brilliant Bob Scott, the multi-talented Zinzan Brooke, has already taken a hammering.

We haven't won a World Cup since 1987. Since then Australia has won two. In 1998 we lost five test matches in a row. In 2001, lowly Argentina went within a whisker of beating the professional All Blacks.

We used to have a massive advantage in rugby. Our players, though amateurs in status, were professional in their attitude. It would be impossible to be more committed than Tremain or McCormick. Other countries were still playing rugby for fun. To the All Blacks, it was at least a life and death issue, if not more important than that (to steal a line originally used by that great American football coach Red Sanders). Now there are many professional teams in the world. The All Blacks don't have that particular edge any more.

That's difficult enough to overcome. But the New Zealand Rugby Union is making things so much worse by placing ridiculous demands on its top players. Does it want them to compromise, settle for 90 percent and an injury-free season? Does it want them to enter a season feeling that even a 70 per cent record of success is acceptable? It's certainly not what the All Blacks' sponsors want.

chapter FOUR

SHOULD THE ALL BLACKS WORK?

JOBS FOR THE BOYS

Of all the changes in New Zealand rugby over the past few years, the one that has most removed the stars from the public is the fact that top players generally no longer do a job outside rugby.

In every sense, top players inhabit a different orbit to the man in the street, the butcher, the accountant, the teacher, the plumber. All Blacks and near-All Blacks earn hundreds of thousands a year and they travel internationally so much that it becomes tedious. So there is already a distance between them and the general public. But it's the fact that the players don't have to "work" for a living that seems to cause the most furrowing of eyebrows.

Down the years, millions of New Zealanders have played, coached, administered and watched rugby for fun. They have fitted in this fun around their working lives. Now top players get paid for playing sport. They don't have to worry about finding a "job". When I listen to talkback radio, or talk to rugby fans, it is this fact which most seems to rankle.

Looked at from the players' point of view, why should they bother to find employment outside their rugby? They are extremely well paid, and can justify themselves by saying they are busy training, playing, recovering, dealing with agents and sponsors, even (very) occasionally attending gatherings like prizegivings for free. Who could blame them if they use their spare time playing golf or computer games?

I think top players today lead an unhealthy existence, and there are lots of people within rugby who agree with me. Top players aren't getting the most out of themselves as people, and therefore as players. Not having regular jobs outside rugby is unhealthy in the sense that it takes away much of the focus from the lives of young people.

Players who also held down fulltime jobs had to lead very organised lives. They put in their day at the office, or wherever, but had to find time to train, with their various teams, and also alone. It seems difficult, but it was no more than New Zealand sportsmen have done for decades.

In 1963–64, Peter Snell was training as a quantity surveyor while building towards the Tokyo Olympic Games. Snell ran in the mornings, at lunchtime and after work as he strove to fulfill coach Arthur Lydiard's 100 miles a week dictum, yet found time to hold down a job. He seemed to manage okay, to judge by his two 1964 Olympic gold medals and the two world records he set immediately after. John Reid worked for an oil company, and later managed his own commercial squash centre in Wellington while he was New Zealand cricket captain.

Fred Allen says that when he was the All Black coach, he would travel the length and breadth of New Zealand selling garments for his women's wear business. "No-one was paying me. It was my job and I did it so I would have money to pay my bills. I selected and coached the All Blacks on top of that. It takes organisation and planning."

Nowadays an All Black with another job is extremely rare. When versatile prop Dave Hewett made his All Black debut at the end of 2001 in John Mitchell's touring side, he was the subject of particular news interest, not so much because of any extraordinary play, but because back home he had a 25-hour-a-week job, as a sales consultant for the Orix financial company. He impressed reporters with his maturity and the perspective he brought to his rugby.

There are many lessons in the Hewett story. For a start, he was never an outstanding schoolboy rugby player. Forget the academies and junior age rep teams. He couldn't even make the First XV at Christchurch Boys High. He was 30 years old, married with two boys, and employed outside rugby when he was selected for the All Blacks. Despite having just two years of top-level rugby behind him, the prop was one of the stars of John Mitchell's team in Ireland, Scotland and Argentina. He was the only member of the 30-strong team who appeared in all five tour matches. He came on as a substitute in the tests against Ireland and Scotland and by the time of the Argentina test, had earned a starting position.

"I feel old from an age point of view, but not a playing experience point of view," he told Kevin Norquay, who covered the tour for the *New Zealand Press Association*. "Greg Somerville, Norm Maxwell and all those guys are younger than me, but have been around for a while now."

In 1997, Hewett played NPC division two for South Canterbury, after telling them he would travel down from Canterbury simply to get the experience. He got two games for Canterbury in the NPC the following year, one a surprise start in the vital semi-final against Waikato.

Hewett said his job gives him a break, enabling him to stop thinking about rugby. "It's great for that. The only problem about having a job is that family time gets compromised. You play rugby on the weekends and work during the week. There are times I wish I didn't work, but it's either that or go home, lie on the couch, and think about rugby — what went wrong, what could I have done? I hate sitting around with my finger up my backside, but I do like to sit down and chill out with the family."

The issue of players having other employment is relevant not just at All Black level, but also in the NPC. Bryce Woodward, the long-serving Northland coach, said that as a rule he liked his players to have other jobs, except late in the season. "It gets a bit tricky as things get hectic near the end of the NPC," he says. "The players are starting to get injuries and need rest and you, as a coach, have a short week anyway between games. In situations like that I'd rather the players stayed mentally fresh. Perhaps a little work, but plenty of time for recovery sessions. It's a balance."

In the 1980s, Andy Haden, typically cheeky, caused outrage when he declared, under "Occupation", that he was a Rugby Player. Now that's just the way it is.

ARE THEY FIT ENOUGH?

Many All Blacks used to be farmers. In fact, for decades, the All Black forward pack was built on the back of farmers like Ian Clarke, Tiny White, Colin and Stan Meads, Brian Lochore, Ian Kirkpatrick and Graham Mourie. Some backs, like Don Clarke, Terry O'Sullivan and Sid Going, were farmers, too. By the late 1980s, that had changed dramatically.

All Black strongmen didn't do their training on farms any more, but in gymnasiums. There has been a smattering of All Black farmers in recent years, including fullback Kieran Crowley, who played for New Zealand until the 1991 World Cup, versatile forward Andy Earl, who played on until 1992 and prop Richard Loe, who lasted until 1995. But they're a dying breed. It is very difficult now to be both a farmer and a fulltime player.

At various times, old players and coaches question the fitness of today's All Blacks. Are they as hard, durable and resilient? I don't think there should be any such question marks. That's not to say Mourie, Lochore, Ken Gray and company weren't fit, but today's players are outstanding athletes. They play the game at great speed, with fewer rest periods. It would be interesting to see how former stars would cope with the demands of today's rugby.

Perhaps the best — Tremain, Meads, Kirkpatrick and a few others — would measure up. But many former All Blacks would be well off the pace. These days every All Black must have handling and running skills and most can kick tolerably well, too. Players like Brian Muller and Graham Whiting, huge props, would really struggle today, when it is not enough to simply lend weight at scrums, rucks and mauls. In today's games, any player — lock, prop, hooker — is likely to find himself between the centre and winger in a sweeping backline movement. He had better know how to handle himself.

When the talk turns to great All Black locks, people naturally choose first Colin Meads. After him, Tiny White, Peter Whiting and Stan Meads are often mentioned. But I think of Gary Whetton, who was extremely tall (6ft 6in), could run like an athlete and had exceptional hands. Whetton, and his successors, Ian Jones, Robin Brooke, Norm Maxwell and Chris Jack, have expanded the role of the lock so that it now calls for a variety of rugby skills.

So no, I don't go along with the oft-expressed theories that today's test players are in some way inferior to those who preceded them. Such a proposition would fly in the face of the evidence of every other measurable sport, where times and scores have improved.

Not all former All Blacks agree. Bryan Williams was discussing this subject one day with Wilson Whineray and some other former All Black stars. "We agreed it was a physically harder game now. There are big hits and the pace is very quick," said Williams. "But then we got to talking about rugby in our time, with the big tours. We travelled and played twice a week. Around our rugby we organised our home life and our jobs. Maybe we were tough in a different way. Players today are more scientifically trained, and there is lot of emphasis on defence patterns. They are good players today. But better? Maybe they simply have different strengths."

WHAT TO DO WITH SPARE TIME

What is unarguable is that modern test stars are struggling in other areas. Rugby is a tough, physical game. A human body can take only so much knocking around. Players might be willing to train or play every day, but they can't do so all day. Training must be divided into sessions — perhaps morning and afternoon, for the keenest. That still leaves a lot of down-time. Are test players filling in their increased spare time well? The evidence suggests they are not.

Some, like Josh Kronfeld, Taine Randell, Anton Oliver, Michael Jones, Daryl Gibson and Mark Robinson have pursued academic careers and emerged with university degrees and double degrees. Unfortunately some others have simply accepted the bucketloads of money coming their way and not gone out of their way to busy themselves. Home videos and video arcades are big attractions.

I heard a slightly sad story from the official of one first division NPC team towards the end of the 2001 season. "We were in Auckland ready for a Saturday evening match," he told me. "On the Saturday morning, we [the team management] had to decide how to fill in the day. A group of us went to Mission Bay and stopped for an hour or so at a café. It was pathetic. Some of the players wanted to be dropped off at a video arcade and a couple who came with us spent much of their time playing with some building blocks in the corner."

These sorts of players aren't exactly stretching themselves. They have the income that enables them to indulge themselves, but that doesn't necessarily prepare them for life after rugby.

Because today's footballers are so well-paid, they sometimes forget what it's like to live in the real world. I like the story of long-time Manly rugby league coach Bobby Fulton, who several times a season would schedule a 5pm training session for a small park slap bang in the middle of Sydney. Fulton wanted his players to be reminded what it felt like to be in a traffic jam, to have to cope like everyone else. A little dose of reality never hurt anyone.

Some former stars leave the game and slip comfortably into other, often rugby-related, roles. Graham Mourie worked for a marketing firm, went back to his farm and then became a professional coach. Grant Fox runs a sports marketing company. Sean Fitzpatrick makes money out of various jobs he does for the Rugby Union, plus speeches. Some, like Zinzan Brooke, have gone off-shore and remained involved in rugby in other capacities, such as coaching and administration. But some former stars do wander about rather aimlessly. I have the uncomfortable feeling that we are going to see more of this in the years ahead.

Dion Waller has realised most of his goals in rugby. When he became an All Black in 2001, the big Wellington lock had climbed as high as he dared dream when he was a schoolboy back in Taupo. But Waller is only too aware of the dangers that lie ahead for him. "I see guys like Mike Edwards, who have been good rep players, struggling once they leave rugby. You have to make sure you develop skills that will help you through life because a career lasts for only a few years."

Having won his All Black jersey, Waller is now weighing up his options. "I could go to Japan. Good rugby players can make $200,000, maybe $250,000 a year over there. Once you become an All Black your price goes up to about $400,000. My wife Sacha is a Japanese English teacher, so the Japanese option is more appealing for me than for many players.

"But ideally, I would like to be able to stay in New Zealand. So I've started my own business. I have designed a lineout machine and am now setting about marketing and selling it. If the business takes off, I will have something to move into after I finish as a player."

Waller says he especially enjoys having something to occupy himself that does not involve playing rugby or training. "Having a job keeps you fresh and gets your mind on other things. I recommend it."

John Hart feels rugby has lost a little through so many top players not having jobs outside rugby. "It's a lifestyle balance," says Hart. "Some players have lost that balance. It's not so bad when they play, but what about afterwards? What skills have they developed? Even when they are in the middle of their careers, they are often bored. Decision-making is an important part of life and the fewer decisions you make, the less your brain is working. That's an issue with top players today."

In previous times, players were incredibly self-sufficient. They had to be, as they juggled work and rugby lives and faced the responsibilities of running farms and other big businesses, and looking after their families. Into the 1980s and even early 1990s, Grant Fox was working fulltime for a sports marketing company, Olo Brown and Terry Wright were accountants, Murray Pierce and John Gallagher were policemen, Alan Whetton was a driver, Greg Cooper worked in sales and promotions for a brewery, the Brooke brothers were building developers. I recall being served in the Manners Street branch of the National Bank by a smiling Alama Ieremia. Pita Alatini worked for a tyre firm when he first left school, then as a bank officer in the Mangere branch of the ASB.

Players like them were used to making tough decisions quickly. It was all part of the rough and tumble of life in the workforce. This spilt over to their on-field play, where they proved themselves independent thinkers. At times of crisis, in those critical dying moments when test matches are won and lost, the All Blacks were the players who remained coolest and got the most out of themselves. Years of training in other walks of life had given them that ability to make important decisions quickly. Until the 1990s, the All Blacks lost very few matches in the dying minutes, perhaps a handful in their entire history.

Chris Laidlaw says that the secret of most of New Zealand's success over the past century has been a simplicity of approach, a focus on

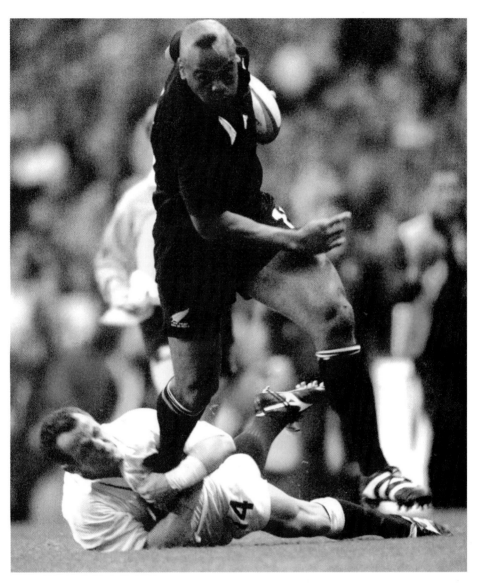

Above: *Jonah Lomu – professional rugby's supernova. If he didn't exist, the PR boys would have invented him. Marketing rule #1: stars sell seats.*

Above: *Goodbye All Blacks, hello Leicester. At the peak of his game, Josh Kronfeld chooses the money over the bag. A portent of things to come.*

Below: *Black day. The blackest AB day ever? John Hart and his coaching team survey the wreckage after France has pasted them in the 1999 World Cup semi-final.*

Above: *Rugby the way it used to be. Brutal, muddy and not a sponsor in sight. A traditional North versus South game boils over: North captain Andy Dalton protests that the South pack have just eaten his first five-eighth.*

Below: *Legends and bellies — Brian Lochore and Colin Meads. No hype, no bullshit, no gimmicks. Their homespun commonsense is what the sport desperately needs.*

Above: *Chris Laidlaw. In a funny sort of way, he started player power. His biography* Mud in Your Eye *lifted the lid on the All Black enigma.*

Below: *Vaguely remember the Bledisloe Cup, but who's the captain again? So many tests are played these days that many All Blacks are anonymous. Even on-field leaders like Reuben Thorne.*

essentials and an innate self-belief by individuals who have had to make it on the basis of their own personal effort. He believes the All Blacks were hungrier for victory because they had more to lose than any other team.

"In the amateur days," says Bob Scott, "we used to fit in our jobs and our rugby. It wasn't hard. We'd look forward to Saturday and would think a lot about the game. It's like anything: the more you practise, the better you get. And we had a lot of practice at thinking for ourselves. It's ridiculous what goes on now, with the constant flow of instructions from the sideline. Why can't coaches and managers let the players think for themselves? If you are used to having discipline and organisation in your working week, you will have the same qualities in your rugby. That's what's missing now. A lot of the players are like robots. They've been drilled and drilled to retain possession at all costs and there isn't the same emphasis on being creative.

"Vic Cavanagh, the great Otago coach, used to say that the forwards win the test and the backs score the tries. Now they don't let the backs perform. They've got forwards out in the backs and it has become a battering sort of game. What a terrible shame that's the way rugby has gone."

THE LOST ART OF THINKING INDEPENDENTLY

The ability to think and act independently is an art that seems to elude some modern players. All Black touring teams used to comprise players, manager, assistant manager (a euphemism for coach) and that was pretty much it. Even medical staff were picked up locally where required.

Now the All Black management is often more than a dozen and includes media officers, managers and assistant managers, coaches and assistant coaches and specialist coaches, doctors, physios, sponsors' reps and more. The players are time-managed to a remarkable degree. Be here then. Talk to the media then. Attend this team talk then. Train then. Get on this bus. Eat then.

There is more money available in All Black rugby now. Players have every whim catered for. It all seems rather unhealthy.

Haden says that despite their incomes, All Blacks should strive to live as normally as possible. "They should be doing all they can to not remove themselves in any way from society. I can't stress enough the importance of maintaining what I call a normal lifestyle — getting up at a proper time to do a job, organising their private lives constructively. Wayne Bennett, the great Brisbane Broncos rugby league coach, says he would never select a player who didn't have a job. I agree with that thinking. Active minds dealing with the normal pressure of life — that's what you want. Those sorts of people are far better at getting something done. If you want something done, give the job to a busy person, not someone who looks to have ample time on his hands.

"If today's players are trying to remove themselves from aspects of society because they are earning a lot of money, they are making a big mistake. I know Rachel Hunter quite well. The All Blacks would love to have as much money as her, yet when she's back here in Auckland, she slips very easily into normal life, driving herself about, shopping at the local supermarket and so on. There's no excuse for players to act any differently. Some, however, think that having a bigger income makes them special. The ones with their feet on the ground know that all sport is about being as normal as you can for as long as you can. It's not a place for prima donnas, preening in front of mirrors inside gyms and getting hair extensions and all that crap.

"They remove themselves in all sorts of ways today. I'll give you an example. They're on the All Black team bus going to the ground. There they are with walkmans on, music blasting in their ears. Sitting next to them are their mates, the guys they will be relying on in a couple of hours' time. That time on the bus is crucial. The odd comment made then can make all the difference during the game. It might be starting to drizzle and a centre might notice that and say to the guy sitting next to him, the winger, that he will chip the ball through on the deck a bit more. Or the lineout guy might say that the ball will get slippery so let's keep the throws slower and more in the air. There's not enough of that going on now. Instead of players inter-relating, they set themselves apart.

"In All Black teams I was in, we had fun. We got up to mischief and had bloody good wholehearted fun. We have reunions now and just carry on where we left off. Will these modern All Blacks be having reunions in 20 or 25 years' time? I doubt it to the nth degree."

The players are now very wealthy, don't play club rugby, and are usually accessible only through their agents. They have minders and helpers coming out their ears. They play well, though they often falter at times of greatest stress. And they are being watched by a different public, people who like to make an occasion out of the day, rather than who necessarily have passion for the All Blacks. It's New Zealand rugby, but is it New Zealand rugby the way we want it?

ARE PLAYERS TOO SELFISH?

Rugby does seem a much more selfish sport at the top level these days. Perhaps because of the money on offer now for All Black positions, players aren't as willing to help each other. They don't take each other into their confidence as much. Sure mates, usually from the same province, will talk among themselves, but there isn't the same sort of opening up. One good example is the issue of pay. Players could help themselves and each other by being honest and up-front about what they are earning and about the special conditions of their contracts — bonuses and so forth. This is just what the employer, the Rugby Union, would not want, because the players would then be able to bargain from a position of collective knowledge. Instead there is a lot of bravado when it comes to pay packets, lots of inflated contract figures. "You look after No 1," was how one All Black explained the situation to me.

Haden says that players not used to getting on with their lives constructively come unstuck on the football field. "How often over the past few years have we seen All Black teams outsmarted in the last few minutes of a match and lose important matches? Their minds seem to freeze.

"I couldn't believe what I saw at the Wellington Stadium in 2000, when the All Blacks played Australia. There we were, with a few seconds to go and the game sewn up. You could see John Eales evaluating the situation, thinking of a way Australia could win. He decided the lineouts were their best chance, as we'd mucked up ours throughout the game. So he forced a lineout down our end. Our guys made a total mess of it. There was panic out there and Eales ended up kicking a penalty to win the match. I felt angry about that. You wouldn't have seen All Black teams of previous eras throwing away a match like that. What our players today are lacking is decision-making ability under pressure. They don't get enough training for it. They aren't doing enough in their own lives and that's why they lose games they should be winning.

"If you trace All Black history, you will find many examples of All Black teams pulling through in the last couple of minutes to win a test match. But you'll hardly ever find an example of the reverse happening. When things got desperate, the All Blacks were always the clearest and cleverest thinkers. They did what they had to do to win. There's no way they'd have shrugged their shoulders and lost. That was not acceptable. Their pride wouldn't allow it. It's one of the changes that've taken place in the All Blacks over the past few years."

John Drake, the former All Black prop, is another who has warned of the dangers of players not working. Speaking to Lindsay Knight of *The Dominion* a couple of years ago, Drake warned that professional rugby was producing too many players who were "brain dead", saying they were not using their minds enough. "They're spending too much time sitting on their bums all day. When I was playing, most of us would go to training to refresh ourselves after working. Now these guys need to go to work to refresh themselves from rugby. People need to go to work, otherwise they go stale."

Drake felt that rather than employing marketing and brand managers, the New Zealand union would be better off having a careers adviser, and the sort of careers players were channelled into should be more mainstream, even trades and manual labour.

Fred Allen also feels the All Blacks were better off when they worked. "They were occupied. Now they play golf. Who'd want to listen to a coach four or five times a week? There's too much time for talking, too much hanging around. I liked it when, as the coach, you'd give one talk, then ask Lochore, Whineray and the rest of them to go out and do it."

Bryan Williams has the impression this problem might be gradually being overcome. "In New Zealand rugby we are trying to get all players to pay attention to the educational side of things," says Williams. "We had a lost generation when the game went pro. The new breed of players is much more mindful of the importance of education. I've noticed that over the past five years. The attitude of players in the early years of professional rugby seemed to be, 'Good, I don't have to work any more.' They seemed to play golf and sleep. Now there's more awareness of the need for a balanced life."

Professional rugby coaches, though older than the players, face the same job versus rugby dilemma. Some choose to make rugby their fulltime job. Others, like Gordon Tietjens, seek to continue with other employment. Tietjens, the successful Bay of Plenty NPC and national sevens coach, applied for the job of Wellington rugby coach in 2001. Though he seemed a good choice, he was turned down because he wanted to continue in his other employment, as General Manager of Bays Engineering. Tietjens said he needed to work to keep a balance in his life, though was prepared to quit his sevens job. Some would have seen his attitude as healthy; Wellington rugby officials chose to see it as an impediment to Tietjens doing the best possible job for their provincial team.

One way where things could be improved, says Williams, would be if the New Zealand union put clauses in its contracts with players to make players more involved in rugby at grassroots level, whether it be with clubs or schools. "The top players would then understand much better the volunteer effort that goes into New Zealand rugby," says Williams. "Perhaps they'd have their eyes opened a bit. That wouldn't do any harm."

Players often complain that their time is too committed for them to take on employment outside rugby. There would certainly be nothing to stop them doing some work in the community, for rugby and outside rugby. Some players, even All Blacks, are terrific in this regard. Others won't lift a finger.

I have some sympathy for these young men. It must be difficult to go from working on a rubbish collection one week to driving a Commodore and having a six-figure salary the next; from anonymity to being a constant focus of attention. It would be hard to keep your feet on the ground; not to develop a swollen head. But the players who manage this best, who keep balance in their lives, are without doubt the ones you would want playing for you in a crisis.

On the matter of accessibility, Keith Quinn feels today's stars do their best to be available, but says the vast increase in media surrounding the All Blacks means that every demand simply cannot be met.

John Hart feels today's top players are under much more pressure to perform than those of earlier eras. "There is much more pressure being an All Black now than back when Colin Meads played. The public scrutiny is intense. Back in the 1960s, players were revered. Now their every move is analysed and criticised. Talkback radio has had an horrific impact; it is one of the worst things to hit New Zealand rugby.

"You hear people hark back to the 1960s and talk about 36-game tours. But what they overlook is that the game was never as physical or demanding as it is now. There has been a dramatic rise in the injury rate. Careers are getting shorter, even as players try to hang on because the pay is so good. The pressure comes at the players from every angle. I'm sure that's the reason why a guy like Josh Kronfeld eventually headed to England, where the game isn't as physical and his life as a player was not placed under the microscope."

THE THORNY QUESTION OF INTELLIGENCE

I do wonder about the intelligence of today's All Black teams. John Eales is a Masters graduate in Psychology from Queensland University and used his intelligence throughout his rugby career. Forty per cent of the Brumbies Super 12 team are university graduates and another 25 per cent are still at university. The Brumbies employ a development officer whose major responsibility is organising team meetings and training around tutorials. The Australians like their players to be busy off the field, working or studying, and reap the rewards in tough, close matches.

All Black teams used to be full of people with all sorts of interests. Lochore and Meads or other farmers might be discussing the correct ratio of sheep or cows per paddock, or the right sort of grass seed to use for different situations. Players took an interest in their surroundings, even to the extent of visiting tourist sites. Earle Kirton still talks about the flight he made from Rome to London with the 1963–64 All Blacks. John Graham, a schoolteacher, got up and told the passengers — his team-mates and other people — that he was about to give a dissertation on Roman history, which had been the subject of his university thesis. He told them to listen, and that he would be asking questions at the end. That speech made a tremendous impression on Kirton and other young All Blacks. It opened their minds, not just because they learned about Roman history, but also because they realised there was a lot more to life than rugby and that they were in a wonderful position to capitalise.

Today's All Black team contains some very intelligent men with degrees or double degrees. But the team culture is vastly different now. It is not just permissible, but almost encouraged, for players to shut themselves off from their team-mates. Imagine a great captain like Wilson Whineray or Graham Mourie letting that happen. It's interesting that when Bobby Simpson took over as coach of the under-performing Australian cricket team, one of his first acts was to ban walkmans from the team dressing room. He wanted players talking to each other and taking an interest in each other and the game. There may be a lesson there for New Zealand rugby.

This is an issue that has been addressed by other sports. As long as a decade ago, the Auckland Cricket Association began helping its leading players prepare for their retirement from playing, encouraging them to participate in a careers assessment programme that identified skills that could be used in the corporate sector and putting more experienced players through a consultancy skills assessment. Interestingly, cricket officials found that they made little progress with 20-year-olds, who were focused narrowly on cricket and unwilling to look beyond their playing days. By the time players got to 28 or 29, they tended to be a lot more receptive to suggestions for a career after cricket. This ties in with what tennis player Chris Lewis once told me: "When you first get on the professional circuit, you are so relieved and so happy, you don't think of anything but tennis. It's only after you've been going several years and start getting the odd injury that your thoughts turn towards what you're going to do after you can't play at the top level any longer."

Bryan Williams: "From my experience of today's players, the longer they have been All Blacks, the more they think about the money side of things. It's their work for five or 10 years. The problem is that when that work dries up, not many of them have had any training to do anything else."

Some unions have been better than others at helping players in this area. Soon after rugby went professional, the North Harbour union, with its then captain Richard Turner leading the charge, tapped into a vast network of corporate supporters to assist with career guidance and introductions to young players. Assistance took all sorts of forms, from introductions to specific employers to running computer literacy courses. Canterbury, too, has shown itself to be forward-thinking in this area.

Many young rugby players have no idea how important it is for them to develop themselves outside rugby. I know of one group of youngsters who attended one of the provincial rugby academies. They were supposed to attend the local polytechnic, but most hardly ever bothered to turn up for their courses. At the end of the year, the academy supervisor asked the tutor if he would give the young rugby players a dispensation and pass them anyhow, and was quite miffed when the tutor would not. In this instance, both the young players and their supervisor were short-sighted. Both could not see further than rugby.

New Zealand players don't get the most out of each other. Why would Andrew Mehrtens necessarily take aside a young kicker in the All Blacks and pass on his knowledge when a specialist kicking coach has been included in the tour party? Will a grizzled veteran of the forwards see it as his job to school up the young locks and props if there are specialist forward coaches? Is the team getting enough out of itself, or is it now relying too much on outside expertise?

There was a lot to be said for being self-sufficient, for coping and relying on each other for help. This instilled tremendous team spirit and independence. From the way the All Blacks have performed at crunch moments over the past few seasons, this is not an area of strength any more. It seems that every season the All Blacks lose at least one match in the last few minutes, usually through bad decision-making at the crunch time. In 2002, the All Blacks lost the test in Sydney, and with it the Bledisloe Cup, by conceding a last minute penalty. All Black centre Tana Umaga was bemused afterwards. "It's the third time they've done that in three years," he said. "They don't make those little errors and that was the difference. We made a couple of errors at important times and that cost us."

Senior All Blacks have always dominated teams. Whether they were Colin Meads-Lochore-Gray-Tremain or Stu Wilson-Mexted-Bruce Robertson-Mourie or Fitzpatrick-Bunce-Zinzan Brooke-Michael Jones, there was always an experienced core. There was good and bad to this, but on balance, it was good. Sure there was a hierarchy that wasn't always healthy. The back seat of the bus was the preserve of the team's most experienced players (until the back seat concept was done away with by John Hart), there were drinking sessions that were virtually compulsory, and there was a definite pecking order in the team. It was almost a boarding school mentality. This wasn't always healthy, but when you look at All Black results down the years, it was mighty effective, for these players set a standard and helped run the show.

While the coach was in charge, the senior players took on a lot of responsibility. It's debatable if that is happening to the same degree now. Since the game went professional and money became a major focus, players have become more self-centred. It was noticeable that when Sean Fitzpatrick, Frank Bunce, Michael Jones and Zinzan Brooke left the All Blacks in 1997, there was no senior core able (or willing) to get the more inexperienced players through. The result was that in 1998 the All Blacks had a horror run of five straight losses.

Back when Fred Allen, Ivan Vodanovich, JJ Stewart, Jack Gleeson and Eric Watson were All Black coaches, they used to despair when trying to prepare their teams for home tests matches. Players were permitted to gather only 48 hours before a game. Trying to get a team to gel in that time, to teach and learn drills and calls, was nearly impossible. Players would often be introducing themselves to each other and the next day would be All Black team-mates. Now they gather days before a game. A media curfew is imposed about midweek. It's all heavy-duty stuff, though I'm dubious some of it helps to produce a better standard of rugby.

I am sure it is to do with the increased money available. Players don't have to strive to cope any more, on or off the field, and that's being reflected in the way a lot of them play.

Great New Zealand Olympians I've spoken to tell me they would get annoyed at team-mates who thought they had succeeded merely by getting to the Olympics. These people forgot that the real job was competing at their best at the Olympics, not just being selected for the team. Similarly, Colin Meads often says his ambition was not just to be an All Black, but a good All Black.

ALL BLACK JOBS

It seems strange to think of the days when All Blacks used to be employed full-time away from rugby. Here are examples of some All Black touring teams:

1953–54 TO BRITAIN AND FRANCE

Bob Scott	Mercer
Jack Kelly	Schoolteacher
Ron Jarden	Oil company clerk
Morrie Dixon	Fitter
Stuart Fairbairn	Chemist
Alan Elsom	Land agent
Jim Fitzgerald	Schoolteacher
John Tanner	Dentist
Doug Wilson	Insurance clerk
Colin Loader	Salesman
Brian Fitzpatrick	Oil company clerk
Laurie Haig	Miner
Guy Bowers	Garage attendant
Vince Bevan	Yard foreman
Keith Davis	Clerk
Bill McCaw	Schoolteacher
Bob Stuart (captain)	Farm adviser
Peter Jones	Farmer/fisherman
Bill Clark	Clerk
Des Oliver	Medical superintendent
Bob O'Dea	Farmer
Tiny White	Farmer
Nelson Dalzell	Farmer
Keith Bagley	Contractor
Snow White	Painter
Kevin Skinner	Grocer
Peter Eastgate	Carpenter
Ian Clarke	Farmer
Ron Hemi	Accountant
Arthur Woods	Farmer

1960 TO SOUTH AFRICA

Don Clarke	Farmer
Tony Davies	Student
Ralph Caulton	Clerk
Russell Watt	Bank clerk
Frank McMullen	Carpenter
Terry O'Sullivan	Farmer
Denis Cameron	Farmer
Kevin Laidlaw	Auto electrician
Terry Lineen	Carpenter
Mick Bremner	Wool buyer
Steven Nesbit	Student
Adrian Clarke	Customers clerk
Kevin Briscoe	Panelbeater
Roger Urbahn	Schoolteacher
Red Conway	Carpenter
Hugh Burry	Doctor
John Graham	Schoolteacher
Dave Gillespie	Truck driver
Rex Pickering	Clerk
Peter Jones	Fisherman
Kel Tremain	Student
Colin Meads	Farmer
Nev MacEwan	Clerk
Ron Horsley	Shopkeeper
Mark Irwin	Doctor
Ian Clarke	Farmer
Wilson Whineray (captain)	Farm appraiser
Eric Anderson	Stock buyer
Roger Boon	Joiner
Ron Hemi	Accountant
Dennis Young	Carpenter

1976 TO SOUTH AFRICA

Laurie Mains	Building developer/real estate
Kit Fawcett	Student
Bryan Williams	Lawyer
Grant Batty	Finance consultant
Terry Mitchell	Carpenter
Neil Purvis	Farmer
Bruce Robertson	Teacher

Bill Osborne	Contractor
Joe Morgan	Fitter and welder
Lyn Jaffray	Lamb drafter
Duncan Robertson	Builder
Doug Bruce	Teacher
Sid Going	Farmer
Lyn Davis	Tomato grower
Andy Leslie (captain)	Mercer
Alan Sutherland	Farmer/shearer
Ian Kirkpatrick	Farmer
Lawrie Knight	Doctor
Kevin Eveleigh	Timber worker/farm contractor
Ken Stewart	Farmer
Hamish MacDonald	Farmer
Frank Oliver	Forestry contractor
Peter Whiting	Schoolteacher/jeweller
Gary Seear	Draughtsman
Brad Johnstone	Builder
Kent Lambert	Shearer
Billy Bush	Meat Worker
Kerry Tanner	Publican
Tane Norton	Banker
Perry Harris	Farmer/insurance agent
Graeme Crossman	Teacher

chapter FIVE
AGENTS — A NECESSARY **EVIL**?

TURN PRO, GET AN AGENT

The advent of professionalism in rugby has led to another spin-off growth industry — that of the rugby agent. I have not heard of any disgustingly bad ones in New Zealand rugby, certainly none who would compare with the conmen who inhabit the world of professional boxing. But still, the performance of some agents here has been mediocre at best.

One All Black who was loath to use agents was Norm Hewitt. He preferred to negotiate with his employers himself. "I liked to be in charge of my destiny," said Hewitt. "If an agent went to negotiate for me, and he had several players on his books, well, he'd want to stay on good terms with the employer, the New Zealand Rugby Union, because he knew he would be back in the room negotiating for his next player. In that scenario, would he push right to the limit in my case? One time I spent three hours bargaining with two New Zealand Rugby Union officials for an extra $30,000 I knew I should be paid. They gave way in the end, but that's the effort it took. Will the agents stay there and fight for you? You really want the Jerry Maguire-type agent, who has just one client and who will die for that client. You don't find many agents like that."

Hewitt feels the area of sports agents is open to exploitation. "There have been some sad cases, and a lot of them involve Polynesian players, who are generally very trusting and open. You'll get an agent taking $5000 as an advance on a contract, then seven per cent of the base pay, and then more money from anything else he negotiates. All the player has to do is sign a bit of paper and all his worries are over. There are rogues out there, and it makes me angry. Agents will target secondary school players, sit down with families and paint a bright, optimistic picture. If they can sign 100 schoolboys and just a few of them come through to become good players, well, that's money in the bank, isn't it!"

Hewitt cited the case of one agent who has several young Wellington players on his books. "He takes seven per cent of their base fee for playing Super 12, seven per cent of $65,000. But that $65,000 is a minimum fee. It does not require any negotiation at all, so why should the agent get any of that money?" This agent, says Hewitt, contracts his players for three years, with the right of renewal for another three years, unless they pull out within six months of their first contract expiring. "Young players are concentrating so hard on playing good rugby, to earn NPC, Super 12 and maybe All Black contracts, that they don't have the time to worry about agents and negotiations and contracts. Because of that, they often get ripped off."

While discussing the less appealing side of agents, three All Blacks mentioned one incident to me as an illustration of how agents put themselves first. The agent in question has many players of international standard on his books, and charges high rates. But, the All Blacks said, he seems little more than a money-gatherer. When one of his players got himself into trouble overseas, and needed some good, professional advice, this agent was nowhere to be seen.

Some rugby agents have a high national profile, like Wellington lawyer David Howman, who has acted for cricketers Stephen Fleming, Martin Crowe, Nathan Astle and Craig McMillan, and All Blacks Greg Somerville, Norm Maxwell, Jeff Wilson, Chris Jack, Mark Ranby and many others. Some have a stable of players; others, like Jonah Lomu's mentor, Phil Kingsley-Jones, look after just one player, perhaps as an extension of a friendship.

Howman, a Wellington lawyer, says it has been interesting watching the development of the rugby agent since rugby went professional in 1995. "There was a big bullrush when the game went professional. A lot of people with questionable credentials tried to get into the business of being sports agents," he says. "Some bad things happened. Trusting players were charged lots of money by people who had done nothing for them. The problem was that people were trying to get into the business for the wrong reasons.

"Since those days, the scene has settled a bit, though looking around it would be fair to say that there are still some agents who are better than others. It's interesting to look at the situation in the United States. I'm not quite sure of the figures, but in American Football there are something like 200 registered agents, but only about 10 work for players who are currently active. The rest have been sifted out."

Do players need agents? "They do and they don't," says Howman. "Top players negotiate their contracts with the Rugby Union once a year, and they certainly need someone to act on their behalf at that time. It's a business arrangement. The players want to get the best conditions they call, and the Rugby Union wants to concede as little as possible. In that situation, players need to be represented by someone who knows what he is doing. It's the players' livelihood and it's important they get it right."

One problem, Howman says, is that some players have tended to be too trusting. "The Rugby Union has over the years tried to say to players that they should trust it, that the union will do what's best. But it's business with an employer and an employee. I think back to what happened in 1995, when some players were well and truly burned. The Canterbury players lost a lot of ground that year by not signing with the Rugby Union immediately. By the time they decided to come on board, the WRC threat had faded away, and the Rugby Union was negotiating from a position of strength. So the contracts offered to the Canterbury players were much less than what had been offered a few weeks earlier to some other players around the country. It took someone like Todd Blackadder about three years to catch up, to get back to a situation of parity. Players can't complain about that sort of thing happening. They have to be smart and act in a business-like manner. So that's a time when they do need to be represented by someone who knows what he is doing.

"But for the rest of the time, most of them don't have much need of an agent. Except for about five players — Jonah Lomu, Jeff Wilson, Tana Umaga, Christian Cullen and Sean Fitzpatrick — the All Blacks have been contracted so tightly that they really couldn't go outside and look for much extra in the way of sponsorship deals."

So why do players retain agents, as nearly all of them do? "Well," says Howman, "it's the cruisey thing to do at the moment. Players think it's cool to have an agent. My advice would be that they be very careful about who they employ, though."

Dion Waller gets twitchy when the subject of agents is raised. "I've seen and heard of some terrible things," says Waller. "Players getting ripped off and used. Young guys are being snapped up and immediately losing a percentage of their income. You need a business person who is a friend. My agent is a friend who is a hairdresser. I don't pay him. He works for me because he genuinely wants to help."

BEWARE THE NEW ZEALAND RUGBY UNION

Waller told of the time he and Norm Hewitt decided to do their own negotiations with the New Zealand union. "We went into the whole thing very thoroughly. We wrote out CVs, prepared mission statements and explained in writing what our goals were and how we thought we could contribute. We put on suits and went in to Rugby Union headquarters to talk. The union people were very impressed with our presentation, but at the end of the day, it didn't help us one scrap. What they wanted was to get our signatures for as small an amount of money as possible.

"The Rugby Union is just like any employer. It wants to get the best labour as cheaply as possible. But in a way the union is worse. Because rugby is a sport, players think they are dealing with people who care about them. They don't. Not at all. The moment you stop playing, or can't help the union any more, they wipe you. I've seen it happen all over the country."

Former All Black lock Andy Haden is New Zealand's best-known sports agent. Haden was heavily involved in the Rugby Wars of 1995 and is a shrewd operator who knows his way around the scene of rugby politics.

His company, Sporting Contacts, goes far beyond sport — Haden is even model Rachel Hunter's New Zealand agent. Haden did work in the 1980s for the Rugby Union, and has from time to time advised all sorts of players. Intriguingly, he has never worked on a paid basis as an All Black's agent.

"I was in a unique position in 1995," he says. "I could have been very heavily involved in representing players, but I chose not to represent any. I think the profession is shonky and the players in many cases were dishonest, untrustworthy, unreliable and lacking in principle.

"The only person I've worked for is Sean Fitzpatrick. When he finished as a player I was very interested in him and have represented him in all his commercial deals since the day he retired, but not when he was playing.

"I have never wanted to discuss contracts. I wanted to stay out of that side of it. Over the years I have given advice to various people, though not in a professional capacity. For instance, I helped [former Australian coach] Greg Smith in Fiji with his contract and have offered advice to some younger players."

Like Howman, Haden feels there has been a degree of weeding out of dubious agents over the past few years. "Some funny things have happened. One day I got a letter from the New Zealand Rugby Union telling me it would deal only with people accredited as agents and inviting me to apply for accreditation. I don't know why the union thought I would want that. Who would want to join a bunch of lowlifes?"

Most agents charge somewhere between the standard Australian Rugby League agent's rate of six per cent and the International Management

Group fee, which can reach 25 per cent. There is a perception that agents are creaming massive amounts of money off the backs of the players. Films like Tom Cruise's *Jerry Maguire* ("Show me the money!") fuel that perception. In fact, in New Zealand, most sports agents generally earn little more than pocket money.

Agents, especially the less experienced ones, can be a pain in the neck. They can be loyal to their player to the point of absurdity, demanding ridiculous fees in such areas as endorsements and book contracts. But like 'em or not, it seems agents are here to stay. Players are constantly reminded to look after their core business, which is playing good rugby, and need an adviser who is financially astute, loyal and able to negotiate skillfully. Hence the arrival of the rugby agent. It seems sad to me that top New Zealand rugby players need an agent. How much better it would be if they could depend upon an astute, trustworthy friend, preferably someone with legal expertise? They need people to assist with life skills management, not managers. Unfortunately finding such people is not easy.

Hewitt says part of the problem is that in his experience the Rugby Union did not negotiate in good faith. "Out in the commercial world, there is usually real integrity. If you do a deal, then sign the paper, that deal is binding. But with the New Zealand Rugby Union, you'd find that the contract, even though you'd signed it, would be open to all sorts of challenges. The union was always trying to change it to its advantage. The Rugby Union treats players like pieces of meat. There is no personal relationship with the employer and maybe that's why the money becomes even more important to the players."

He cites the case of Christian Cullen. "At the end of 2001, Cully was not chosen for the All Blacks' end-of-year tour. Coach John Mitchell announced Cully had not been selected because of injury. Within a couple of hours, he changed the story and said Cully had been dropped. It was a very important difference because it meant Cully was either paid as an All Black, or not. Cully had to take legal action to get the money he was owed. There wasn't a scrap of goodwill from the Rugby Union."

Another dispute surfaced in June, 2002, with the news that former All Black loose forward Ron Cribb was suing the New Zealand Rugby Union for more than $100,000 to help with his recovery from a knee injury. Cribb claimed he was entitled to rehabilitation payments because at the time he first suffered his knee injury, in September 2001, he was an All Black and was therefore entitled to payments under his All Black contract. The Rugby Union refused to pay, disputing Cribb's claim that he would have made John Mitchell's end-of-year All Black team in 2001. It seems we are going to see more of these sorts of disputes in the years ahead.

Hewitt: "I spoke to Josh Kronfeld when I was in Europe and he told me how relieved he was to be out of New Zealand so that he didn't have to put up with all that crap from the Rugby Union. Josh told me how, once he told the Rugby Union that 2000 would be his last year in the All Blacks, it wiped its hands of him, to the extent that he found he was not being paid his full year's pay. He said once his All Black commitments finished, the union was reluctant to pay out the remaining money he was owed.

"I hear the same story all the time from players who are sick to death of the way they're jerked about by the Rugby Union. Most players come to realise the union doesn't give a stuff about them. There are some exceptions. If Jonah Lomu has a complaint about his contract, he'll be invited to meet with the union like a shot. It'll do all it can to accommodate him. He's one of their stars. But if a fringe All Black has a legitimate gripe, he'll find it much, much harder to get a hearing."

part THREE

THE DOMESTIC GAME

chapter SIX

THE **CLUB** SCENE

THE TIMES THEY ARE A-CHANGIN'

In 1954, it was announced that just-retired All Black fullback Bob Scott was moving from Auckland to Wellington and would be joining the Petone club. There was pandemonium. On the morning of the announcement, the reserved seats in the Petone Recreation Ground grandstand were booked out for the season. The Petone Borough Council complained of rudeness by rugby followers who telephoned too late and missed out on getting a season ticket. The owner of the menswear shop Scott was to take over had an interesting morning as people continually put their heads inside the door and asked when Bob Scott would be arriving. For three seasons, the Petone Rec was full. People would say: "I'm off to see Bob Scott play today."

In 1999, Jonah Lomu, the most famous rugby player in the world, announced he was moving from Auckland to Wellington. While this news caused Hurricanes and Wellington representative fans to froth with excitement, it had no impact on the club scene. Eventually the Wellington union allocated Lomu a club — struggling Wainuiomata — and the big winger has turned out for the club a couple of times since, drawing several thousand spectators on each occasion. There were jokes in the capital the first time Lomu was to play for Wainui that he would need a map to find his club headquarters.

The changing face of the club rugby scene in New Zealand is well illustrated by the examples of Scott and Lomu. In the 1950s, All Blacks played club rugby each Saturday afternoon and were big crowd-pullers. By the end of the century, the All Blacks and club rugby inhabited separate orbits.

I want to examine the state of New Zealand provincial rugby, but it is pointless to talk about the National Provincial Championship, the Ranfurly Shield or even the Super 12 without first putting the microscope on club rugby. For a century club rugby has been the lifeblood of New Zealand rugby, a vital training ground for players, coaches, referees and administrators. With the heavy emphasis on the professional game these days, club rugby is floundering. In every main city, clubs are withering and dying and the club competition is becoming increasingly insignificant.

There was a time, not that long ago, when club rugby was a prime focus of the sport in New Zealand, and a very important part of the social fabric of the country. The major club matches in the bigger towns would draw thousands of spectators each week. And no wonder — there was far less representative rugby and all the country's top players turned out each week for their clubs. If you wanted to see top rugby, you went along on a Saturday afternoon and supported your local club. Club loyalties were very strong.

Afterwards, club players and supporters would get together. In the 1960s it became fashionable for clubs to have their own clubrooms built and the 6 o'clock closing law made clubrooms even more attractive. Previously club players tended to meet at local pubs — in Wellington, Wellington College Old Boys converged at the Pier Hotel, Wellington club players at the Carlton, Marist went to Barrett's; in Christchurch, Linwood players drank at Cokers, Marist at The Dominion; in Auckland the Gluepot became linked with Ponsonby and so on. But energetic club committee members set about raising funds and having rooms built. It became the thing for most clubs to have their own clubrooms and these used to buzz with activity on a Saturday night. Beer would flow, and so would rugby stories.

Each club had its own special flavour. In Wellington, Marist and St Pat's, which in 1971 amalgamated, were the Catholic clubs. Petone was a genuine suburban club, with working class members. Wellington was a city club and people worked in town, then travelled through the Hataitai tunnel to train and to meet in its clubrooms. University (as with University clubs all over the country) was a curious mixture of the scholarly and the slightly off-beat — Mick Williment played for University, and so did Mark Sayers. Wellington College Old Boys was said (by those in other clubs) to fancy itself as a glamour club, well to-do and with a certain style that didn't always go down well elsewhere.

These club identities were to be found all around New Zealand. Phil Gifford's Loosehead Len used to call the Grammar club in Auckland "Glamour" and it was a good tag. Like Wellington College Old Boys in Wellington, Grammar players, coming out of the prestigious Auckland Grammar School, were said to rate themselves a bit. Ponsonby was working class, Waitemata out in Henderson was very close to the Dalmatian community, Otahuhu was situated in the middle of a strong league area.

In Christchurch, Linwood was very strong and had a similar feel to Petone and Ponsonby, Christchurch, which attracted former students from private schools Christ's College and St Andrews, was very different. Marist was the big Catholic club in Christchurch. High School Old Boys was similar to WCOB in Wellington and Grammar in Auckland.

Down in Dunedin, Southern, the club that produced the famous Cavanaghs, was a good, strong workingmen's club, closely linked to the Railways workshops. Kaikorai at the northern end was more middle class, as was Pirates, the club of Charlie Saxton and Kevin Skinner.

Just as every club had its own identity, so top players were closely associated with particular clubs. For more than 80 years from the turn of the 20th century, All Blacks looked forward to club rugby and were proud of their clubs.

ALL BLACKS AND THEIR CLUBS

Way back in the early years of the 20th century, the famous All Blacks were proud club members. Dave Gallaher, the 1905 Originals captain, was one of the stalwarts of Auckland's mighty Ponsonby club. His vice-captain on that tour, Billy Stead, was the Invercargill Star club's shining light. Multi-talented Wellington back Billy Wallace was a Poneke man, as was Tom Ellison. Jimmy Duncan was a proud member of Kaikorai in Dunedin. Halfback wizard Freddie Roberts played for Wellington's Oriental and winger George Smith, one of New Zealand's most remarkable sportsmen, turned out for City in Auckland.

The first Ranfurly Shield match was not played until 1904 and because of the difficulties of communication and travel, provincial rep programmes were extremely thin. In 1899 Wellington played nine rep matches and Auckland just four. In 1911, Wellington's rep programme still comprised only nine matches, and Auckland's had risen to six. In that 1911 season, Wellington played their first rep game on June 22, while Aucklanders had to wait until July 29 to see their rep side in action. But it didn't matter too much because the interest in club rugby was so intense.

Club affiliations remained just as strong after the First World War. The Brownlie brothers, Laurie, Maurice and Cyril, All Blacks all of them, represented the Hastings club, as did winger Bert Grenside. Jack Griffiths played for Wellington's Poneke club, while the three Nicholls brothers, Doc, Ginger and Mark, all All Blacks, were staunch Petone men. Freddie Lucas, one of the 1924 Invincibles, was a Ponsonby man. His captain on that tour, Cliff Porter, represented Athletic in Wellington, as later did halfback/first-five Eric Tindill. Jack Manchester, captain of the 1935–36 All Black team to Britain, turned out for the Christchurch club. Ron King, the strong man of the All Black pack just before the Second World War, was the pride of the West Coast and proudly informed people that his club was Hokitika Excelsior.

Throughout New Zealand the association of the leading players and their clubs was well-known. Rep rugby was still not the dominant part of the season. In 1932, Auckland played 12 rep games, including a Ranfurly Shield fixture against Canterbury. The team's first outing was not until June 3, the traditional King's Birthday fixture against Waikato. Wellington played 13 rep games that season, the first, against the New Zealand side that was to tour Australia, taking place on June 15.

The emphasis on club rugby continued after the Second World War and through the 1950s. To cite just a few examples, Ponsonby boasted Eric Boggs, Bob Scott and Johnny Simpson; University in Wellington had Ron Jarden, Bill Clark, Jim Fitzgerald and Brian Fitzpatrick.

Has Catley played for Taupiri in the Waikato competition. Just along the road, the five rugby-playing Clarke brothers, with All Blacks Don and Ian in the vanguard, were nationally associated with the Kereone club. Nearby, hooker supreme Ron Hemi represented Frankton. Tiny White played for Gisborne High School Old Boys. Kevin Skinner played for Pirates in Dunedin and Peter Johnstone for Taieri.

Ivan Vodanovich was a big figure in Wellington's Marist club, but no bigger than Bob Stuart at the University club in Christchurch. Stuart's provincial team-mate, Pat Vincent, turned out for Christchurch High School Old Boys. Another All Black, Morrie Dixon, played for Sydenham, while hooker Dennis Young played for just the one club, even if it did undergo various name changes – Christchurch Technical Old Boys from 1948–59, Technical College Old Boys Shirley from 1960–61, and Shirley from 1962–63.

Peter Jones was the pride of the north, playing for Awanui and earning the club national recognition. Another of Northland's famous sons, Johnny Smith, played for Kaikohe.

These players were farmers and fishermen, teachers and shop managers. All of them not only found time for, but eagerly awaited, midweek club training and club rugby on Saturday afternoon. To them club rugby was not an imposition but a delight. They loved the football and thrived on the camaraderie.

The last of club rugby's halcyon times were the decades between 1960 and the early 1980s. Club loyalties remained, and money had not yet really entered the equation.

Bob Barber and later Brian McKechnie played for Star in Invercargill. Jack Hazlett gave another Invercargill club, Drummond, equally yeoman service. Staying with the deep south, Leicester Rutledge played for Wright's Bush and Ken Stewart for Balfour. In fact, Stewart was known throughout New Zealand rugby as Balfour.

Grant Batty travelled south from Wairarapa to play in Wellington, first for University and then for Marist St Pat's. A few years later Stu Wilson made the same trek, but chose Wellington College Old Boys. Joe Karam, Batty's good mate, played for Marist and then, after the club amalgamation, Marist St Pat's. Wilson's partner for Wellington and New Zealand, Bernie Fraser, played for Hutt Valley Marist throughout his club career. Big lock Nev MacEwan secured good lineout ball for Wellington's Athletic club for years.

University clubs remained strong. Bob Burgess, with his long hair, drooping moustache and brilliance at first-five, was the quintessential University player, and turned out for the Massey branch of the club in Palmerston North. Gerald Kember, Mick Williment and Mark Sayers belonged to University in Wellington. Tony Davies played for University in Auckland and then in Dunedin, where he was a team-mate of Chris Laidlaw and Earle Kirton. Grahame Thorne was for a time Auckland University's major star.

Billy Bush was a staunch Belfast club player in Canterbury. Across town, Kerry Tanner was a big name in the New Brighton club. Down in Dunedin, Laurie Mains was a Southern man, in every sense of the word. Most clubs had a big name — Bruce Hunter played for Pirates, Duncan Robertson for Zingari-Richmond and Bevan Wilson for Matakanui.

In Manawatu, John Callesen turned out year after year for Palmerston North High School Old Boys, as did Mark Donaldson. Ken Granger played for Freyberg Old Boys, which was to be Bruce Hemara's club a few years later. Sam Strahan was Oroua's claim to national fame. In the south, Brian Ford was the pride and joy of the Kaikoura club.

The big clubs had plenty of drawcards. Petone boasted Ken Gray, Ian Stevens, John Dougan and Allan Hewson. Ponsonby had Bryan Williams, Andy Haden,

Malcolm Dick, Ron Rangi, Keith Nelson, Peter Whiting and Terry Morrison. Marist, another powerful Auckland club, had in their ranks Des Connor, Terry Lineen and Paul Little. Frank McMullen, Peter Murdoch, Ron Urlich and Waka Nathan were backbones of the Otahuhu club. Gary Cunningham played for North Shore. Mac Herewini gave good service to two Auckland clubs, Otahuhu from 1958–66, and Manukau from 1967–70. Grammar boasted All Black captain Wilson Whineray, while Northcote had Snow White throughout his record career.

In Northland, Bevan Holmes, who played 31 times for New Zealand but never in a test match, played for Kamo throughout the 1970s. A decade later it was Ian Jones, another big forward, who gave the club international recognition. Jones, in fact, was known throughout the rugby world as Kamo. Joe Morgan was Northland's Mid-Northern club star. The fabulous Going brothers, including All Blacks Sid and Ken, were Mid Northern players through and through.

In Taranaki, Ian Eliason provided valuable lineout ball to the Kaponga senior team for a decade. Graham Mourie, when he wasn't a student in Wellington, was an Opunake club man. Hulking prop Jazz Muller played for Eltham and hasn't strayed far since.

In Canterbury, Fergie McCormick and Tane Norton were Linwood men. Alex Wyllie was the pride of the Glenmark club. Bruce Watt and Richard Wilson were Christchurch club players. Stu Cron and Lyn Davis played for Suburbs in Christchurch. Davis' namesake, Bill Davis, was a Taradale player, while his Hawke's Bay and New Zealand midfield partner Ian MacRae turned out for Marist.

Andy Dalton turned out each year for Bombay in the Counties competition, while Bruce Robertson opposed him many a time while representing Ardmore College. All Black hooker Bruce McLeod played for Manurewa in the Counties competition. Bob Lendrum gave the Papakura club great service as a back and a kicker.

In Wellington Ralph Caulton played for Poneke, while the Wellington club boasted All Black forward Ron Horsley, then, a few years later, Graham Williams.

This is just a smattering. You could name any All Black of the post-war period through to about 1985 and see that he was closely linked with a club. It didn't matter if it was an urban or a rural area. Away from the big towns, Ian Kirkpatrick and Lawrie Knight played for Ngatapa, near Gisborne, Kel Tremain for Napier High School Old Boys. Brian Lochore played for the Masterton club for 15 years. Was there ever an All Black more associated with a club than Colin Meads was with Waitete? Not just Colin, either. His brother Stan, another fine All Black, was a stalwart member of the club, too.

The situation changed during the last 15 years of the 20th century. Now often players wanted to be paid to play club rugby. Some were less keen to turn out at any level below representative. Auckland did a better job than many areas in maintaining links between All Blacks and clubs, even if rep players appeared increasingly infrequently at club level. Thus the Brooke brothers, including All Blacks Zinzan and Robin, were associated with Marist, as were Inga Tuigamala, Terry Wright, Bernie McCahill and John Kirwan. Ponsonby had Olo Brown, Joe Stanley and Carlos Spencer; University had Grant Fox, Sean Fitzpatrick, David Kirk and John Drake; Brad Johnstone played for North Shore; Michael Jones was a Waitemata man and Gary and Alan Whetton were affiliated with Grammar.

In Wellington, Michael Clamp played for Petone, Brian McGrattan for Marist St Pat's, Murray Pierce for Wellington, Tana Umaga for Petone. In Christchurch, Andrew Mehrtens turned out on occasion for High School Old Boys, Wayne Smith for Belfast and Warwick Taylor for University.

Taranaki fullback Kieran Crowley played for Kaponga, and was known as the Kaponga Kid. Andy Donald, the under-rated Wanganui halfback, played for Ohakune from 1976–83, then Ohakune-Karioi until 1986. Dave Loveridge played for Inglewood, John Mitchell for Fraser Tech in Hamilton, Hika Reid originally for Ngongotaha in Bay of Plenty. Doug Rollerson played for University in Manawatu, Wayne Shelford for North Shore, Jamie Joseph and Stu Forster for Southern.

THE PAYMENT PROBLEM

In the 1980s, as the game moved into its "shamateur" stage, money became a factor. Some leading players began seeking payment before they would play for a club, and even for those who still valued club rugby, the huge increase in representative matches began to squeeze their availability.

In 1987, Grant Fox explained the predicament. "There's too much first class rugby," he said. "It works to the detriment of club rugby, which is sad because that's the bread and butter of New Zealand footie. Now, unfortunately, the top guys aren't able to play any club footie. I've played three games in two years for my University club, which is horribly wrong, and I've made myself available whenever it's humanly possible, without trying to physically run myself into the deck. We're playing about 35 games a season at first-class level. A fitness expert like Jim Blair believes about 30 is the maximum for any guy at the top level, not only physically, but mentally."

And that was in 1987. Since then the situation has only become worse, with the introduction of the Super 12 competition and the expansion of the international season. Look at today's All Blacks. Who can say which is Christian Cullen's club? (As a matter of interest, Cullen has been linked with Paraparaumu, Kia Toa in Manawatu and Northern in Wellington.

In 2002, he finally played his first game for Northern, at the strong direction of All Black coach John Mitchell.) His club affiliation means nothing. But it's not just Cullen. Do we really link Reuben Thorne, Caleb Ralph, Pita Alatini, Kees Meeuws, Roger Randle and other leading players with clubs?

Club rugby used to really mean something. Rep teams were picked on club form and with about 10 weeks of club rugby, uncluttered by rep commitments, players had the time to press for higher honours. Murray Mexted transferred from second division Tawa to high-flying club team Wellington because he was looking for a better standard of football. Ken Gray did the same thing, switching from Paremata to Petone, and Ron Jarden moved from Woburn (formerly High School Old Boys) to University. Frank McMullen moved from Eden to Otahuhu and later Lindsay Harris moved from Eden to Waitemata, all of them knowing that if they moved to a strong club side, their chances of earning rep selection would be increased. Players would go to the King Country to play with the Meads brothers. An Australian, Andy McGeogh, made a point of joining the Waitete club in 1970 for just that reason.

Club rugby results were important, and clubs would go to some lengths to secure good players. In Wellington in the 1980s, Hutt Old Boys were known as "cheque book Hutt". They boasted a whole swag of big names, including Hika Reid, Steven Pokere and coach Mark Shaw. A decade earlier, Naenae and Avalon, who eventually amalgamated, were reputed to be willing to buy in talent. In Auckland at the same time, Roskill were not averse to spending some money to ensure they kept hold of their best players and lured others to their club. Pakuranga were happy to buy players of the calibre of Pokere, Reid and Steve McDowell. Silverdale were known as Silver Dollar for obvious reasons. In Christchurch, Merivale-Papanui were said to be good payers. Once payment to players started, every leading club was placed in a quandary: either start paying or lose good players and status. Would they pay and remain in the senior grade, or refuse and be relegated?

In earlier times, other clubs were more inventive. For instance, Athletic in Wellington had a system for attracting talent. Officials in their club owned a rubbish collection round and people coming to the club could get a job collecting rubbish, as did All Blacks Tom Lister and Terry McCashin, and other solid players like Gary Catley.

All Black legend Colin Meads says: "Paying club players used to happen in the big centres before the professional era started. The gossip line started and we knew the top clubs in the big cities were paying money to players. It is still going on and is killing country rugby." Meads, who has belonged to Waitete all his life, says his club will never pay a player. "There are other clubs in the King Country paying players. It should stop. You shouldn't be paid anything until you are a provincial player."

It beggars belief that clubs are prepared to pay players. The clubs are in desperate financial straits, kept alive primarily by revenue from pokie machines. (Ironically, some club officials blame the pokie machines for luring club members from clubrooms into pubs on a Saturday evening, and therefore adding to the struggles clubs have to keep their rooms financially viable.) Club players are not the top tier and very often not even the second tier. There is declining interest in club rugby. Yet some stupid club officials continue to buy players from other clubs and offer as much as $500 a game.

Paying players is very short-term because you do not buy loyalty. The massive Pakuranga club in Auckland has had three All Blacks in its history — Pokere, Reid and McDowell. All three were really fly-by-night players in terms of club rugby, looking for the best deal they could land. Significantly, all three later played in Wellington, where they were among the highest paid club players. In cases like these, it is the money, not the club, which means more. James Arlidge is of infinitely more value to Pakuranga. He has been a Pakuranga player since he first laced on boots as a little boy. He has progressed through the ranks of junior rep teams, NPC and now Super 12 and is a real club hero. Arlidge is the sort of hero clubs need. Tana Umaga fills the same role for Petone in Wellington.

It's a moot point whether provincial unions can outlaw the practice of paying club players, as rugby is now a professional game. But several major unions have drawn up a charter that they have asked clubs to sign voluntarily, to keep club rugby amateur. Clubs have willingly signed the charter, but indications are some of them are still paying.

Colin Meads says the decline of club rugby started in the country areas about 12 years ago and has now spread to the cities as well. He says the club scene is different from what it was in his playing days. "Young people have got many other things on their plate today. The footie club used to be the community meeting place in our district for everything from dog trials to a meeting of the women's division of Federated Farmers." He believes fervently that club rugby is necessary to keep All Black rugby strong. "Where are the kids supposed to start? How do they become All Blacks if club rugby isn't strong? If it hadn't been for the Waitete club, I might never have become an All Black. The club gave me a start. I learned most by playing rugby with guys who had been playing 10 or 12 years. They kept my feet on the ground. Without a good club standard, players will go from schools to junior rep teams and will miss a great part of what New Zealand rugby is all about."

Clubs have always been very proud of their All Blacks and when a New Zealand team was named to tour overseas, they would organise fund-raisers if one of their members had been included. These donations were often substantial and in the days when players were paid a pittance while on tour, were important considerations for players intending to be away for months without pay while trying to find money for their family and to meet house mortgage repayments. This white envelope, as it was called, was part of New Zealand's rugby scenery. For instance, in 1979, the Hutt Valley Marist club presented All Black winger Bernie Fraser with a cheque for $9000 before the All Blacks' end-of-year Northern Hemisphere tour. This was a very large amount back then and must have been a boon for Fraser, who was an owner-driver of a truck and basically lost his job while on tour.

Many All Blacks faced similar problems, especially farmers, who were always well represented in New Zealand teams. Some city players had jobs such as teaching and were either paid or part-paid while on tour, but who was going to run the farms? Things got so dire in 1974 that All Black coach JJ Stewart arranged for Sid Going's farm to be managed while the team toured Britain.

Before the professional era, All Blacks had always struggled for money. We read stories of how during the 1905 Originals tour of Britain, France and North America, Canterbury centre Bob Deans, who came from an extremely wealthy family, used to give some of his financially strapped team-mates money to get them through the tour. But there weren't many Bob Deans about. Usually it was the player's club, and sometimes his community, that raised money to help him tour.

Clubs no longer organise fund-raisers for their All Blacks. The practice began to die out when All Black tours became annual events. And nowadays, players don't need it — they are earning hundreds of thousands of dollars a year. Anyway — why fund-raise for a player you seldom see?

THE VANISHING ALL BLACKS

It wasn't long ago that All Blacks not only played rugby for a club, but were full club members. Virtually all of them paid their own club fees.

Certainly they spent their Saturday evenings in the clubrooms and filled normal club duties, including serving behind the bar, helping out at fund-raisers and working bees. Just as Peter Snell, Bill Baillie and Murray Halberg were proud members of their athletics clubs in the 1960s, and John Reid, Bert Sutcliffe, Dick Motz and Jack Alabaster took part in club cricket, so the All Blacks got the most out of their association with clubs. They enjoyed the competitive and the social elements and were very much part of the club scenery. In 1972, Colin Meads broke his back in a car accident while driving home to his farm after painting the Waitete clubrooms. The chances of an All Black being involved in a club working bee these days are almost nil.

If we fast-forward to the modern era, we can see that club rugby means virtually nothing to most All Blacks. Yet there's evidence of how important club rugby can still be. Late in 2001, Carlos Spencer had occasion to play some club rugby in Auckland and even appeared in the Gallaher Shield final, helping Ponsonby to a 31-13 win over Otahuhu. He seemed to thrive on the experience. His clubmates, who had previously regarded him with suspicion and treated him more like a guest on the odd occasion he had turned up at the club, were impressed by his attitude and became much more accepting of him.

During 2001, Andrew Mehrtens was dropped from the Crusaders and found himself turning out for the High School Old Boys club. He even kicked the penalty that enabled High School Old Boys to win the Christchurch club title. It was freely stated that his All Black career was over. The very idea of a current All Black playing club rugby was preposterous. The odd exception arises when a player, on the comeback after injury problems, will have a game at club level to confirm his fitness.

As a gesture, a major provincial union may assign some of its All Blacks to clubs. Thus Jonah Lomu is a member of the second division Wainuiomata club. Early in 2001, Lomu was "rotated" out of the All Blacks for the season opener against Samoa. So, while Anton Oliver and his men demolished Samoa 50-6 at the North Harbour Stadium, Lomu turned out at suburban Lyndhurst Park to play against Tawa. Several thousand spectators turned up to watch. If Lomu hadn't been playing, there wouldn't have been 100. It was all a bit artificial, though. While Wainui loved being able to have big Jonah turn out for them, he didn't know many of his team-mates' names and had no particular link with them.

The pity of it is that any players, whether they are All Blacks or just good honest club toilers, should love playing club rugby. It was interesting that when Mehrtens kicked that winning penalty for High School Old Boys, his team-mates included Ben Hurst, Aaron and Nathan Mauger and Daryl Gibson, all of them Canterbury reps or better. There has always seemed a desire by the players in Canterbury to remain part of the club scene. Is that a reason why Canterbury and Crusaders teams do so consistently well, and why there is such good spirit year after year in Canterbury rugby?

Wellington club rugby, by contrast, is all over the place. While administrators pay lip service to club rugby, their actions betray them. The 2001 Wellington Jubilee Cup club final was between Poneke and Marist St Pat's. The Wellington union ruled that for the most important match of the season, each team would be denied two of their best players, to save them for the NPC. By taking out two stars from each team, the Wellington union believed it was acting fairly. In fact, it was continuing to do all it could to kill club rugby.

"It was lunacy," says Brian McGuinness, who stood down recently after 10 years as Chairman of the Marist St Pat's club. "Poneke couldn't play David Holwell and Sam Johnstone and MSP couldn't play Semo Sititi and Lome Fa'atau. How can that be said to be administering in the best interests of club rugby? The union said it was evening it out, but it was pathetic. Nearly all the rep players wanted to play in that final. They're good men with a bit of club loyalty. But the union is their employer and wouldn't let them. That's how highly the union valued its club final, the so-called showpiece of its club season.

"Any feeling our rep players still had for club rugby was getting killed. The Wellington union didn't want the rep players injured before their NPC matches. Poneke and MSP joined forces and met Malcolm Holmes of the Wellington union. We begged him to let us make the best players available, but he wouldn't wear it. It was another nail in the coffin of club rugby. As it was Wellington went out and lost to Bay of Plenty in the NPC! It's odd the way things work."

Despite all the fine words, many administrators continue to overlook the importance of club rugby. It was telling that when the Boston Report was drawn up in 1994 and accepted in 1995, there was no mention in all its pages of club rugby. The report offered a review and revamp of New Zealand rugby, bringing the game into the modern era and all those fine phrases. Yet club rugby was ignored.

It may soon be too late. There were 230 teams playing senior club rugby in Wellington in 1970. Now there are 148, including eight women's sides that never existed three decades ago. The number of players has declined nearly 40 per cent in that time. In 1970, there were 31 rugby clubs. Now there are 18.

Bryce Woodward, who has coached Northland for several seasons, says the standard of club rugby in the province is much lower and the number of players is also down hugely. "We've had so many players head off overseas. Who can blame them?" he says. "Clubs are generally holding up not too badly in Northland. What's noticeable is the makeup of the senior sides. There are a few old guys in each team, players aged about 34 or 35, who a decade or two ago would not have been playing top grade rugby. Then the rest of the club side will be made up of youngsters, players hardly out of their teens. There are very few players in their mid to late 20s."

There are lots of indicators as to the declining standard of club rugby. In Manawatu, the Palmerston North Boys High School First XV plays in the under-21 grade. "When I arrived in here in 1987," said Palmerston North Boys High principal Dave Syms, "if we won half of our games we'd be delighted. In some years we won only three or four. For the past five years we realistically wanted to win every game. The standard of the under-21 grade, as with all grades of club rugby, has declined. It used to be unheard of for players to go from the First XV straight into senior rugby. Now it happens on many, many occasions."

You can't blame just the administrators. The attitudes of the players themselves, even the rather mediocre players who a decade or two ago would have struggled to make senior level, have changed dramatically. These days, club players seem to expect everything to be provided by the club — transport, drinks afterwards, gear. The suggestion of the player coughing up with an annual subscription fee would be met with bewilderment.

The pity of it is that there is still much support among New Zealand rugby followers for club competition. People like having a local club to support. In 2001, the North Canterbury club final between Glenmark and Oxford drew 5000 spectators. The Gallaher Shield in Auckland, the Jubilee Cup in Wellington, The Telecom Trophy in Christchurch, the Gallaway Trophy in Dunedin . . . the finals always draw well.

(In 1975, the Canterbury club trophy name was changed from the Harewood Trophy to the Canterbury Savings Bank Trophy and now sponsors rule. They have tried elsewhere. In 1994, Lion Brown insisted that the Lion Brown Trophy replace the Jubilee Cup in Wellington. It didn't work. Supporters still talked about the Jubilee Cup and players strove to win it. New sponsors DB accepted this reality and the Jubilee Cup was reinstated five years later.)

Club finals are special occasions, reminders of what club rugby used to be like every week. Generally, though, the downturn in spectator turnout has been vast, the more so when it is considered that it used to cost spectators an attendance fee to watch a big club game. Club rugby is usually free now for the smattering of spectators who can be bothered attending.

This decline in playing numbers and strength is reflected in the decrease in media coverage of club rugby. Whereas there was once detailed reporting of all club matches down to perhaps the senior third grade, now some papers do not bother running club reports at all, preferring to list just the scores. Others run abbreviated accounts of just the top grade.

One of the most famous New Zealand short stories was AP Gaskell's *The Big Game*, an exciting story about the club championship final in Dunedin between long-standing rival clubs Southern and University. This wonderful story explores inter-club rivalry and its effects on a city. Such emotions have, apparently, gone forever.

DECLINING STANDARDS

Clubs have suffered hugely from losing the top tier of stars. It was terrific for rugby followers to know that if they turned up on Saturday, they might see a match involving some All Blacks and other leading provincial players. Now, the standard of club rugby has dropped alarmingly and the flow-on effects are starting to be noted in the international arena.

Not only are the top players missing, but also the next level down aren't as good because they haven't been exposed to the very best week after week. It's not just the All Blacks who are absent. Over the past 10 or 15 years thousands of good players, some provincial and many just good, solid, senior club standard, have headed overseas. They are travelling either because they are New Zealanders in search of OE, or they have managed to secure a playing contract overseas, be it Italy, Spain, Japan, France or Britain. New Zealanders love to travel, more so traditionally than South Africans, and a New Zealand passport enables a person to gain entry relatively easily into many European countries.

When you take away thousands of the leading players from the club scene, you can quickly see how much this has affected the standard of club rugby. The best club players have been peeled away, and what we now see passing for top club rugby would probably have been Senior B in decades past. The average age of a senior club team has dropped from

28 to about 22 in a quarter of a century. It is not unusual, even in the main centres, to find players in their teens playing the top level of senior club rugby, and not just in the backs, either. Once, when a teenager was selected for his club's senior side while still in his teens, it signalled the arrival of an unusual talent; now it probably means the club is struggling desperately to fill its ranks.

The expectations of the young players are different, too. These days, a promising youngster expects to have cracked the club's top premier side within about a season of leaving college. If he hasn't, he gets twitchy, looking around at other clubs or perhaps overseas.

It is easy to understate the turnover in good club players. Here is one example, which I believe is no different from that which would be found in many big clubs throughout New Zealand. In Wellington, Marist St Pat's won the Jubilee Cup in 1996. Within three years, just two of that champion side were still playing rugby. Three had retired, but it was the exodus overseas that really ripped apart the champion team. Kelly Rolleston went to Italy, John Daniell to France, Gordon Simpson, Isaac Feaunati, Richard Denhardt, Brendan Reidy and Damian Geraghty to Britain, Andrew Gallagher and Richard Higgs to Japan. A London club signed one player for the equivalent of $NZ197,000, plus win bonuses, match fees and all expenses paid, including a car and a flat. This was not an All Black, but just a top club player. Marist St Pat's officials estimate that at present they have the equivalent of two Jubilee Cup champion teams playing overseas.

Brian McGuinness: "The money that has come into rugby has eroded the loyalty factor. Players are now just waiting for the next phone call, the chance to get overseas and make some money. Fifty per cent of them don't have any particular skills apart from rugby, so it's understandable. Club rugby is like a revolving circle. Guys are leaving all the time, and some are coming back. You get lots who can't be bothered playing club rugby after they return from overseas, but a few are good club men and get back into it. Even so, you'd have to say the social culture of rugby has been corrupted by the dollars that have come into the game. We will never regain that voluntary die-on-the-sword feeling. It's getting increasingly harder to get good club administrators.

"Because the club scene is so transitory now, clubs don't develop their icons and heroes and youngsters have difficulty associating themselves with the stars. The cracks in the club veneer are showing everywhere now."

The sad thing, says McGuinness, is that the Wellington union is desperately suspicious of its clubs, particularly the stronger ones. "MSP did some work a few years back to introduce a notice of motion at the Wellington union's annual meeting calling for the separation of the amateur and professional arms of rugby administration. It was so obviously the way things should have been, but we had a huge battle getting that through. Another one: for the club championship final, we wanted the game to be played on a Sunday and the union wanted it on a Friday night. Sunday is so much better for clubs because they can have a luncheon and build up to the game properly, make something of the day. Again, we had a real fight persuading the union on that. It's a constant problem in being a club administrator. You try to take a holistic view, but the Wellington union fights you every step of the way. It's so suspicious. In the end you just run out of puff. You just get tired of arguing with guys who have a different agenda."

Players seem to decide earlier that it is time to concentrate on their business careers. And those who have been contracted overseas for hundreds of thousands of dollars a year are not likely to be attracted to playing rugby for nothing more than a free sub on their return.

Former All Black captain (and member of the Petone club in Wellington since he was seven) Andy Leslie says coaches of senior club teams today have to do a lot more "coaching", as opposed to planning and organising. "The coaches I speak to tell me they are having to coach basic skills that should have been taught at under-18 or secondary school level. The standard of senior club football is much lower now than it was before professional rugby arrived. It would be fair to say that the NPC is about the standard that good club footie used to be.

"It's a different scene now. I remember being selected to play for the Petone senior side and Bob Scott congratulating me and telling me that I was now only one step away from the Wellington rep team. He said if I kept my head down and tried hard, I could make the reps. Club rugby isn't the same stepping stone now. Perhaps one or two players in each club side have ambitions to play rep rugby. The rest are playing just for fun.

"Club rugby doesn't provide the base of the rep team any more. How can it when players are either brought into the area, or ushered through the academy system? It all undermines the club game.

"Sometimes I hear administrators talk about how important it is to look after the grassroots of rugby, but the problem is that they're often talking about the NPC, whereas I think they should be talking about club rugby."

It has always been said the club rugby is the lifeblood of the sport in New Zealand. Indeed, there was club rugby in New Zealand at least 20 years before the founding of the New Zealand Rugby Football Union, in 1892. Where do the NPC, Super 12 and All Black players come from? The feeder system has been weakened considerably. Young forwards are no longer exposed to those grizzled veterans of the tight five. Instead they attend the rugby academies that have sprung up around the country and cater to those players who have been earmarked as having talent worth fostering. But the actual on-the-job learning takes place now during rep matches, not in club play.

Norm Hewitt, who on arriving in Wellington joined the Wellington club as a favour to his former New Zealand Colts coach, Graham Williams, said he was shocked at the attitude of some players in the club's top side. "I'd turn up at club training and there would be only seven or eight of the team there," he said. "I'm not saying it was like that in every club, but it was at the Wellington club at that time. To me, it signalled a general lack of enthusiasm in the club. Wellington used to be a really strong club team, but it has struggled over the past few years. No wonder."

WHY CLUBS ARE DYING

Clubs are struggling all over New Zealand. Saturday evenings used to be big money-spinners for the clubs. Clubrooms would be packed, full of members, and members' wives and girlfriends, having fun, spending money, enjoying each other's company. Now many clubs no longer have clubrooms as such. They do a deal at the start of the season with a pub and that is where their members converge on Saturday evenings. The cost of keeping clubrooms running outweighs the financial benefits of opening them.

To cite one city as an example, in Palmerston North, big clubs like High School Old Boys, Queen Elizabeth College Old Boys and Kia Toa have all closed their clubrooms.

There have been other factors. The increased emphasis on drink-driving laws has altered the social habits of New Zealanders, who these days do not tend to drive to their local clubrooms, drink all evening, then hop in their cars and drive home.

In addition, the major cities now offer an amazing variety of popular cafes and restaurants, and many players and their partners find they prefer to spend their Saturday evenings there, rather than in the less inviting clubrooms. Another point: there will often be a big Super 12 or international match on a Saturday evening. To judge by television viewing figures, rugby followers apparently prefer to watch these games on television from the comfort of their lounge, rather than in clubrooms or pubs.

And, as John Hart points out, attitudes to rugby have changed. "Since the game went professional, there have been fewer and fewer volunteers available. People look around and see that so many people are getting paid for their involvement in rugby. Now people are less inclined to be unpaid workers for a club."

There used to be an expression in rugby that it was a game for life. It meant that once youngsters were lured to rugby, they would remain involved in the game, as players, administrators, coaches or supporters for the rest of their lives. This is no longer the case. One factor that is driving players away from all sport, not just rugby, is student loans. Young men in their early 20s are emerging from university with huge student loan debts — often $50,000 or more. They want to get cracking and cut down or wipe off that debt. Playing sport on weekends and training during the week eats into their work time. It becomes a matter of prioritising, and often sport drops down the pecking order.

All this has had an effect on clubs, whose membership numbers are declining anyway. Many clubs are folding, others are amalgamating and most of the rest are struggling financially. Clubs that took out mortgages to build their clubrooms are often really hurting.

It's not just under-performing clubs in small towns that are struggling. The mighty Ponsonby club, which has produced dozens of famous All Blacks down the years, from Dave Gallaher to Carlos Spencer, was perilously close to folding a few years ago. "In the late 1980s, early 1990s, Ponsonby nearly went under," says club stalwart Bryan Williams. "But we have been innovative and have fought back, so that today we have never been stronger. We had to take some drastic measures to survive. We sold our clubrooms and now lease rooms at Western Springs, so that the Auckland City Council is responsible for looking after our grounds.

"Our clubrooms weren't mortgage-free and the debt was rising while the value of the building was falling. Things looked very grim. Then we had a bit of fortuitous timing. Ponsonby became a trendy suburb and the value of our property rose, so we were able to cut our debt. A lot of very hard work was put in by some dedicated Ponsonby club supporters, but it was a close thing."

In late 2001 Williams was appointed Director of Rugby at Ponsonby, which has given the club a more professional and effective administration. Williams' salary is part-funded by the money the Auckland Rugby Union gives clubs.

Williams says clubs aren't getting enough support from provincial unions. "There are so many new people in the game at the administrative level, lots of marketing types with no background in rugby. They don't realise the culture of the game. They seem to inhabit ivory towers and view things academically and don't care about the rest. You need some dyed-in-the-wool rugby types, people with genuine passion for the game."

Williams is emphatic that not enough of the millions and millions of dollars pouring into rugby goes into the bottom end. "I think a lot of administrators work on the trickle down theory, but there's not much trickling down, sometimes. If it weren't for the pokies, many rugby clubs would be dead."

Lin Colling was Chairman of the Ponsonby club for several years. He says clubs need to define their position and understand what they are trying to achieve and who they represent. The fundamental problems, he says, are lack of profile, poor playing standards and insufficient funding.

Like many club administrators, Colling believes too much emphasis has been placed on New Zealand's rugby elite, citing Ponsonby's situation as an example. The *Otago Daily Times* ran a superb series on the state of rugby in 2001. In the segment on club rugby, Colling told Alistair McMurran: "We are the second-biggest rugby club in Auckland, behind Pakuranga. We have 47 teams, 17 of them at senior level. It costs us about $6000 to run a team." To run the club, he estimated, costs $250,000 a year.

"That's only the salary, or part of a salary, of one All Black. We want a more equitable distribution of the funds coming into the game at the top. The grassroots — the clubs — have been left to their own devices. I would like to see some of the funds distributed to clubs." Colling estimated that if the New Zealand union made a distribution of $1000 to a senior team and $500 to a junior team, it would put clubs in a more viable financial position and would cost the union about $5 million.

FLAWS IN THE ACADEMY SYSTEM

Colling also pointed to the decline in club rugby as one of the reasons New Zealand's coaching is suffering. "The career path from junior club coach to premier club coach to provincial coach that has underpinned New Zealand rugby for more than 100 years has been blocked. Coaches and players are being fast-tracked through high schools, academies and development squads, not serving any form of apprenticeship at different levels of the game. Coaches at the academies have academic qualifications such as a degree or diploma in sport, marketing or management, but lack hands-on experience at club level. We are developing cloned coaches and players. A lot of coaching is from the manual. And we get a dumbing-down of player intelligence."

The decline in the great clubs is nationwide. Petone has been a marvellous Wellington club. It has boasted the mighty Nicholls brothers, Bob Scott, Ken Gray, Andy Leslie, Allan Hewson, Tana Umaga and other famous All Blacks. Around Wellington, the suburb is known as the Village and there is a great pride in the area's clubs — rugby, soccer, workingmen. In 2002, the Petone club fielded just eight Saturday afternoon teams, and eight primary school teams, down from the heyday of 15 senior teams and 10 schoolboy teams. Upper Hutt, another strong Wellington club, was down about 100 players for the 2002 season. Those sorts of player declines can decimate a club in no time.

Leslie agrees with Colling about the academy system. "I'm not a fan of the current system at all," he says. "They identify the guys very young and then what happens is the slower-developing players get left out. They might be 15 or 16, give it another year, then flag away the game because they're not in the system.

"Rugby officials have to cater for the slower maturers, especially the forwards. When I think back to players of my time, lots of the best players did not make their college First XVs. They developed later. Players like Ken Gray, Murray Pierce and me would not make it in the current system. You can't have a system that overlooks players who mature more slowly. We are trying to recognise players younger and younger, but if boys get overlooked early on, they tend to move away from rugby. It is important for rugby to retain its huge player base. I hope it does not develop like gridiron has, where once a player has reached college level and hasn't made it, he gives up. But it looks like it could go that way here. We don't want to become a nation of watchers. That would be tragic. They should have one junior rep grade, under-23, and leave it at that. There are too many at the moment and it means players don't bother with club football."

Colin Meads agrees. "I have played with players who became All Blacks at the age of 27, 28 or 29, who never played First XV rugby. Some of them became the best All Blacks. Under the present system they would not become All Blacks."

Another former All Black captain, Tane Norton (he succeeded Leslie in the job in 1977), stresses the effect weekend work has had on club rugby. "It means players aged over 25 are being forced to choose between supporting their family or playing rugby. The boss is not so sympathetic to rugby players today," says Norton. "If he plays football and gets injured, he could lose his job."

Like most wise old rugby heads (but apparently not those at the New Zealand union), Norton is wary of the dangers of fast-tracking promising players. "We have excellent props at Linwood and I have seen them in other clubs, too, who might not come of age until they are 25 or 26. Everyone expects them to be a top prop at 22 and they can't do it. On the other hand, players who are selected for the New Zealand under-17, under-19 and under-21 teams are often not heard of again. They think they should become All Blacks the next year, but they aren't quite ready for it. They presume they will be picked for a top team when they are 19. When they get knocked back and are told they won't be in a team, they chuck the game.

"Once upon a time, a player could be picked, and dropped, picked again and dropped again. Although it hurt, it did his character a lot of good. He learnt to take those knocks."

As Reuben Thorne, the 2002 All Black captain said shortly after being appointed: "I know that some people seem to go automatically from New Zealand Schools on to Under-19s and Colts, but, with hindsight, it might not be a bad thing to sometimes miss out. It makes you a bit more determined to prove that you are as good or better than those picked ahead of you." Thorne, 27 when named All Black skipper, was not an early developer himself. He was in the New Plymouth Boys High School First XV that was coached by Jed Rowlands and included future Super 12 players such as Daryl Lilley, Michael Collins and Campbell Feather. But Thorne, though chosen for various Taranaki age rep teams, never did make the national Colts, Secondary Schools or Under-19 sides.

The plethora of various age rep teams now is ironic, given that there was a time when the New Zealand Rugby Union refused to have any. "I had to plead with the New Zealand union to have an under-23 game," says Fred Allen, All Black coach during the 1960s. "Out of that game — against Taranaki, it was — came players like Peter Whiting and Ian Kirkpatrick. You need to have a bit of age stuff, but not all these age teams they've got now. It's ridiculous. A lot of promising players are tied up in academies while the clubs have got kids playing for them in the senior grade."

Brent Anderson, the New Zealand Rugby Union's community development officer, takes a slightly different angle on this issue. He agrees there are dangers in selecting players too young. "If you select 20 or 30, you are sending a signal to the rest that they won't make it," he says. "Why not spread the net and pick 50 and coach them all and then see who comes through? You have to be careful about the message you are sending to the kids who miss out. Bay of Plenty have addressed this issue and they are doing away with their under-13, under-14 and under-15 rep programmes and instead have instituted a rugby extension programme. Northland are going the same way."

Brian Cederwall, Wellington's rugby development officer, says: "You have to beware of overkill. There is a balance that must be struck. The bottom line is that for youngsters, including those in rep teams, rugby must still be about having fun."

DON'T THEY REALISE WHAT'S HAPPENING?

Club officials throughout New Zealand remain unimpressed with the attitude of the New Zealand union towards club rugby. In Dunedin, the proud University club has been critical of the high-performance policies of the New Zealand union. "The All Blacks in 10 or 20 years may be struggling to qualify for the quarterfinals of the World Cup," University club president Ross Brown warned in another story in the *Otago Daily Times* series. "The resources being put into high-performance rugby should be redirected into club rugby. The policy of the New Zealand union in identifying talented players while still at school has led to a plethora of colts and academy sides that are set a training and playing schedule that eats heavily into the club season. The high-performance policy is saying in essence that the traditional method of developing rep players — via club rugby — is no longer good enough."

In his 2000 annual report, Brown said the high-performance policy of the New Zealand Rugby Union posed a threat, possibly mortal, to club rugby. "Club rugby is going to be squeezed out the way things are going. You're going to have All Blacks sides in the future which won't even know what the club culture is all about."

In the same University club report, club captain Bill Thompson said: "I am yet to be convinced the NZRFU is even listening to clubs, even though it gives lip service to how it sees club rugby being so important to the future of the game. I get the distinct impression that the game has been taken over by people who have never served the game at grassroots level, and they appear to be on NZRFU staff."

But it's the provincial unions, even more than the national union, that should come under fire if club rugby is not being administered properly. In Wellington, MSP's Brian McGuinness fears the worst. "The writing is on the wall for club rugby. Money has corrupted the game. In New Zealand, rugby has been interwoven with our culture, but since the money came in and people started getting paid, it's become harder to find grassroots volunteers, those people who year after year did the hard graft.

"The professional-amateur thing has really hurt club rugby. In Wellington, you've got the Wellington union running a business, and the clubs running an add-on. The clubs are different animals. One's a business; the other's an amateur game. I wouldn't say the clubs haven't had financial assistance, but by and large they are left to look after themselves. No-one knows the problems of club rugby better than the various club administrators, yet in my time as Chairman I never felt we were really listened to. It was more like we were tolerated. Basically, it was an attitude of, 'Here's some money. Now get on and look after yourselves.' But it's not that easy. And the Wellington union sometimes makes it even harder.

McGuinness says the Wellington union paid little heed to its clubs. "The union has no real understanding of its club scene. David White, when he was CEO of Wellington, said to me, 'You guys are strong enough anyway.' He had no idea how much of a struggle it is for clubs, even the strong ones."

There were more alarm bells about Dunedin club rugby in 2001 when Taieri, a club formed in 1883, announced it could not field a premier team for the first time. This was Taieri, which had fielded All Blacks James Allan, Peter Johnstone, Arran Pene and John Timu; which had the biggest schoolboy club in Otago, and which organised one of the country's biggest annual schoolboy sevens tournaments. In 1955, Taieri shared the senior championship with University A and in 1995 those players held a reunion. There were many happy memories shared that day.

Within a few years, the club had been forced to forfeit its premier status. After finishing fifth in the Dunedin championship in 1999, following a top-three placing the previous year, it seemed Taieri was secure. But during the summer before the 2001 season, several key players were lured away by other clubs and suddenly coach Brian Johnson realised he couldn't field a competitive team. He had the names of 18 members of the previous year's squad and 16 of them had gone elsewhere.

There were many reasons for Taieri's decline. There was a lack of good club administrators. Nine players from the previous year's senior side had headed overseas and there had been no premier colts team over the previous two years. Other Dunedin clubs had lured away Taieri players. But Taieri's problems are far from unique.

Eastern withdrew from the Dunedin premier competition in 2000, creating a bye for the first time ever in the top grade. They returned to the premiers the following year by amalgamating with Dunedin to form the Eastern Sharks.

The plain truth is that the strength of Dunedin senior rugby has declined so much that there is no longer justification for 12 top sides. For 2002, the top club competition comprised just 10 teams — Taieri were still out, and the Sharks did not field a senior side. With all the departures overseas and early retirements from experienced club players, there are enough players to justify perhaps eight premier teams. Until a few years ago, most premier teams comprised mainly players drawn from their area. Now university students comprise the bulk of many premier teams. It reinforces just how important Otago University is to Otago rugby. But having students dominate the premier club scene has other drawbacks. With the academies and various age rep teams now taking priority, club coaches find it increasingly difficult to organise their teams for each week. A couple of seasons ago, University A used 43 players during the season, many of whom were youngsters who were far from ready to play top grade club level.

Waitete used to be the proudest club in the King Country and, because of the Meads link, world famous. Now even Waitete is struggling for numbers. Colin Meads has an interesting theory on this. He feels that the mechanisation of farms is one reason why so many rural clubs are struggling. Whereas previously farmers needed to employ young lads to do jobs around their farms, now farm bikes and farm machinery have taken away the need for much of the human toil. With fewer jobs available, the boys have tended to leave the area, robbing it of potential rugby players.

THE AMALGAMATION GAME

Amalgamation has become the name of the games as clubs battle for survival. There have always been amalgamations. In Dunedin, way back in 1887, Zingari (formed in 1878) and Richmond (1884) linked. In 1899,

Caversham (1884) and Pacific (1884) amalgamated to form Southern. In Wellington in 1932, the Melrose and Selwyn clubs combined and became United. That club became defunct in 1938. (All that remains now is the gymnasium, an old building in the zoo grounds behind Newtown Park.) But the pace of amalgamation has increased rapidly over recent years, a sure sign that clubs have been struggling.

Great old club names are vanishing every year.

AMALGAMATE OR DIE

In Wellington, Karori, Athletic and Onslow combined to form Western Suburbs. Victoria University and Wellington College Old Boys linked to form Harlequins, or Old Boys-University, as it is now known. Taita and Naenae are now Avalon. By mid-2002, Avalon was set to vanish. Poor administration plus falling numbers meant the club faced financial ruin and even a plea to the business community in the area did not provide enough assistance to guarantee Avalon's future. Hutt Old Boys was founded from an amalgamation of Hutt and Hutt Valley High School Old Boys. It later joined with Hutt Valley Marist to form Hutt Old Boys Marist. Earlier Marist and St Pat's Old Boys became Marist St Pat's and Oriental and Eastern Suburbs became Oriental Rongotai. Northern United sprang out of Porirua and Titahi Bay.

In Auckland, Grafton and Cornwall amalgamated in 1982, to form Carlton which, a few years later, became Grammar Carlton. In 1985, Teachers, previously known as Teachers College, and Eastern, formerly Eastern Suburbs, combined to become Teachers Eastern. Roskill Districts takes in Roskill and Hillsborough.

In Christchurch, Merivale and Papanui combined to form Merivale-Papanui which, on amalgamating with Lincoln College, became Merlins. Marist, founded in 1910, and Albion, founded in 1885, became Marist-Albion. Sunnyside Spreydon became Suburbs and now Hoon Hay. Technical Old Boys became Technical-Shirley and is now Shirley.

Besides the Zingari-Richmond and Southern club amalgamations, Otago has Alhambra-Union, which grew out of Alhambra, founded in 1884, and Union, founded in 1872, and Harbour, formed in 1992 when Port Chalmers (1884) joined Ravensbourne (1887).

The situation has been replicated outside the main centres. In provincial unions like Waikato and Counties, the sub-unions, formerly so strong, have almost disappeared, certainly as a force. In other areas, such as Bay of Plenty, clubs are now sports clubs. Clubs such as Te Puke Sports, Tauranga Sports, Opotiki Sports involve several sports, which combine to share premises, administration and other costs.

In Hawke's Bay, two strong Napier clubs, Marist and High School, became

Napier Old Boys Marist. Just as incredible, Hastings Old Boys and Celtic, once thriving clubs, also amalgamated. In Masterton, Red Star and Masterton are now Masterton Red Star.

In 1978, Taranaki had 18 clubs. By 1998, that number had nearly halved. Ukato, Rahotu and Opunake had combined to form Coastal; Manaia, Okaiawa and Hawera Athletic had become Southern; Patea and Waverley were now Border.

And so it goes. There have been many amalgamations, even between once seemingly thriving clubs, in every area of New Zealand. With each amalgamation, a little of what made New Zealand rugby special is lost.

A CASE OF WRONG PRIORITIES

Former All Blacks look at what's happening and shake their heads. "The whole thing is the wrong way round," says Bob Scott. "You can't have all the money going to the top and not enough to the base. It's not healthy for the game overall. They have destroyed a lot of the game by letting this situation develop with the demise of so many clubs.

"I feel sorry for the top players. They will miss out on the after-match evenings at the local club. It was a wonderful feeling. I loved my club footie. I played for Ponsonby and for Petone. I'd line up each week against other strong club teams and often our games would attract crowds of 20,000 or more. There'd be several All Blacks on the field, the standard was great, and you had a very satisfying game. Afterwards you mixed with your opposition and later with all the members from your club, not just players, but club officials who might run fund-raising raffles, organise teams or whatever.

"Club rugby was one of the most enjoyable aspects of my rugby career. I wouldn't have missed it for anything, and I couldn't imagine deliberately missing a game if I could play in it."

Scott feels administrators have not acted in the best interests of rugby. "The game has been taken away from New Zealanders. I'm very hot on what's happened. They have sold the game down the track by taking it away from the ordinary people."

Fred Allen feels the same. "It's heartbreaking. You spend 65 years of your life and then this happens. Clubs used to be the cornerstone of rugby. Club rugby was what provided the basis of the All Blacks. Youngsters would get into senior rugby, learn their trade from the experienced players in the team, and in the opposition, and, if they were good enough, go on to play rep rugby. There was huge club rivalry and the crowds were sometimes enormous. I have played a club match on Eden Park in front of 28,000 people. You still see some old-fashioned club volunteers, some real rugby people, full of enthusiasm for club rugby, but the more you hang around, the more you realise so much of the talk is about money, money, money. If you can get a leading player to turn out for a club, chances are he'll shake hands at the end of the game, then bugger off.

"I played for Grammar and later I coached the team. We'd play the game, then all head off to the Captain Cook and be with the other team and enjoy each other's company. Now they can't get out of the place quick enough."

It's the provincial unions that must take primary responsibility if their clubs aren't being well enough looked after. Their job is to distribute funds and assistance where necessary and appropriate and to oversee all rugby under their jurisdiction.

I was surprised to find the New Zealand union's Brent Anderson relatively unconcerned. "Some clubs are good; others are finding it a battle," he says. "I went down to the club finals in Wairarapa last year and the standard that day was as good or better than the six finals I played in during the 1980s. And that's real rural heartland.

"Sometimes an amalgamation is a sign of club strength, not weakness. Why have two struggling clubs when you can have one strong one? Talent and resources can be more concentrated."

Anderson says it's an unavoidable fact of life that some clubs will have to battle and stresses that the New Zealand union does what it can to support clubs. "We acknowledge the importance of club rugby and try to schedule fixtures during a club 'window', allowing the spotlight at certain times to fall on club rugby. Two unions, Taranaki and Northland, have appointed club liaison officers with New Zealand Rugby Union assistance. And let's not overlook the money that goes to clubs through provincial unions. In 2001, the Hurricanes franchise paid $400,000 to clubs. That's a huge income for clubs."

Be that as it may, it's hard not to agree with *Otago Daily Times* sports editor Brent Edwards, who has been reporting rugby for more than 30 years. In examining the state of New Zealand rugby in 2001, he wrote: "While the NZRFU continues to make soothing noises and voice its commitment to club rugby, the standard of and numbers playing the game at that level continue to decline. The simple fact is that there is too much rugby now and that the game at club level has suffered the most from the professional era."

All Blacks from more isolated areas, such as Tiny White in Gisborne, will talk about how the Super 12 has taken all the good players away from rural areas and placed them into the five Super 12 franchise areas, severely hurting club rugby in many smaller towns. The 1949 team to South Africa included three players from South Canterbury, brothers Maurie and Jack Goddard, from Timaru, and Lachie Grant, from Temuka. Imagine that happening now!

On the other hand, if you talk to today's All Blacks, they will shrug their shoulders and ask what they are supposed to do. They are so committed to Super 12, NPC and international programmes that they simply don't have time for club rugby, even if they have the will.

Before his move to Wellington, Pita Alatini belonged to Dunedin's University club for three seasons, from 1999–2001. But he did not play once for the club. "I'd love to play some club rugby — it's fun — but the way the schedules have been, I haven't been able to," Alatini explained in the *Otago Daily Times* during 2001. "It's hard to cope with all the demands. It's really unfortunate that club rugby does have to suffer, but that seems to be the reality of it.

"Club footie's fun, but it can also be quite demanding because there are players who want to prove themselves against you. You've got to make sure you maintain your standards, so that you come off the field satisfied the guy you've just marked says, 'I've just played someone who deserves to be at a higher level.' "

Dion Waller says he enjoys his association with the Tawa club, but can understand why top players are reluctant to play club rugby. "There's always the worry that you'll cop an injury. And when the All Blacks do play club rugby, they become targets. You get guys who like to take them on and sometimes get a bit nasty about it. Often, especially after the Super 12, you just feel like a bit of a rest from playing rugby. But I really enjoy my association with the Tawa club. It's a bit of rugby down time, when you can get on the piss with the boys and relax. The guys at the club like it when I get out there, and if I'm able to pass on some skills, well, that's good."

Waller makes the point that club rugby is losing numbers not just because professional rugby players are excluding themselves. "It's professionalism in all forms," he says. "I've got a mate who is a plasterer and he is thinking of giving up club rugby because he wants to concentrate more on his job. It just seems more people find reasons not to play club rugby these days."

Former All Black winger-fullback Jeff Wilson joined the Harbour club when he moved from Invercargill to Dunedin after the 1992 season. It is surely revealing that over the next eight seasons, Wilson played 71 games for New Zealand, 60 for the Highlanders, 64 for Otago and just 15 for his club. It's been the same for his New Zealand team-mates from Otago. Carl Hoeft, a member of the Pirates club since 1997, turned out just 14 times for the club in five years, but that was a better ratio than Kees Meeuws managed. Meeuws had three outings for Southern in four years, while Anton Oliver had seven games for University in eight years.

DOES CLUB RUGBY STILL HAVE A ROLE?

John Hart can see the dilemma, and says one mistake people make when looking at club rugby is to compare it with the days of 20 or 30 years ago. "I hear former players like Colin Meads talking about club rugby with great nostalgia, and I understand what they're saying. I played club rugby and I loved it. And I agree that it would be good if club rugby was as strong as possible. But we're in a different era now.

"There is another tier in our rugby now, with the Super 12. You'd probably be better to equate the NPC today with the club rugby of days gone by. You will never get All Black or Super 12 players back in club rugby. It can't happen, except perhaps for the odd game, because the players are so committed to top rugby. They are professionals and club rugby is an amateur game. Top players play so much big rugby now, and it takes such a toll on their bodies, that club rugby is not an option. But All Blacks should all still have an affiliation with a club. If All Blacks could still go along to a club and see the kids, attend the prizegiving, do a bit of coaching, that would be of immense value.

"Rugby officials have to put it into context and ask professional players to be givers, not takers. Gordon Hunter used to call today's top players bankers, because their major concern was their bank account.

"There is no reason why NPC players can't play club rugby and those who choose not to are remiss. It would help their rugby if they played for clubs and it would certainly lift the standard of club rugby if all the NPC players turned out."

Hart feels there are many reasons why club rugby is struggling so much. "Lack of volunteers is one problem," he says, "but there are others. "The game is too complex. It is so difficult to coach that people don't step forward to coach as much. I know of 40-year-old guys who won't coach because it's too difficult. That's a big reason why teachers won't coach. There are too many interpretations and Joe Blow can't coach it.

"Clubs have to be run better, and there is a need for paid administration at club level. If professional rugby wants to help amateur rugby a good way would be to pay for administrators to help club rugby and then tie those clubs back to schools. If I look at Auckland as an example, I would appoint 15 CEOs and pay them $60,000 each per year and they would share time and grow club administrations, then seek out sponsorship. They'd be dealing for the clubs as a group and would have more purchasing power."

Given that the nature of senior teams has changed so much in terms of a younger average age and fewer rep players, Hart feels the standard is fairly good. "Obviously we are missing the experienced core of players who either retire younger to pursue their business careers, or are off overseas playing. But the senior players I watch now are still pretty good, surprisingly good, actually."

Most clubs would be sunk without the money that filters down to them from above. Clubs in the areas of Super 12 franchises receive a payout. In 2001, clubs in the Hurricanes catchment area received up to $28,000 each as a payout, manna from heaven for clubs in today's scene.

Still, only the really pro-active clubs are thriving these days. A strong, vibrant club membership can no longer be taken as a given, even in large suburban areas. To survive, clubs have to be increasingly wise. For instance, Marist St Pat's decided in the early 1990s to mobilise its Catholic business links to help rescue a shaky financial situation. In Wellington, rugby followers said MSP was calling on the Vatican Army. The Shamrock Club was set up and a package offered to companies connected to the club. Fifteen businesses signed up straight away, and that number has increased to more than 50, which contribute more than $20,000 annually to the club coffers, about a fifth of the club income. The club also opted to share their facilities with the St Catherine's Old Girls netball club. The idea was that netballers would mingle with rugby players, after-match speeches would acknowledge players of the day from both codes and everyone would gain. This concept has not worked quite as well, partly because the netballers finish their games at different times and don't often go back to the clubrooms, whereas all the rugby matches finish in late afternoon.

Even MSP, though, finds it hard graft just treading water. Brian McGuinness: "There is still a bit of heart pumping in club rugby, but the signs are not good. It's not what it was and will never return to those days. Even with all our fund-raising, we desperately need the income from the pokies. That provides us with about a fifth of our income and we'd be pretty sick without it."

For decades, energetic and loyal administrators propped up clubs. There are still some such people about, but their numbers are dwindling. Not only is theirs an increasingly thankless task, but many must wonder why they should bother devoting so much time to the game for free when so many others throughout the country are being paid vast sums to be professional administrators.

The New Zealand union, through its much-increased revenue over the past few years, now distributes much bigger sums to provincial unions. In 1995, the 27 provincial unions split $2.1 million between them. In 2001, that figure had risen to $15.7 million, including both direct cash distribution and other resources. This money should, in theory, greatly benefit club rugby, if the provincial unions use it well. But what club rugby needs is players. If it can't get the stars, and the next tier are all heading overseas or quitting rugby in their mid-20s, clubs will continue to struggle.

It's hard not to agree with Meads when he says: "Without club rugby, New Zealand rugby is down the tubes."

chapterSEVEN
PROVINCIAL RUGBY

WHAT PRICE LOYALTY?

It was the decision of Wellington centre Paul Steinmetz near the end of the 2001 season that rammed home to me how much the provincial game has changed since the advent of professional rugby. Steinmetz, who had battled for some seasons to establish himself in the Wellington representative lineup in the face of opposition from such talented midfielders as Alama Ieremia, Jason O'Halloran and Tana Umaga, staged a one-man strike at a critical point in the season because he wasn't happy with the way his contract negotiations were going.

Steinmetz, then 24, having seen off O'Halloran and Ieremia to Japan, felt he fairly much had a starting position locked up for both the Hurricanes and Wellington for the 2002 season. But he was disturbed to learn that the Wellington union had signed All Black second-five Pita Alatini from Otago for 2002, which in all probability would leave Steinmetz on the reserves bench for much of the representative season.

After consultation with his agent, David Monnery, Steinmetz then withdrew his labour. He refused to play in Wellington's make-or-break match against Auckland, hoping to put more pressure on the Wellington union. He was seeking a release from the contract he had signed not long before, so that he would be free to seek his fortune elsewhere, probably in Otago.

Wellington lost comprehensively to Auckland, which effectively ended their title hopes for the season. The Steinmetz negotiations rumbled on. Finally the player was granted a partial release by Wellington and was able to play his Super 12 in 2002 for the Highlanders, while continuing with his NPC commitment to Wellington.

This sort of action by a player has been virtually unheard of in the history of New Zealand rugby. Generally, players have been at pains to represent their province. In previous eras, players would even turn out for their province the day after playing a test match. In 1981, All Blacks Stu Wilson, Bernie Fraser, Allan Hewson, Murray Mexted and Gary

145

Knight all played in the Wellington-Manawatu NPC match just 24 hours after taking part in one of the most epic test matches of all time, the infamous "flour bomb" test at Eden Park, when New Zealand beat South Africa to win the series 2-1.

But Steinmetz turned his back on his team-mates and on thousands of Wellington supporters. His action is a direct result of rugby going professional.

To get an idea of how incredible was Steinmetz's decision, imagine Colin Meads refusing to make himself available for King Country for any reason — money, too many other good players in the squad, not a comfortable enough team bus. Or Brian Lochore turning his back on Wairarapa-Bush. It would have been unthinkable.

In the pre-professional days, players cherished the opportunity to represent their province. Such allegiances and loyalties are vanishing fast, for Steinmetz is surely not a lone case. Others will follow as players make it ever clearer that they are there more for the money than for the honour and glory of representing their province.

Already it is increasingly difficult to get some All Blacks to play at national provincial championship (NPC) level, let alone appear in club matches. It was noticeable during 2001 that after the international segment of the season finished, several All Blacks cried off NPC matches because they were "stale" or needed time to recover from "niggling" injuries. What was equally noticeable was the swift return to the playing field of several players once the All Black coach's job moved from Wayne Smith to John Mitchell and it became clear they would have to justify to a new coach their place in the New Zealand side.

This reluctance to turn out for their provinces is a huge change in attitude for the All Blacks.

There are two major competitions that currently fall under the umbrella of the term Provincial Rugby — the Super 12 and the National Provincial Championship. There is also the Ranfurly Shield, a competition with a century of tradition, but one that is struggling to maintain its relevance in New Zealand's crowded domestic rugby calendar.

It could be claimed that the Super 12 is an international tournament, as the teams it involves come from three countries. However, each team is drawn from enlarged provincial lines, and in New Zealand Super 12 selections tend to roughly mirror NPC selections. Initially it was called the International Provincial Competition (IPC).

THE NPC'S EARLY DAYS

The National Provincial Competition was introduced, belatedly, in 1976. Quite why it took the New Zealand union so long to launch a national championship is puzzling. Soccer's version had been running well for six years, and team sports such as cricket and softball had for many years run national championships. In the late 1960s, the representative rugby season remained fragmented. Air travel was by then commonplace and a national championship seemed a natural progression. Yet rugby administrators in the game's amateur era were generally excessively cautious. Certainly neither Jack Sullivan nor Ces Blazey, the New Zealand union's Chairman and his deputy, was initially enthusiastic about the prospect of an NPC, fearing it would hurt club competition. There were also concerns that the NPC would undermine the Ranfurly Shield.

Especially after soccer had successfully launched its national league, calls for rugby to follow intensified. Auckland rugby administrator Barry Smith led the charge, and there was a feeling throughout the country that some sort of national competition was needed. Some felt a national club competition would be the answer (remember, in those times club competition was a much more significant part of the rugby landscape than it is now). But this proved impractical, so attention turned to a national provincial championship.

This would not only give more focus to the rep season, but had the potential to provide the New Zealand union and its provinces with a guaranteed and sizeable income.

Eventually approval for the launch of the NPC was gained at the New Zealand union's 1975 annual meeting, exactly 100 years after New Zealand's first interprovincial match, held in Dunedin, which was between combined Dunedin clubs and combined Auckland clubs. It was a long process. Besides the energetic Smith, other key people along the way had included Bob Stuart, Ron Don, Peter Wild, Russ Thomas and JJ Stewart. At the 1975 annual meeting, those backing the NPC asked Wanganui delegates Buddy Stevenson and Paul Mitchell to formally make the proposal. Wanganui at the time held considerable sway throughout the country because JJ Stewart, the All Black coach, came from there and Bob Stuart, former All Black captain and leading administrator, was Wanganui's nominee on the New Zealand union executive. It was felt that it was better for the NPC proposal to come from an area like Wanganui than from one of the country's biggest rugby provinces.

It was decided that there would be a first division of 11 teams, plus second divisions that would be split on an island basis. The first division sides were determined after studying teams' results over the previous five seasons. The first division teams were Auckland, Bay of Plenty, Canterbury, Counties, Hawke's Bay, Manawatu, Marlborough, North Auckland, Otago, Southland and Wellington. Only Auckland, Canterbury, Otago and Wellington have never been relegated. The initial format was far from perfect (main complaints being that there was no final, the mandatory South Island quota system that ensured at least four South Island teams were in the first division, and the fact that some provinces had sometimes played up to half their matches before others had even started), but it was exciting for rugby to at last have a national championship.

The winners of the inaugural first division title in 1976 were Bay of Plenty, though it should be remembered that that season the All Blacks were on tour in South Africa for much of the winter.

The NPC has evolved over the years. Protection for South Island teams was maintained until 1984, and a split third division was introduced in 1985, though after a year a standard three-division format was adopted. Most significantly, a play-off system of semi-finals and final was introduced in 1992.

The NPC format now is a good one, which players and public like, though that didn't stop there being various reviews throughout the 1990s, and suggestions of enlarging the first division and combining some unions. Despite pushing from the New Zealand union, such suggestions generally met with a cool reaction from provincial unions and have not been persevered with. Any problems with the NPC have nothing to do with the format.

These days provincial rugby is split into the haves and the have-nots. Only six of the NPC first division's 11 teams are genuine title contenders. The teams in the second and third divisions are feeders to the bigger centres.

The advent of the NPC signalled the gradual erosion of the traditional rep calendar, where major unions like Auckland would play some lesser games against neighbours like Thames Valley and Wellington would play Wanganui and Wairarapa-Bush midweek. Queen's Birthday Weekend would generally signal the start of the serious rep games, such as Auckland-Waikato and Wellington-Manawatu. By then there would have been 10 weeks of club rugby, during which the best players in an area strove to earn and justify inclusion in the rep side. The rep season would run until the end of September.

The NPC's arrival was a good thing. It gave the rep season structure and more of a point, for it enabled a champion team to be found. It managed to thrive without killing off the Ranfurly Shield, though the utter dominance of Canterbury then Auckland through the 1980s did lessen interest in the Shield.

Through its first decade, Bay of Plenty, Canterbury, Wellington, Counties, Manawatu and Auckland all won the NPC first division. Interest was spread and the NPC became a top-class competition.

THE IMPACT OF PROFESSIONALISM

Things changed dramatically after 1995, when rugby officially went pro and the Super 12 franchises totally altered the landscape. Proud provincial unions suddenly saw their best players disappearing. Trying to counter the exodus, two such unions, Manawatu and Hawke's Bay, formed the Central Vikings, who won the second division title in 1998 but were denied access to the first division, not because they didn't deserve promotion, but because they didn't meet some of the Rugby Union's financial requirements. It became increasingly more difficult for strugglers like Southland and Bay of Plenty to score consistent success against the super powers.

These days Northland and Taranaki are hanging on as genuinely competitive first division teams by a combination of judicious talent-scouting, the fierce pride of the players, local support and unrelenting determination. Everybody knows the NPC is flawed these days because of the concentration of rugby talent in a few areas.

In 2001, Northland stunned Auckland 44-43 after a magnificent match. "That was a huge result for New Zealand rugby," says Northland coach Bryce Woodward. "I received dozens of phone calls of congratulations in the days afterwards, from people all over the country, from the top of the New Zealand union down. They thanked us for breathing some life into the NPC by proving that anything was possible. Northland and Taranaki have risen above the odds over the past few years. If they hadn't, the competition would have looked pretty sick. As it is now, I've no doubt the NPC has lost something with the power bases now found at the Super 12 franchise headquarters."

Keith Quinn, who has reported the NPC for Television New Zealand since its inception, says the standard recently has declined noticeably. "The flood of players going overseas has hurt. In the first division now, there are four teams who are generally well off the pace. The NPC can be a good competition, but if it becomes less of a priority for All Blacks, it would be disastrous."

Quinn is right about the exodus of rugby talent. The 2002 *Rugby Almanack* listed the names of no less than 119 New Zealanders, who had played the game at first class level in this country, and who were playing overseas in 2001 — in Argentina, Australia, Canada, the Cook Islands, Croatia, Denmark, England, Fiji, France, Germany, Hong Kong, Ireland, Italy, Japan, the Netherlands, Papua New Guinea, Samoa, Scotland, Spain, Tonga, the United States, Wales and Zimbabwe. And that's only the first class players, quite apart from the thousands of good club players who are now playing their rugby overseas.

(It's not just the players who are heading overseas. In 2002, some very good New Zealand coaches, such as Wayne Smith, Tony Gordon, Peter Thorburn, John Kirwan, Leicester Rutledge, Wayne Smith and Warren Gatland, were based overseas.)

Other things have further undermined the NPC's integrity. The way players are lent to other unions has reduced the competition to farcical proportions. In 2001 James Arlidge, a promising first-five, was not required by Auckland, who lent him to Northland. Arlidge proved a class player and ironically won the match for Northland over Auckland soon after with his superlative play and accurate goal-kicking, contributing four conversions and two penalties. He played all Northland's NPC games, tallying 118 points, and was then drafted into Auckland's ranks for their final two games of the season.

Bay of Plenty were a good example in 2001 of a union benefitting so much from the loan system that their NPC results became rather mean-ingless. Among the 42 players they used that season, two were on loan from Auckland, three from Waikato, one from Wellington, two from Canterbury and one came from Queensland. It was the same throughout the country. Buller used 38 players, including two from Wellington, three from Nelson, seven from Canterbury and one from Auckland. East Coast, whose second division performance was so celebrated, were a champion borrower, using six Hawke's Bay players, five from Wellington, one from Poverty Bay, one from Auckland and one from Bay of Plenty — 14 temporary imports on a roster of 33 players. Much of the borrowing was justified on the grounds that the players hailed from the Ngati Porou tribe, though I cannot find any mention of tribal affiliation in the New Zealand Rugby Union handbook.

King Country, Marlborough, Mid Canterbury, Poverty Bay and Wanganui also borrowed players from at least four different unions.

Canterbury and Auckland acted as feeder unions to all the lesser unions surrounding them, as well as to some further afield. Altogether 67 Canterbury players appeared in NPC matches in 2001, 38 for Canterbury and another 29 for South Canterbury, Mid Canterbury, Buller, West Coast, Marlborough, Nelson, Bays, Southland and Bay of Plenty.

When players are able to switch about from union to union so freely, it undermines the integrity of the competition. For instance, how could East Coast truly claim to have beaten Manawatu when so many of their players were supplied by other provinces?

Many provincial coaches don't agree with me on this. Bryce Woodward: "I support the lending of players. In Northland we have a policy that we try to minimise loaned and outside players, but in this professional era, we find our home-grown talent is ripped away from us. We can't afford to buy a $20,000 player off another union. It's a bit frustrating. There are Northlanders playing good rugby all over the country. The days of Northland keeping a player like Sid Going are gone. We find that when we do get hold of some talented youngsters, they make good progress with us. James Arlidge is an example. We try very hard to make all our players, including the loan players and those from overseas, understand what the Northland community is about. There's a definite feel to rugby in Northland, and when they understand that and make a proper commitment to the area, they play better. You get the odd player not interested in that side of things. They get found out very quickly. From our point of view, if there were no loan players, it would play even more into the hands of the wealthy unions."

Woodward says the argument continues to be waged. "Ken Going came out strongly against loan players. He wants home-grown players representing Northland. Ken is from the old school. He didn't like it that we had a couple of Fijians playing for us because he felt the community wouldn't buy into a Northland team with the talent imported.

"I know what Ken was getting at, but in this professional era, it's not realistic. Northland has to aggressively chase every scrap of talent it can get its hands on. As it is, the deck is stacked against provinces like Northland, without getting too noble about only playing home-grown players."

As the *Rugby Almanack* noted in 2001: "Success in the NPC is no longer a reflection of a strong, healthy club competition, but a reflection of the most active unions making maximum use of spare talent from a metropolitan union. Rural club players, disappointed at being omitted from their NPC squad because of a loan player being preferred, head off overseas, which further reduces player numbers and club teams."

This all impacts on the supporters of various unions. In much the same way as English soccer is now all about supporting the jersey, rather than the player, so it is with New Zealand provincial rugby. In England, clubs seldom field more than a couple of local players.

Provincial fans are being asked to support not the local blokes made good, but the results of a shopping spree, players who could be gone in two or three months' time and have little affinity with the area.

It's not that players in New Zealand never used to swap provinces. Kel Tremain and Wilson Whineray moved about the country, playing their rugby for whichever area their work or study took them to. Stu Wilson and Grant Batty moved from Wairarapa to Wellington in their late teens. Graham Mourie, Taranaki born and bred, played for Wellington for a couple of years while studying at Victoria University, then returned to Taranaki. Fred Allen played first for Canterbury and later for Auckland, Kit Fawcett for Otago, then Waikato.

But these moves were not made primarily for rugby reasons. Young men might go to Dunedin or Wellington to study at university, then move on. Or their jobs would force them to move from one city to another. They seldom transferred because they were lured by a province seeking to enhance its rugby team. Many players — for example, Tiny White, Allan Hewson, Doug Rollerson, Fergie McCormick, Colin Meads, Bryan Williams, Laurie Mains, Brian Lochore, Joe Stanley — played for one province throughout their long careers.

Now, with rugby a professional sport, players have licence to hawk off their services to the team that will pay the most. It doesn't happen just in rugby; mercenary players have similarly spoiled netball's national competition. But in rugby, where there is so much more money on offer, the situation is more dire. Provincial loyalties have been blurred.

The New Zealand Rugby Union seems to have grasped the danger. For the 2002 season it introduced new eligibility rules, restricting the number of overseas players a team could field to two (which still means up to 54 for the competition), and also limiting the number of players able to be imported from other provinces. The changes help a little, but they don't go far enough.

For all its high profile, sponsorship and television exposure, the NPC is in danger of becoming a second-class competition. When the New Zealand Rugby Union permits its employees — the players — to bypass many matches on flimsy grounds, when it allows a loan system that undermines the integrity of the competition, when only a few teams are capable of winning the major trophy and when players are now willing to boycott matches to give their pay and contract negotiations greater leverage, then there is something rotten at the heart of the competition.

FINANCIAL CHAOS

There's worse to come, I fear. The drums are still beating for the Super 12 competition to be extended, which would cut further into the domestic season, and give players even more excuse to claim tiredness or injury recuperation time. The NPC, even though it is the greatest national rugby competition in the world, will continue to be chipped away and undermined.

The problems with the NPC are reflected in the parlous financial state in which some provinces now find themselves. While the super unions are doing very well, elsewhere some are on the brink of financial disaster. There may be a good case for amalgamating some — West Coast and Buller, with struggling club competitions, could profitably unite.

But it's not just isolated unions like Buller and West Coast that have struggled. In 1997, the New Zealand union had to bail out four provincial unions because, according to then Chief Executive David Moffett, they were "in a perilous financial situation", having each recorded losses of between $148,000 and $220,00. The main problem was payments to players, which had drained provinces of financial resources.

The New Zealand union had to provide special financial support to the four to prevent them from going bust, a situation created mainly by their fight for promotion — or against relegation — in the NPC.

Perhaps more startling was Moffett's other revelation that year that only the four main test-venue unions (not coincidentally, all were Super 12 franchise headquarters) had solid profit balances for 1997. The other 23 unions did not. Half the unions traded in the red. But for the New Zealand union's direct support grants of $70,000 per union, 24 of the unions would have been in debt.

Over the past few years, many provincial unions have run into major financial trouble at one time or another. Bay of Plenty, Counties-Manukau, North Harbour and Poverty Bay are four of many. Generally, the financial plight of these provincial unions can be attributed to poor management. There may be insufficient sponsorship, and ineffective relationships with existing sponsors. The problem could be not enough improvements to the union's major ground, meaning too small a spectator capacity. A poor performance by the provincial team, perhaps through lack of attention to player development policies, or not enough emphasis on improving coaching standards, could be the problem. As a rule of thumb, you will find that a provincial union that is performing poorly in administration will also return below-standard results on the field. When teams start to punch above their weight in the NPC, there will almost inevitably be a link back to a much-improved administrative structure.

A union like Counties-Manukau is probably typical. It's ironic that Jonah Lomu is the richest rugby player in New Zealand, a multi-millionaire, while the union that produced him is virtually insolvent. Worse for Counties, in 2001 they were relegated from the NPC first division, after three seasons of struggling to hold their head above water. For a province that produced All Black greats like Bruce Robertson and Andy Dalton, and that in the 1970s and '80s, under the coaching of Barry Bracewell and Hiwi Tairoa, was very fashionable, it was a real fall from grace.

Well into the mid-1990s, Counties looked very healthy. They had in Mac McCallion a forthright coach who could get the most out of his team, and players like the emerging Lomu and Joeli Vidiri, who drew crowds with their exciting running and try-scoring ability. In the first two years of Super 12, they were beaten NPC finalists, but as super unions have siphoned off their strength, they have struggled increasingly.

But it all unravelled surprisingly quickly. Counties' identity was submerged by Auckland in the original Blues franchise. They lost good players to the two surrounding super-provinces they border, Waikato and Auckland, while Lomu went to Wellington. The Counties area produces outstanding teenaged players, but many have been lured away, notably by the Otago union offering inducements for boys willing to travel south. Crowds at the Counties home ground, the Lion Red Stadium in Pukekohe, diminished as the rep team's results got worse. For 2003 the major stadium in the area will be the Pacific Arena in Manukau. It is by no means certain that the change in location will help Counties' fortunes.

Counties may well have been partly responsible for its own problems, with a quick turnover of people in key positions such as rep coach, union board Chairman and Chief Executive, and a less than concerted approach. But it is an example of a casualty of the professional area, one of the have-nots in an era of haves and have-nots.

Even unions that on the surface look to be thriving are nervous about what lies ahead. John Hornbrook, who has been Chief Executive of the Otago union since 1985 (when there were four fulltime staff, compared to 15 now, plus the Highlanders staff), was recently asked by *Otago Daily Times* Sports Editor Brent Edwards how he saw the state of club rugby in 10 years' time. "Unless Dunedin grows significantly and the tertiary institutions get bigger, we'll struggle to maintain the number of teams we have," he said. One of the major concerns for clubs, he said, was their debts. "They have large clubrooms, which cost them a lot of money to keep up to scratch. One of our main goals is to get our clubs debt-free. To do that we need to be making a surplus ourselves to help our clubs."

What professionalism has done is add a huge expense to every union's costs — player payments. As John Hart says: "New Zealand isn't big enough or rich enough to be able to afford to have hundreds of professional rugby players. I believe contracts should be offered to players who reach Super 12 level. Below that — NPC, club, youth — there shouldn't be payments. It's bad for the game. I say leave the NPC as an amateur competition, with the carrot being a Super 12 contract for players who excel in the NPC."

THE RANFURLY SHIELD

The Ranfurly Shield, for so long the premier trophy in New Zealand, has been terribly affected by the advent of professional rugby and rugby's move to the big towns. The Shield has been contested since 1904, when Wellington beat Auckland and became the first successful challenger, and there have been some magnificent eras, dramatic matches and memorable pieces of individual brilliance since.

Auckland held the Shield from 1905–13, setting a record with 23 successful defences. Along came Hawke's Bay after the First World War, and, with superstars like the Brownlie brothers, Bert Cooke and George Nepia leading the way, held the prized log o' wood from 1922–27, repelling 24 challenges. Southland enjoyed a reign that endured nearly 10 years — from 1938–47, but involved just 11 successful defences.

Otago, coached by the inimitable Vic Cavanagh, took forward play to another level and dominated the Shield from 1947–50, through 18 defences. Later in the 1950s, it was Canterbury's turn, and they held on for 23 defences. Fred Allen got hold of Auckland and guided a team stacked with good players through 25 successful defences from 1959–63, in so doing, setting a new benchmark.

Hawke's Bay enjoyed their second golden era in the late 1960s. Canterbury had another three-season reign and still teams like King Country, Southland, Wairarapa-Bush and Counties could challenge with realistic hope of success.

In the 1960s and '70s, Taranaki, Hawke's Bay, Marlborough, South Canterbury, Manawatu and North Auckland all won the Shield, and therefore spread interest in the competition throughout the country. But since 1980, only Waikato, Wellington, Canterbury, Auckland and Taranaki (for a fortnight) have held the Shield. Taranaki's effort was an aberration — it won the Shield in 1996 off a second XV from Auckland and lost it a couple of weeks later to Waikato.

The age of areas like Marlborough, South Canterbury, Hawke's Bay or Manawatu holding the Shield has gone, and with it the special magic of the competition.

Older footie fans feel real nostalgia for the log of wood. The Ranfurly Shield has given New Zealand some of its most famous games. The tempestuous Battle of Solway, between Wairarapa and Hawke's Bay, in 1927. Otago's come-from-behind win over Auckland in 1947. The Canterbury-Auckland "match of the century" in 1985. Great players have established their reputations in Shield games. We think back to a young loose forward named Waka Nathan, urged on by Wilson Whineray, doubling round to score under the posts to help earn Auckland a nerve-jangling 19-18 win over Canterbury in 1960. That match signalled the arrival of a world-class flanker.

With the advent of pro rugby and the confining of New Zealand's leading rugby talent to just a few major unions, the Ranfurly Shield has slipped a long way. It doesn't mean there aren't still some cracking Shield games. Wellington lost a dramatic challenge to Canterbury in the dying moment in 2001. Afterwards there was huge anguish in the capital and irate Wellington fans complained about the refereeing of Steve Walsh. A normal NPC match that ended the same way would not have generated the same after-match heat. So the Ranfurly Shield still means something. But its importance has undeniably diminished.

Back in the late 1960s, Colin Meads' King County team staged a formidable challenge against Kel Tremain's Hawke's Bay side. It was a stirring match, fiercely contested all the way. Meads and Tremain, team-mates for a decade and firm friends, battled each other to a standstill and entreated their troops for ever greater efforts. It was during this match that Tremain is said to have turned to the referee and asked him to count the number of Hawke's Bay players on the field, claiming: "I think Meads has eaten one of them." The country followed the challenge on the radio. For an hour or two it was the only thing happening in New Zealand. Imagine that today: the country held spellbound by a torrid Hawke's Bay–King Country rugby match. Times have changed.

As with the Ranfurly Shield, so with the inter-island match. This fixture was once an eagerly-awaited part of the rugby calendar, but looks to have vanished forever. It was played each year until 1986, but has been held only once since, in 1995. Australian rugby league has done brilliantly by promoting its annual State of Origin encounters. New Zealand rugby already had a similar competition, but has thrown it away.

chapter EIGHT

AND **THEN** CAME THE **SUPER** 12

ORIGINS OF THE SUPER 12

The Super 12 arrived in 1996 with all the bells and whistles of a new competition backed by blanket television coverage. There are many who can claim some credit for devising the competition, but it seems that in late April, 1995, the CEOs of the New South Wales, Queensland and Australian Rugby Unions, — David Moffett, Terry Doyle and Bruce Hayman — sat in an office at Ballymore and built the Super 12 from its foundations.

From their deliberations a revolutionary new competition emerged. It eventually comprised five teams from New Zealand (Auckland Blues, Waikato Chiefs, Wellington Hurricanes, Canterbury Crusaders and Otago Highlanders), three from Australia (Queensland Reds, New South Wales Waratahs and Australian Capital Territory Brumbies) and four from South Africa (Natal, Transvaal, Northern Transvaal and Western Province). Since those days, the New Zealand union has tried to emphasise the franchise, rather than the provincial element of the competition, so the geographic names Auckland, Waikato, Wellington, Canterbury and Otago have been dropped. After two years, the South Africans changed tack. After initially involving their top four Currie Cup teams in the competition, they introduced regional teams from 1998 and the South African teams are now called the Bulls, Cats, Sharks and Stormers.

It was planned that the Super 12 would involve the top 150 or so of New Zealand's players, spread out among five franchises so that teams were evenly matched, and that a draft system would operate. But there were early misgivings about the competition.

It was hoping for a lot to simply announce a new competition and then expect it to immediately be a huge hit. It lacked tradition, and there was simply a pot-pourri of rep players bought, sold and exchanged, then thrown together to form a "team". The blending of various provinces into one team had to be a worry.

The franchises were initially broken down like this:

Auckland Blues
Auckland, Counties-Manukau

Waikato Chiefs
Northland, North Harbour, Waikato, Bay of Plenty, King Country, Thames Valley

Wellington Hurricanes
Wellington, Manawatu, Hawke's Bay, Horowhenua, Wairarapa-Bush, Taranaki, Wanganui, Poverty Bay, East Coast

Canterbury Crusaders
Canterbury, Marlborough, Nelson Bays, Buller, West Coast, Mid Canterbury, South Canterbury

Otago Highlanders
Otago, Southland, North Otago

Understandably, Northland and North Harbour were unhappy about being lumped in with Waikato. Would Taranaki, Manawatu, Hawke's Bay and other southern North Island provinces be happy to be a feeder for Wellington? Would Otago totally dominate the proud Southland area? Changes have been made. Now Northland, North Harbour and Auckland make up the Blues, and Counties-Manukau has moved to the Chiefs. The Hurricanes situation works tolerably well (though in 2002 both the Manawatu and East Coast unions claimed their players were not getting a fair go at selection for even the Hurricanes' development squad), and it does seem that Otago has indeed utterly dominated Southland in the Highlanders franchise. In 2002, there were 22 Otago players, two from North Harbour, one from Canterbury and one from Wellington in the Highlanders' original 26-man squad. No-one from Southland was chosen.

The fact that there was no promotion-relegation element was another concern. Once teams could no longer make the top four semi-finals, the danger was that their effort would fall off appreciably. What did it matter if they finished sixth, ninth or eleventh?

Then there was the question of what the competition would do to New Zealand provincial rugby, for it seemed obvious that it would concentrate talent in a few key cities. Already the trend was for promising or ambitious second and third division players to move to first division areas, where they might better catch the eyes of the national selectors. Thus players like Steve McDowell and Adrian Cashmore moved from Bay of Plenty to Auckland in the early stages of their careers. Would the Super 12 spell the end for areas such as Hawke's Bay, Southland, Northland, Taranaki and Bay of Plenty as significant powers in domestic rugby? And who would even care about second and third division rugby?

Finally, the Super 12 was scheduled to begin at the start of March. This would stretch the season greatly. Would it mean there was too much rugby and not enough of a break for top players and for the rugby public? New Zealanders love their rugby, but would this be overkill?

On the face of it, it could be claimed the Super 12 has been a dazzling success, despite these initial reservations. It provides three months of good rugby between the top players from the three major southern hemisphere rugby powers. Especially in its first two or three years, the Super 12 brand of rugby was highly entertaining, with the emphasis on running the ball and scoring tries.

The competition draws very large crowds and even bigger television viewing audiences. In 2002, the unbeaten Crusaders drew an average of 27,666 spectators to their home matches and a total attendance of 160,186, almost 5000 more than the record, set in 1998. New Zealand's total Super 12 attendances in 2002 also smashed previous records — the average crowd of 22,887 was almost 1000 up on 1998, which had been the year for record attendances.

HOW THE SUPER 12 HAS HURT NEW ZEALAND RUGBY

Sadly, there is a downside. What's great for the crowd may not be so good for the future of the sport here. If it wasn't for the commercial aspects — the television revenue from the competition largely funds the professional side of New Zealand rugby — I feel the competition would be altered dramatically, or even scrapped.

There can be little doubt it has hurt New Zealand provincial rugby. Any good players from areas like Poverty Bay, King Country or Marlborough will quickly be snapped up by a Super 12 franchise and, chances are, will play their NPC rugby for the base of that franchise. Leon MacDonald learned his rugby in Blenheim, but it is Canterbury and the Crusaders who get the benefits. Buller's Ben Blair was also drawn to Christchurch. It should be noted that the Crusaders and Canterbury seem to make visiting players feel extraordinarily welcome. Others who have transferred to Canterbury in recent years through their Super 12 connection have included Mark Robinson, Greg Feek, Norm Maxwell, Scott Robertson, Caleb Ralph, Justin Marshall, Reuben Thorne and Greg Somerville.

When the first serious All Black team of 2002 was named, there was widespread comment and some criticism because John Mitchell named 13 Crusaders in his starting XV. A closer inspection showed that many of the so-called Crusaders were not actually from Canterbury. The All Black team (the last 13 of whom were Crusaders), with the province where each player learned his rugby:

Christian Cullen (Horowhenua)
Doug Howlett (Auckland)
Caleb Ralph (Bay of Plenty)
Mark Robinson (Taranaki)
Aaron Mauger (Canterbury)
Andrew Mehrtens (Canterbury)
Justin Marshall (Southland)
Scott Robertson (Bay of Plenty)
Reuben Thorne (Taranaki)
Richie McCaw (Otago)
Chris Jack (Canterbury)
Norm Maxwell (Northland)
Dave Hewett (Canterbury)
Mark Hammett (Canterbury)
Greg Somerville (Hawke's Bay)

In fact, Mitchell picked a team that was drawn from most parts of New Zealand. It's just that because of the Super 12 competition, the Crusaders had acted as a magnet for many of them to move to Christchurch.

But for injury, Leon MacDonald, another Crusader, would have been fullback instead of Cullen. MacDonald's original province was Marlborough.

It hasn't happened just in Canterbury. Paul Miller, the All Black No 8, moved from Invercargill to Dunedin to play for the Highlanders and now plays for Otago, too (though he was loaned to Southland for the 2002 NPC). Another of the crop of new All Blacks, first five-eighth David Hill, was one of Marlborough's pride and joys. He went south to get first division exposure with Southland, was then snapped up by the Chiefs and now turns out for Waikato. Brendan Laney was a South Canterbury representative who was lured south and finished his New Zealand domestic career by playing for the Highlanders and Otago. There are many similar examples; the players can't be blamed for what is, the way things are now, a commonsense attitude.

The strong keep getting stronger. The Blues have gained Joeli Vidiri, Justin Collins, Justin Wilson and Nick White, all of whom also turned out for Auckland. The Chiefs have gained Roger Randle and Mark Ranby, to Waikato's benefit. The Hurricanes have gained David Holwell, Jonah Lomu and Tony Coughlan, all of whom then bolstered the Wellington team. The Highlanders have gained Neil Brew and George Leaupepe, who became Otago players.

We won't see such things as Tiny White living in Gisborne and being a leading All Black. Or Colin Meads spearheading the King Country season; Alan Sutherland and Brian Ford turning out in Marlborough colours. Phil Gard played for the All Blacks in 1971–72 while representing lowly North Otago, an unthinkable scenario today. Even in the 1980s, it wasn't vital to come from a major union. Andrew Donald was an All Black halfback while representing Wanganui. Brett Harvey, Marty Berry, Brent Anderson and Rob McLean all became All Blacks in 1986 or '87 while representing Wairarapa-Bush.

Because this doesn't happen now, the NPC is weakened as a competition, with the first division strength centred on six or seven teams, and the second and third divisions containing no top players.

A by-product of this trend is that leading coaches and would-be leading coaches must also all base themselves in the main rugby centres. You won't very often find cases such as those of Ted Griffin (Northland), Colin le Quesne (Hawke's Bay), Brian Lochore (Wairarapa-Bush), Peter Burke (Taranaki), Jack Gleeson (Manawatu) and JJ Stewart (Wanganui), who coached provincial teams outside the main centres with great success and, in many cases, moved from there to national selecting and coaching prominence.

It seems that the Super 12 and the Tri-Nations competitions are regarded by the New Zealand union as sacrosanct because, even though they cause all sorts of problems in the New Zealand season, they generate the money that sustains professional rugby. By way of contrast, the NPC, though a wonderful competition, is not as profitable. Because the Rugby Union funds all travel for competing teams, the provincial unions make a profit out of the NPC. But it costs the New Zealand union money. To the bean counters, concerned with balance sheets, profits and losses, this must be painful. But surely money that sustains the NPC is money well spent, helping to foster the game nationally. It's an investment.

WHAT'S MORE IMPORTANT: THE SUPER 12 OR
ALL BLACK VICTORIES?

Former All Black captain John Graham told *Sunday Star-Times* sports editor Duncan Johnstone in 2001 that the Super 12 should be scrapped in the interests of saving All Black and New Zealand rugby. He felt the Super 12 hindered the All Blacks from performing at their peak for test rugby, pointing out that All Black rugby had not significantly improved since the introduction of the Super 12, while the NPC had lost its edge and club rugby was failing.

"I can't see how any professional rugby players can play to their best when they have Super 12, NPC, Tri-Nations, overseas touring sides here and an All Black tour," said Graham. "Our All Black brand will continue to suffer if the players are not at their peak when they play for the All Blacks. There is no earthly point in hearing about our players being stale without doing something to fix it. Players see the All Blacks as the pinnacle, but there is so much pressure on them to produce the goods early on that the Super 12 has become the more important mission."

Graham accepted that the Super 12 would probably remain because it was the money-raiser that kept the game afloat, but said interest in making money had become more important than the success of the All Blacks, which had to be of grave concern for the game. The tough-talking former headmaster said the New Zealand Rugby Union was at the crossroads in shaping the country's rugby future: to continue with its Super 12 commitment, or seek to restore the All Blacks to No 1 in the world. "If a brave union said it wanted to nurture the game in this country to protect the All Black brand, which is the competition that should go? I don't have any doubt about that at all. It's the Super 12."

In 2001, *New Zealand Rugby Almanack* editors Clive Akers and Geoff Miller lamented the state of New Zealand's club and domestic rugby competitions: "Sadly New Zealand domestic rugby is at the mercy of the Sanzar partners and the IRB, who are looking at developing a global rugby season. The game is now top-heavy with administrators searching for the ideal global game, and the New Zealand Rugby Football Union will have less control over the old-fashioned, but hugely succession chain of club competition, NPC and national teams.

"Our Sanzar partners are keen to expand the Super 12 which, in turn, pushes the Tri-Nations further into the NPC season. The more our international partners can interrupt our successful domestic competition, the more advantage they hold at international level. The more our All

Blacks are restricted from NPC participation, the less effective they will be in international rugby."

Norm Hewitt, the former Wellington and Hurricanes captain, says that having the Super 12 is like playing a test match every weekend. "It's extremely hard on the players physically. They get hammered, even before the test matches roll around. And it's also a bit of overkill. I mean, during the Super 12 season, it's like there's five test matches being played per weekend. It's too much, and it starts to turn people off."

What is interesting is that the New Zealand Rugby Union's stated No 1 goal is All Black success. That is a foundation belief of the union, for everyone realises that if the All Blacks lose, everything else — commercial opportunities, spectator numbers, playing numbers, income — drops away. Murray McCaw, when presenting his Chairman's report at the 2002 annual meeting of the union, cited "ensuring the All Blacks are the best in the world" as an area that the union intended focusing on strongly.

With that in mind, how does the union then justify continuing with the Super 12 in its present form? Players, coaches and all concerned are adamant that the Super 12 is raising the standard of Australian rugby, but hurting New Zealand's. If the No 1 New Zealand union goal is All Black supremacy, is it not impossible to justify continuing with the Super 12?

Those who think about the game in New Zealand worry about the way test football has been downgraded and how the NPC and club football are being affected. Murray Mexted, former All Black great and current Sky Television commentator, told the Wellington *Evening Post* during the 2002 Super 12 season: "It's imperative that we retain the strength of our various competitions, and I'm talking about club rugby and the NPC . . . The moment you tinker with that, you are limiting the future longevity of New Zealand rugby as a world force. You change that at your peril."

Lindsay Knight put it well in his introduction to *NPC — The Heart of Rugby* when he wrote: "The money interests now running the game believe that the only competitions for top players now should be the Super 12 and internationals. Yet that presents a catch-22 . . . the Super 12 might be needed because of the money it generates to pay for professionalism, but the NPC, where professionals merge with semi-professionals and amateurs, remains for New Zealand the most important competition. It may be a conflict caused by the NPC representing the heart and soul of New Zealand rugby, but the price of the move to professionalism in the mid-nineties was that a good part of that soul had to be sold."

Players and coaches know what effect the Super 12 is having. Going into the 2002 season, All Black centre Tana Umaga called for the scrapping of the Super 12. He said in *The Dominion* newspaper he thought it made more sense for the top players to play more club rugby, as that would help raise the standard of play throughout New Zealand.

"The Super 12 starts too early for us, and every year they seem to want to start earlier. I would rather push out the Super 12 and just have club rugby, the internationals and the NPC," Umaga said. "That's the way it used to be, but there are not many of us traditionalists left."

The Super 12 will remain at least until Sanzar's contract with News Ltd expires in 2005. I would expect it to continue after that. The New Zealand union needs vehicles to generate money to cover its costs, including player contracts, and the Super 12 is a big profit-maker.

Those who defend the Super 12 point to the money it can make for provincial unions. Some of New Zealand's Super 12 franchises — generally the Hurricanes, Crusaders and sometimes the Highlanders — are able to make big payouts each year to their member unions because of the income they get through gate receipts and marketing. For the franchises that aren't as financially successful — the Chiefs and the Blues — it's bad luck for their member unions. Thus Wairarapa-Bush does very well out of the Hurricanes, but Bay of Plenty misses an equivalent cash handout because the Chiefs have not proved very profitable. This distribution is seen by the provincial unions who are missing out as unfair and is the cause of much griping.

It would require a good deal of bravery to turn away certain income, but surely the New Zealand union must at some point heed the pleas from players like Umaga. "It's going to come to the stage where rugby administrators have to be honest about it and admit there is just too much rugby," says Umaga. "I'd like to see club rugby becoming stronger, with us going back to our clubs and then to the provinces. It makes us rely on ourselves and makes us stronger. We are helping other countries become stronger by playing against them all the time. I'd rather look after ourselves first."

One Super 12 player I spoke to said he was disappointed by Umaga's comments: "It's easy for Tana to say that. He's an All Black, so he's getting plenty of coin. What about those of us who aren't All Blacks, but are trying to make a living out of professional rugby? We need the Super 12."

Umaga's Hurricanes and All Black team-mate Dion Waller says most players can see the good and the bad in the Super 12. "We like it because it gives us the chance to play against the best players from Australia and South Africa," says Waller. "It pays good money, too. But on the other hand, it's a very tough competition and there's no time to recover from injury. In the 2002 Super 12, I broke my hand, partially tore a calf muscle and pulled a hamstring. I had to battle through as best I could. As a player, you get selfish — you don't want somebody else taking your place in the team. He might play well, and keep you out."

Waller said he was in no doubt that the All Blacks would play better if the Super 12 didn't exist. "I've seen it myself in the All Blacks," says Waller. "You have players who are carrying injuries that haven't had the chance to recover. They think they are giving it 100 per cent, but they are really only at 80 per cent because that's all their bodies will allow.

"I do agree with Tana that the country the Super 12 is really helping is Australia, and that overall it's hurting our top players."

THE AUSSIES LOVE IT, OF COURSE

The Australian view of the Super 12 is, of course, vastly different from New Zealand's. Respected Australian journalist Greg Growden, writing a 2002 Super 12 preview article in the *Sydney Morning Herald*, had this to say: "As the Super 12 heads into its seventh season, the competition remains the Southern Hemisphere rugby jewel. It commands as much interest as the domestic test series, generates capacity crowds and continues to be the real international trendsetter. It remains vibrant, ever changing, ever alive. It brings in the fans because it appeals to their sporting instincts. It is a simply devised and easy to understand tournament that encourages and rewards those who seek to be different and adventurous. Everything else in rugby basically follows the Super 12."

That view is fairly representative of the Australian attitude to the Super 12. The success of the competition across the Tasman has meant that the number of union players is rivalling the number of those playing league there. In 2001 there was a seven per cent increase in rugby union player numbers, to 136,000. That's up from just 86,000 back in 1996 and represents an overall increase of 58 per cent. League stars like Lote Tuqiri, Andrew Walker, Wendell Sailor and Mat Rogers have switched to rugby union. For Aussies, the Super 12 has been a saviour.

The Australians have no state championship to speak of, so the Super 12 gives their test hopefuls the chance to get tough, high-quality international competition before the Tri-Series. On the other hand, the South Africans have not really responded to the Super 12 challenge — just witness the lowly finishing positions of the four South African franchises in the 2002 Super 12 for confirmation. It was amazing that South Africa would be pushing, as it was, for a fifth Super 12 team when clearly the four teams already there weren't making a competitive go of things.

New Zealand teams have done exceedingly well in the Super 12. The Blues won it in 1996 and '97, and the Crusaders in 1998, '99, 2000 and 2002. It wasn't until the sixth year of the event that a team from another country claimed the trophy. The Crusaders, the Blues, the Highlanders and even the Hurricanes have had great moments in the Super 12. The least happy franchise has probably been the Chiefs, who have yet to make a semi-final, but their record is as good, if not better, than some South African teams. The success of the New Zealand sides is not surprising. We take our rugby seriously and have embraced this new competition. The players and their fans are proud of any win over Australian or South African opposition. Over a series of a dozen matches, New Zealand teams will generally perform with distinction.

But this success has been at a price. It means our domestic season is now absurdly long, stretching from February (the Super 12 start has been brought forward by several weeks since the competition's early years) until October; it means players are much more likely to get hit by both physical and mental fatigue. And it means there is almost no chance of top players playing club rugby, which unfortunately is almost an irrelevance these days. It wasn't that long ago that there used to be what was termed a silly season, a period of a few weeks between the finish of the winter codes and the start of the summer, or vice versa. I wonder when players get married now that the silly season has disappeared! (Keith Quinn made doubly sure he missed no rugby. He was married on Friday, April 3, well away not only from rep matches, but also from Saturday club play.)

It's a vicious circle. If the Super 12 competition was reduced in length, perhaps by forming two pools with the winners to play off, it would give players more time to rest. But it would also mean less income through television because there would be fewer matches played. With less income, the players would be paid less. They would then be more likely to head overseas and chase bigger cheques. If that happened, Rugby Union officials would have to relax the current rules, which bar players based overseas from being considered for the All Blacks. But then, once those overseas-based players became eligible to represent New Zealand, there would be even less incentive for good players to remain in this country, and the domestic competitions, such as club rugby and the NPC, would be utterly undermined. That's the conundrum New Zealand rugby officials face, balancing the demands of raising money to fund the game with those of allowing the players to run on to the park in the best possible condition.

Super 12 defenders said that by putting in place this sort of international provincial competition, and bringing in lots of money, administrators would have enough money to be able to stop top players from heading overseas, even if it seemed their All Black days were over. The reverse seems to have happened. Players who have been dropped from the All Blacks use the fact that they are still competing at Super 12 level to broker lucrative financial deals in the northern hemisphere and are lost to New Zealand rugby. Todd Blackadder, Jon Preston, Ofisa Tonu'u, Andrew Blowers, Craig Dowd, Filo Tiatia, Jason O'Halloran, Alama Ieremia, Adrian Cashmore, Norm Berryman, Shane Howarth, Frank Bunce, Richard Loe, Lee Stensness, Glen Osborne, Isitola Maka, Mark Mayerhofler, Stephen Bachop, Stu Forster and Tabai Matson are among dozens who fit into this category. That's a lot of expertise for New Zealand rugby to lose, temporarily or permanently, in just a few years.

These sorts of players, dropped from the All Blacks, are less inclined to stay and try to fight their way back into the national side. In days past Kevin Briscoe, Neil Wolfe, Earle Kirton, Laurie Mains, Greg Cooper, Zinzan Brooke and many others have been dropped from the All Blacks for quite some time before regaining their places. Now the temptation is to simply pull up sticks at home and chase bigger money overseas.

Other players, non-All Blacks with good Super 12 records, also decide to skip off to greener financial pastures overseas while the going is good. Better to go while still of Super 12 level, than hang on too long. So we've also lost the likes of Glen and Tony Marsh, Willie Lose, Gordon Simpson, Glen Metcalfe, Reuben Parkinson, Brendan Laney, Finau Maka and others this way. The Super 12 hasn't been enticing enough to hold these players, but it has helped them make more money overseas.

Bryan Williams says there have been pros and cons for New Zealand as far as the Super 12 goes. "It has played havoc with our club and provincial rugby," he says. "The timing is a difficult issue. Players are finishing an end-of-year tour, then having to start training for the next Super 12 season almost immediately. It's too tough. But on the other hand, spectators are able to watch good rugby in February, March and

April. It's great for them, especially as the weather then is good, which makes it even more enjoyable."

In the end, the debate about the Super 12 boils down to this: are rugby officials going to chase the dollar or endeavour to do their best by the NPC and the All Blacks?

part FOUR

TRENDS

chapter NINE

THE **BROWNING** OF NEW ZEALAND **RUGBY**

WHITE FLIGHT

The face — more accurately, the colour of the face — of New Zealand rugby has changed dramatically over the past decades, and more especially since the game went professional in 1995. Whereas until about 1980, New Zealand rugby was generally, though certainly not exclusively, a white man's game, the opposite is now the case.

These days ever more Maori and Pacific Island boys are taking up the game. On the face of it, that should be healthy for New Zealand rugby, because it is clearly now appealing to a segment of the population that was not nearly as committed to the game previously. However, there has been an exodus of white boys away from the game that is more than counterbalancing the incredible increase in brown-skinned players.

It is not difficult to understand why this is happening. I have heard a few people describe this white flight from rugby as racism, but that is not the case at all. What happens is that boys, and their parents, are intimidated by the size of the Maori and, particularly, the Polynesian boys of the same age.

You do not need to be a scientist to know that an eight-year-old, 12-year-old or 15-year-old Polynesian boy will almost inevitably be much bigger than a white boy the same age. He has an inherent genetic advantage. This has become a huge problem for rugby.

Dave Atkins, coach of champion Auckland club side Ponsonby, explained the problem well in a fine John Matheson article called "So What's the White Answer?" published in the October, 2001 issue of *New Zealand Rugby World*: "It generally comes back to one thing — the sheer athletic ability of the Polynesian versus the European. A 14-year-old Polynesian will almost always shit all over the white kid.

"Look at the choice he has. The young white kid can say to himself, 'I am a skinny little kid. I am 13 years old. I can go and play with my skateboard or I can go and run against that 80kg Polynesian guy and get absolutely hammered.' Why would he want to play rugby? The kids see it; so do the parents."

The disparity in size does not matter nearly as much, if at all, in hockey, soccer, squash, mountain biking, rock climbing or many other winter sports. But it is critical in rugby. In junior teams, one outsize boy can not only have a major impact on the result of the game, but can do serious physical damage.

To get around this problem, junior rugby administrators sensibly divide grades by weight, not age. But this is only possible where there are enough boys to form both open and weight grades. What about smaller towns, where the number of boys playing means this is not possible?

Having weight-restricted grades only partially solves the problem, though. In an under-60kg team, the Maori and Island boys might be 58 or 59kg, whereas white boys could be 46kg. This is still a whopping difference. And to play against boys their own weight, the Polynesian players in particular often have to be in grades where the white boys are three or four years older. Bearing in mind such issues as peer pressure and social considerations, how much fun is that?

What many junior rugby club officials, especially in parts of Auckland and Wellington, have found is that the sport is losing vast numbers of white boys, who prefer to play a sport like soccer, where they begin the game without a physical disadvantage and can end it without having been smashed about by a much bigger opponent.

It is easy to see the impact Maori and Pacific Island boys are making at major colleges. The Wellington College First XV in 1970 contained no Maori or Polynesian boys. In 1971, one boy was Samoan, the rest white. In 1972 one boy was a Maori, the rest white. In 2002, of the squad of 23,

12 were white, four Samoan, four Tongan and three Maori. This trend is replicated through many of the bigger North Island boys secondary schools.

In some areas there has been such an exodus of white boys over the past few years that the situation may now be settling somewhat. In the *New Zealand Rugby World* article, Pakuranga Rugby Club Chairman Greg Kasper pointed to the influence of Polynesian boys as being the major factor in the club's huge drop-off in junior numbers. Pakuranga, New Zealand's largest rugby club, lost 12 per cent of its juniors in 2000 and 15 per cent in 2001. But new club Chairman Don Adamson says the situation seems to have stabilised now. "We've about held our junior numbers in 2002," he says. "Maybe there's a drop of a couple of per cent, that's all. We're still fielding more than 50 teams where the children are aged 15 or under.

"I don't think the white flight thing is so much of an issue now. The weight grades have really helped. There was definitely a large exodus of white boys from rugby there for a while. Maybe now the people for whom that was going to be a factor have gone, and so the numbers are settling down again.

"You still hear complaints about the size of some of the Polynesian boys, but it's not a persistent problem any more. Having said that, there's no denying soccer is booming in our area. Pakuranga is about 20 per cent Asian, and we don't have any Asians in the rugby club. There are a lot of South Africans in the area, too, and not many of them seem to be drawn to rugby, either. That might be a reason why soccer's numbers have grown so much. From what the Manukau City Council tells us, the soccer numbers out our way are vast. They can hardly find grounds for all the soccer teams for Saturday competition."

Adamson says the biggest reason that junior rugby has suffered a big drop-off in numbers, certainly in Auckland, is the lack of success of Auckland, the Blues and the All Blacks. "The role model factor cannot be overlooked. In the 1980s and early '90s, when Auckland were so strong, and then when the Blues kicked off the Super 12 by winning the first two tournaments, rugby was very big with the kids. They wanted to be like their rugby heroes. But when the Auckland teams and the All Blacks start losing, and that hero factor fades, kids look at other sports or ways of spending their time."

The remaining problem that the white flight has caused in Pakuranga, and in most clubs, has been in administration. "We are a very big club and we struggle to get enough rugby administrators anyway, but not one administrator in our club is a Polynesian. They are all white. This reluctance of the Polynesian people to get involved with running the game is the area that is hurting us as a club the most."

A POLYNESIAN AIRLINES PASSENGER LIST

Ken Laban several times covered the New Zealand regional college rugby finals for TelstraSaturn television. Teams are divided into Southern, Central and Northern A and B, and players basically are drawn from college First XVs. Since the tournament began in 1985, Northern Region teams have won it 14 times, Central twice (in 1988 and '90) and Southern once (in 1996). "The two Northern teams and Central read like passenger lists from Polynesian Airlines," says Laban. "Traditionally the two Northern teams would thrash out the final. All the teams were big, but the Northern teams were that much bigger again. Coaches hadn't chosen their team by colour, but they had gone for size, and what is inevitable, if they are focusing on size, is that Polynesian kids will dominate."

This dominance of brown-skinned players is carrying through to club and rep rugby. The Wellington and Auckland rep teams (I choose those two cities, rather than, say, Christchurch or Dunedin, because they have bigger Maori and Pacific Island communities and so the issue is much more relevant) are these days dominated by brown-skinned players.

The Wellington representative rugby squad in 1970 contained 62 players. Of them, 54 were white and eight Maori. There were no Polynesians. In 2001, Wellington used 36 players, of whom 13 were white, 15 Polynesian, eight Maori and one South African.

In Auckland the numbers corresponded almost exactly. In 1970, 47 players were used. Of them, 39 were white, five Maori and two Polynesians. By 2001 the figures looked vastly different. Auckland used 36 players, of whom 10 were white, 19 Polynesian, six Maori and one French.

Maori and Polynesian boys now provide just under 60 per cent of all the contracted Super 12 and NPC players.

The situation is replicated with the All Blacks. The 1905 Originals contained one Maori — Billy Stead (from Invercargill) — and the other 26 players were white. The 1924–25 Invincibles contained three Maori — George Nepia, Jimmy Mill and Lui Paewai — and the other 26 players were white.

In 1928, when the All Blacks were to tour South Africa, two very prominent Maori players, Nepia and Mill, were excluded because of the wishes of the South African Government. Other Maori who may have come into contention were Jack Blake, Wattie Barclay, Dick Pelham, Bill Rika and Albie Fellwasser. Perhaps Maurice Brownlie's 29-strong team would have eventually included three or four Maori, but for racial considerations in selection.

There was a strange quirk in 1947 when New Zealand, for one match in Australia, fielded an inside backline of Vince Bevan, Ben Couch, Peter Smith and Johnny Smith — all Maori. But this was very much an aberration, as was revealed by the fact that for the 1949 team to South Africa only three prominent Maori players — Johnny Smith, Couch and Bevan — were considered likely selections, but for the colour issue. Others Maori who were mentioned as possible selections were Peter Smith, Kiwi Blake and Ron Bryers. Again, though, the team would have been made up almost entirely of white players, colour bar or not.

In 1960, when New Zealand again decided to pick a whites-only team (in misguided deference to their hosts), only two Maori players — Tiny Hill and Pat Walsh — were even close to contention, though it seems Wilson Whineray's team would have been all-white regardless of racial issues.

In 1970, when dark-skinned players were finally included, just four were chosen — Sid Going, Buff Milner, Blair Furlong and Bryan Williams — the first three Maori, the fourth Samoan. Four in a team of 30. How things were soon to change.

Now fast-forward to the modern era. In 2001, the All Blacks called on 44 players. Of them, 13 were Maori, seven were Polynesian and 24 were white. In several recent years the percentage of Maori and Polynesian players has been even higher.

The trend is obvious. The number of Maori players making rep and New Zealand teams is rising, but nowhere near as fast as the Polynesian representation. Back in 1992, when the All Blacks took the field for the test against South Africa (the first in 11 years), winger John Kirwan joked that he should be nicknamed Chester. He was the only white in the New Zealand backline. At the time Chester Williams was the only black in the South African backline.

Sometimes the question of what constitutes a player who is Polynesian or Maori is tricky. Does he have to be full-flooded Maori or Pacific Islander, or half, or quarter? Because of such considerations, it's possible to quibble slightly with the numbers I have quoted, but the trend is unarguable.

The really big difference is in the explosion in the number of Polynesians not only playing rugby, but playing it incredibly well. Since the Pacific Island countries gained their independence from New Zealand and were granted free access, the scene has changed dramatically. Now families move to New Zealand seeking a better life, or their children might grow up here. Either way, the pool of Polynesians in New Zealand is increasing significantly all the time.

The first Polynesians to play for the All Blacks were the Solomons, Frank and David. Frank was born in Pago Pago, American Samoa, in 1906 and David in Levuka, Fiji, in 1913. Frank played nine matches for New Zealand in 1931–32 (and made an appearance for the New Zealand Maori in 1927!); David made eight appearances in 1935–36. But the Solomons were way ahead of their time.

Fijian Arthur Jennings played six matches for New Zealand in 1967, but it wasn't until the All Black debut of the brilliant Auckland winger, Bryan Williams, in 1970, that the arrival of Pacific Islanders as significant factors in the All Blacks was really noted. Since then, the Polynesian influence has become ever stronger at all levels of rugby in New Zealand.

WHAT THE 2001 NEW ZEALAND CENSUS SHOWED

The ethnicity of the New Zealand population has changed significantly in recent times. According to the 2001 New Zealand census, one in five New Zealanders was born overseas, compared to one in six just a decade earlier. In Auckland, the figure is one in three; in Southland it's one in 15.

In the 1950s and '60s, 60 per cent of the immigrants were from Britain (and nearly all the rest were from Europe, the United States and Canada), and the immigrants were overwhelmingly white. Now British immigration accounts for less than 25 per cent. Asians make up 40 per cent of immigrants and there is a significant number of Samoan, Cook Island and Tongan immigrants. The Pacific Island population in New Zealand increased 39 per cent from 1991 to 2001. All these trends — an increase in Polynesian and Asian immigration and a decrease in European immigrants — will affect the makeup of future All Black teams.

In 2001, one in seven (526,000) New Zealanders was Maori, one in 15 (240,000) Asian and one in 16 (232,000) from a Pacific Island nation. Statistics New Zealand predicts that in a decade, 21 per cent of the population will be Maori and 8.5 per cent Asian.

BIRTHPLACE OF NZ RESIDENT POPULATION (2001 CENSUS)

1. NZ   2,890,869
2. England   178,203

3.	Australia	56,142
4.	Samoa	47,118
5.	China	38,949
6.	Scotland	28,680
7.	South Africa	26,061
8.	Fiji	25,725
9.	Netherlands	22,242
10.	India	20,892
11.	Tonga	18,054
12.	Korea	17,931
13.	Cook Islands	15,222
14.	United States	13,347
15.	Taiwan	12,486
16.	Malaysia	11,463
17.	Hong Kong	11,301
18.	Philippines	10,137
19.	Japan	8382
20.	Canada	7770

NEW ZEALAND CITIES WITH THE LARGEST POLYNESIAN POPULATION:

1.	Manukau City	72,300
2.	Auckland	47,600
3.	Waitakere	23,200
4.	Porirua	12,200

HEADS IN THE SAND?

Oddly, some rugby administrators are surprisingly loath to concede that there has been a trend towards the browning of rugby. I cannot understand why this should be so, but perhaps it is part of the habit of administrators generally to paint as rosy a picture as possible.

Brent Anderson, the New Zealand Rugby Football Union's community development officer, said to me: "There is some anecdotal evidence that there is a concern [of white players leaving the game because of the dominance of Pacific Island and Maori boys]. But I don't have the data base information to make an absolute judgment." While conceding that "the balance of numbers is swinging more Polynesian", Anderson said he was unsure if that was causing a trend of white flight in rugby. "You would have to ask them. We haven't surveyed," he said.

Brian Cederwall, the Wellington union's director of rugby development,

Above and Below: *Spot the difference. Rugby and brown. Soccer and white. The racial divide happens as early as primary school.*

Above: *Rugby is diversifying. We're the best sevens players in the world and that 2002 Commonwealth gold could soon be turned into an Olympic equivalent.*

Below: *And our women are world champs too. The women's game is also overwhelmingly Polynesian.*

Left: *The long and the short, the thin and the stumpy. Rugby may still be a game for all shapes but the sizing is all XXOS. Wellington's Dion Waller and Norm Hewitt have a hug on their way to winning the 2000 NPC title.*

Right: *Not so much affection. Players agent Andy Haden lectures the* New Zealand Herald *rugby writer Wynne Gray. Gray has been a leading critic of the NZRFU administration and so too Haden.*

Above: *Paul Steinmetz. Otago or Wellington? An ominous symbol of player power.*

Below: *The real threat to rugby. NZ Soccer CEO Bill MacGowan is plotting the take-over right now.*

said: "There is a problem in open grades only. The set-up in the weight-for-age grades doesn't work too badly. Players have to play one grade above their age [if they are too heavy for their age]. There is the odd case of another Jonah, but it generally works well." Cederwall concedes that by promoting Polynesian kids above their age, other problems are caused. "You take them out of their peer group and that makes it tough."

Cederwall doesn't feel there has been any great trend in Wellington towards white kids fleeing to soccer in the face of oversized Polynesian rugby players. "Perhaps when the boys get into open grade rugby on leaving school, this becomes a problem, but otherwise there hasn't been a big drop-off in numbers. In Wellington there are 5500 Saturday morning kids playing rugby and another 2800 at secondary school."

Mark Fairmaid, a Wellington junior rugby referee and a long-time official for the Norths club, supports this observation. "I hear about the trend, the Polynesian boys pushing the white kids away from rugby, but to tell the truth, I haven't noticed it very much. There are a few examples, but not a massive white flight sort of thing. Our junior club is down three teams on last year, but that's about the same as in the past few years. There's been no regular dip in numbers. Some clubs, like Upper Hutt, have lost big numbers, but I don't think it would necessarily be correct to attribute that just to the influence of the Polynesian boys."

I listen to these people, good people who care passionately about rugby, and I am astounded. They are not describing what I am seeing. When I go to rugby grounds on a Saturday to watch junior rugby, the percentage of Polynesian and Maori boys playing is striking. In some teams, the odd white boy stands out as being different. I walk along the sidelines at junior soccer games, and parents will tell me their boys have left rugby because of the size disparity. I look at the names of various rep rugby teams — First XVs, secondary school selections, age-sides — and I see that they are often crammed with Polynesian and Maori boys.

In my opinion, the blasé attitudes of some rugby administrators on this issue flies in the face of the facts.

Norm Hewitt, an All Black who captained the New Zealand Maori, says: "It's undeniable. The Fijians, Samoans and Tongans are big lads. As kids they dominate the little white boys, who are about half as big. The white dads will often encourage their kids to have a go anyway, but the mums look at the Polynesian boys and say: 'They're giants. Let's find another sport.' The Island boys all look up to Jonah Lomu, and they want to play like him. They get the ball and want to run over their opposition."

Mothers get a lot of blame for the white drift away from rugby. Soccer New Zealand's Bill MacGowan feels mothers have been great friends to soccer. Northland and New Zealand under-21 coach Bryce Woodward feels the same, but unlike MacGowan, he isn't too happy about it.

"We've got a very fast-growing Polynesian population in Northland. The Maori boys are generally a bit bigger than the white boys, but it's with the Polynesians that the difference is really noticeable. I have mates whose kids play soccer. I can't believe it. When I ask why, they invariably say it's their wives. It's because of the politically correct world we live in. The fathers can't speak up any more.

"Mothers sow the seeds of doubt and then a lot of kids pick up on that and are encouraged to change codes. It's hurting rugby, and it annoys me because I think the environment has been created where kids who might play and love rugby are pushed quite vigorously towards soccer."

Brent Anderson of the New Zealand union: "There is a safety issue at primary school level, but rugby is as safe or safer at primary school than it has ever been."

There are stories of coaches of some junior teams protesting at the size of some of their opposition players and of rugby officials turning up with scales to see if players are fulfilling weight restrictions. Brian Cederwall: "We have to go around with scales sometimes. Kids can outgrow a grade during the season, though we give a three or four kilogram allowance and kids seldom outgrow that."

Yet Cederwall himself has seen the difference in weight of college boys the same age. "One of my own boys was 30kg when he started college. His classmates were as heavy as 110kg. Obviously you couldn't let boys with that weight disparity be on the same team."

John Hart, who has seen more rugby than most, says it can be terrifying for a parent to watch his son taking the field with much bigger Polynesian boys. "I look at my young fellow. He was playing at first five-eighth in the under-21 grade. I shuddered when I saw him out there, a little white kid up against some huge Polynesian players. I don't blame parents being worried about the size disparity, especially as rugby has become so physical these days, and I can well understand why, in those situations, a sport like soccer would appeal to many parents and boys."

Chris Laidlaw has watched — as a parent and a television and newspaper media man — the colour of New Zealand rugby change and wrote, for the December, 1999 issue of *New Zealand Books*: "More and more school and age group teams are reliant on youthful

Polynesian vigour to make the difference. Hulking youngsters dominate the landscape at almost every game. Fifteen-year-olds weighting 100kg, and playing at centre, have become the norm. It is an arresting sight, not least for the modestly-proportioned Pakeha lads who get run over every Saturday and wonder how many more times they must be offered up as a human sacrifice."

Some people defend this situation. Willie Jackson, for one, can't see what the fuss is about. Jackson, who entered Parliament in 1999 as an Alliance MP, said in the *Rugby World* article that until 1970 there was a history of racism towards Maori players from the New Zealand Rugby Union. "It owes Maori an apology. Many Maori players missed their chance to wear the All Black jersey because of decisions made by the New Zealand union."

Jackson says he hates the fact that when the All Blacks perform poorly, the brown-skinned players are blamed. "This is what happens," he told *New Zealand Rugby World* magazine. "When the All Blacks start losing, they start blaming all the darkies. Listen to talkback . . . the callers want to know why there aren't more Canterbury farmers in the team. They say things like, 'We need more Pakeha players in the side.' I can't believe the crap I hear, but if you listen, you'll hear them blaming the pollywollies."

Jackson cites the outstanding All Black teams of 1995 and '96, both of which were predominantly Maori and Polynesian. "What's wrong with these people? Have they got amnesia? Think back to those teams. Can't they remember the teams were stacked with pollywollies? That's what irritates me about the attitude against the darkies. We will get blamed because the All Blacks are going through a rough patch, but at the same time it seems to have been conveniently forgotten that when the All Blacks were winning, the majority of the team were Polynesian. That's the hypocrisy of this."

But this over-simplifies the issue. Maori and Pacific Islanders have been much less inclined to become coaches, referees and administrators than have white people. I don't say it never happens. Bryan Williams has done an incredible amount of work for rugby in general, and Samoan rugby in particular, since he closed his long and distinguished playing career in 1984. There have been other fine Maori and Polynesian administrators over the years.

But these people are still in a small minority. Polynesians and Maori do not generally seem as keen to sit on committees. They like to get out there and do things. Perhaps they are happiest when playing a sport, not administering it. "Polynesians make good administrators," says Ken

Laban, "but they prefer to administer for their own groups — for example, an Islands rugby team. It's actually a real challenge for the New Zealand and provincial rugby unions . . . the demographics of New Zealand are changing, with an increasingly strong Asian and Pacific influence. Rugby officials must realise that and know how to get the best out of those people for the good of their game."

As the percentage of Maori and Pacific Island people in New Zealand continues to grow so much faster than Pakeha people, this situation is going to become more marked.

It is easy to listen to this and say, "So what? Aren't there as many people as ever playing rugby?" But that is too simplistic.

The All Blacks have always represented New Zealand; they are the sports team that New Zealanders have identified with. I wonder if all New Zealanders still feel that the All Blacks are representative of New Zealand in general, when half of them (sometimes more) are brown-skinned. Where are we going with this? Will New Zealand rugby at national and international level comprise of a group of brown-skinned players playing, being cheered on by white spectators and television viewers? That's certainly been the trend in some of the professional sports in the United States.

THE JONAH FACTOR

Is there one factor that explains why rugby is these days so much more appealing to Pacific Island and Maori boys than in previous years? Yes, without question. Money.

It's a situation that is comparable to the lure of professional sports like boxing and basketball in the United States. Black boys growing up in the poorer areas of some of America's major cities face a terribly difficult task gaining an education and acquiring the academic qualifications to land themselves high-paying jobs through their adult lives. It's not impossible, but for a variety of reasons — family circumstances, poverty, peer pressure — the odds are stacked against them. Boxing and basketball, where black boys can use their physical skills, offer the most appealing way of earning big money.

As John Hart says: "Some families would say that professional rugby is the best chance their boys have to make money. Look at Tana Umaga. He used to play rugby league, but he went for the money and turned to rugby union."

New Zealand doesn't have the major ghetto problems of the bigger

American cities. Even so, a parallel — though not as severe — problem exists. Bryan Williams is in no doubt that many Polynesian boys see excelling at rugby as a way forward.

"The money is a real lure and Jonah is the role model. I don't doubt that the increasing domination of the Polynesian boys is causing spin-off problems. The white boys have trouble. There are weight-restricted grades in some areas, but there isn't enough emphasis put on that. It's bad enough at college, but you really notice what happens in the 17-21 years bracket. That's when a lot of white boys are lost to the game."

Clubs and provinces have not been slow to realise the impact a couple of big, athletic Polynesians can make to their teams and there are innumerable stories in rugby of young Pacific Island boys being offered packages including accommodation and jobs to get them to commit to a team. Sometimes a boy's parents are offered a house.

While conceding that the Polynesian influence is causing a definite browning of rugby in some areas, Williams is unsure if that should be classified as a problem for rugby. "It's a difficult one. I don't have a definite view on that. But we should look at what's happened in the United States. The Polynesians here are not very inclined to get into coaching. In the US, it seems the coaches are white and the players are black. Maybe that's the way it's going here. It's certainly something the New Zealand Rugby Union should be thinking about."

Over the past five years, many provincial unions, especially those in the North Island, have adopted senior weight-restricted grades. In Wellington, there is an under-80kg grade that involves 26 teams split into three divisions. The overwhelming number of players in these teams is white. They play skilful, attractive rugby, but are unable to play un-restricted weight rugby because the big Polynesian and Maori players would hammer them. The appeal of the 80kg grade in Wellington is replicated elsewhere, including in Auckland and Canterbury, where the unions have tried 75kg and 85kg grades, with success.

White players are now in a small minority in terms of senior rugby, certainly in Auckland and Wellington. Fewer than 20 per cent of the players in Auckland's Gallaher Shield competition now are white. The figures are similar in Wellington. Auckland champions Ponsonby fielded a team comprising 11 Polynesian or Maori and four white players to start their 2001 Gallaher Shield final against Otahuhu. The dominance of brown-skinned players even led to a joke within the club, with the senior side being labelled the Mighty Whities.

Williams also says coaches need to respond to the challenge of coaching Polynesians. "They have different body types and need work on the conditioning side. They are big boys and don't train as well. On the other hand, they thrive on the team element. Coaches have to know how to work with their Polynesian players to get the best out of them. It's a different challenge for coaches."

Some coaches have failed notably to bring out the best in their Polynesian and Maori players. Probably the most glaring example was the first coach of the Auckland Warriors league team, Australian John Monie, who was well off the pace in this regard. However, he was far from the only one. For instance, Norm Hewitt, in his book *Gladiator*, was critical of Hurricanes and Wellington coach Graham Mourie and felt Mourie did not have a good understanding of how to deal with the Maori and Polynesian players in his squads.

On the other hand, Dion Waller, one of the Hurricanes' and Wellington's best forwards, points to players like Tana Umaga, Jerry Collins and Rodney So'oialo, all Polynesians whose rugby flourished under Mourie. "With the academy system, and all the various junior rep teams they have these days, all the players pretty well know the ropes by the time they get into NPC or Super 12 teams," says Waller. "It doesn't matter if they're Polynesian, Maori, white or whatever, they know the sort of training that's required and they usually fit in fine."

A strong, athletic Pacific Island or Maori boy will find he is able to totally dominate junior rugby players his age. Why not try to turn that situation to his advantage by seeking to play rugby professionally and chasing a lucrative NPC or Super 12 contract?

That line of thinking has clearly appealed to thousands of Pacific Island and Maori boys. They see a player like Jonah Lomu, a talented teenaged rugby player with no more than normal academic qualifications, now earning millions of dollars a year to play sport and wonder why that can't be them.

Norm Hewitt says the Jonah factor has been a recurring theme in the "dozens and dozens" of visits he has made to secondary schools over the years. "I talk to these boys and their attitude is always the same. They expect to be able to leave school and basically go straight into professional rugby, where they know they can earn very big money."

The processes are certainly in place now in New Zealand. There is a large amount of recruitment of big Polynesian boys, not just from other colleges or areas, but even from the Pacific Islands. In the late 1980s, Scots College in Wellington began recruiting huge Fijian players, prop Bill Cavubati among them. That was an early example of a trend that has become more widespread: colleges buying in talent from the Pacific Islands.

Besides the scholarships that some colleges offer, various provincial unions have talent scouts hell-bent on identifying any talented teenagers, more often than not Polynesians, who might become outstanding rugby players. The boys, and their families, quite reasonably see a career as a professional rugby player as a good option, a chance to get ahead financially. The situation is exacerbated by the recruitment policies of some unions. For instance, during 2001, the Otago union caused ructions when it basically signed up the entire Wesley College First XV from Manukau, not the first time Otago had pursued that sort of course.

The Wesley College boys therefore had the chance to stay with their mates, continue playing rugby and quite possibly land themselves professional rugby contracts. Good for them. It's a snowballing process — other boys around the country would have looked at the Wesley situation and taken heart, knowing there must also be opportunities for them somewhere along the line, too.

White boys, on the other hand, face two obstacles, if that is the right word. First, they generally start behind the eight ball because they are not as imposing physically. How do the predominantly white Otago boys feel when their provincial union hauls in the Wesley College First XV? It's hardly a vote of confidence in home-grown talent. Secondly, white boys often feel they have more career options outside sport.

Ken Laban feels there needs to be a rethink on this issue. "We are a Polynesian country with a growing Polynesian population," he says. "That's fine, but we have to make sure that academic achievement receives the same sort of kudos as sports achievement. At the moment my feeling is that academic excellence isn't celebrated nearly as much as rugby excellence, yet it should be the other way around.

"It's the emphasis that's important. I would like to see minimum academic qualifications put in place for any first XV players — three or four subjects in School Certificate, or whatever today's equivalent is. That would remove the idiot factor from the game and sow a seed of academic requirement."

Laban says there are plenty of examples in the Polynesian and Maori rugby communities for youngsters to follow. Alama Ieremia is a good case. He was born in Apia, Samoa and came to New Zealand initially as a volleyball and cricket player. He was in the top 10 per cent of his seventh form and went on to Victoria University to do a geography degree. He played under-21 rugby for the Wests club in Wellington and ended up very quickly rising through the ranks to represent Manu Samoa and then the All Blacks. His background of academic study always stood him in good stead.

"There are lots more examples — Jeremy Stanley is a doctor. Taine Randell, Daryl Gibson and Michael Jones have double degrees. It's important that today's teenagers have these sort of examples placed in front of them, so that there is some focus on the academic side, rather than simply rugby achievement."

IS IT WHAT CORPORATES WANT?

Before leaving the subject of rugby and white flight, here's a thorny question: what will happen to the commercial side of the All Blacks if they start losing more often? Will corporate sponsors and advertisers be equally happy to be associated with the brown-skinned All Blacks as they have with the New Zealand teams of the past?

I'm not sure. Certainly while the All Blacks continue to win well and win often, the situation will be fine. Over the past year or two, the superstars of New Zealand rugby, the players sponsors would have clamoured to sign, have been Jonah Lomu, Christian Cullen, Tana Umaga, Jeff Wilson, Andrew Mehrtens and Anton Oliver. Half of them are part or fully Maori or Polynesian. There has been no sponsor resistance to chasing Maori or Polynesian players, far from it.

But what if the All Blacks lose more? What if they not only can't land the World Cup (which we haven't won since 1987), and not only continue to lose often to Australia and South Africa, but also start to get beaten by England, France and other Northern Hemisphere teams whose standards have improved since rugby went pro?

How keen will those sponsors be to be associated with a losing All Black team full of brown-skinned players? It's not a problem at the moment. In fact, says New Zealand Rugby Union Commercial general manager, Trevor McKewen, the mix of different backgrounds and cultures is one of the attractions of the All Blacks for sponsors. "If the All Blacks ever became perceived as a team that loses, then all bets are off," says McKewen. "Winning is absolutely critical."

In my experience, sponsors look for two things: they want a healthy commercial return, and they want a business relationship they are comfortable with. adidas sponsors the All Blacks because it thinks it'll make money out of them. The local butcher sponsors the schoolboy rugby team in the area not because he's necessarily going to sell more sausages, but because he wants to lend a bit of a hand, or because he's a parent of one of the schoolboys, or a friend of the schoolboy team's coach, or some such.

Until the past few years, I felt golf the world over did extraordinarily well out of sponsorship because it was a sport played and run by white men, and therefore appealed to big corporates, whose shakers and movers are generally white men. It was a comfortable, empathetic relationship. But then along came black American Tiger Woods, who blew my theory out of the water. Woods had such appeal that prize-money and sponsorship for the American pro tour multiplied several times over almost solely because of him.

If the All Blacks start losing more often, they'd better find someone with Woods' appeal.

chapterTEN
WHAT **PRICE** TRADITION?

PINETREE? . . . WHO'S PINETREE?

Jonah Lomu has developed from a wide-eyed, rather innocent teenager into a world rugby superstar who gives New Zealand a huge amount of reflected glory. Lomu has been paid very well to play his rugby in New Zealand — upwards of $1 million per year, when endorsements and other commercial opportunities are taken into account — but if he'd been of a mind to, he could have perhaps doubled that income by hiking off overseas.

Such is Lomu's pulling power that he is big news in Italy, Spain, Argentina and other non-rugby countries. When the All Blacks hit town, he is the major attraction. It is to Lomu's immense credit that he has remained modest, and as accessible to the public as is practicably possible. He's always professed to be honoured to be able to play for the All Blacks and his every action since he made his test debut in 1994 has reflected that.

There were several senior All Blacks through the mid-1990s who were more than happy to grab the piles of money World Rugby Corporation was offering and abandon ship. It has always seemed that the All Blacks meant more than that to big Jonah. He seems to be mindful of the associated traditions.

Asked about his thoughts when huge amounts of money were offered to the All Blacks in 1995, Lomu told Keith Quinn in *Legends of the All Blacks*: "I was sceptical in lots of ways. We would have been giving up a fair bit of history with the All Blacks. A lot of people didn't know that I was the only one in the room who didn't sign on the dotted line. I just didn't want to leave New Zealand. I had a lot of things I hadn't achieved and more I wanted to do in that black jersey. Sure, there was crazy money in it, but at the end of the day, you have to be happy in what you do. I was glad everything was sorted out and we carried on for the All Blacks."

Some All Blacks, on the verge of brilliant careers, initially signed for WRC after being pushed and prodded by their more senior team-mates, then had misgivings. Eventually two, Josh Kronfeld and Jeff Wilson, decided they wouldn't be going the WRC way. Their defections caused a rethink. Veteran All Blacks, fearing big paydays were going to be taken away from them, seemed to be more concerned with the money than with their provincial team-mates and the All Black jersey. Zinzan Brooke later said he would like to get Wilson at the bottom of a ruck. He claimed it was said in jest. But there was a sting in the comment. Kronfeld said in his book he'd been given a hard time by his room-mate, Richard Loe, on subsequent tours. Again, it was "all good fun".

When we consider Lomu's obvious respect for the All Black jersey, it's incredible to think that as an outstanding teenaged rugby player, he had no idea who Colin Meads was.

"I remember an under-16 tournament in Te Kuiti. Everybody kept talking about 'Pinetree' and 'Pinetree Country'. They said, 'Jonah, you're going to be playing against Pinetree's son.' Finally I said, 'Who's this Pinetree?' The room just went quiet. I suppose that was the start of my initiation into the All Blacks and All Black traditions. I had a crash course in history."

I mention this story not to disparage Lomu, who has done the All Black jersey proud. But I want to emphasise how easily traditions, even famous, long-standing traditions like the All Blacks, can be lost.

Colin Meads is one of the great figures in New Zealand history. Never mind rugby history, or sports history, but New Zealand history. His name, his nickname and his face are as recognisable as the Auckland Harbour Bridge or Christchurch's Cathedral Square. He has been one player who transcended generations. As he played his last test match in 1971, anyone younger than 40 would have no memory of watching him take on the Springboks or the Lions. Yet he is an iconic figure.

His first biography, *Colin Meads All Black*, published in 1974, sold 61,000 copies. Publishers scrapped for years for the right to publish a second Meads book, which was eventually written in 2002 by Brian Turner. *Meads*, as the second biography was called, had a first print run of 40,000, a huge number for New Zealand. Such is the stature of Meads.

It is amazing that any young kid who was as good at rugby as the teenaged Lomu would not know about Meads. Yet I don't believe the Lomu case is unique.

Some people are interested in history. They read dusty old books and modern versions of old stories. They are as fascinated by what went on half a century or a century ago as they are by the goings-on today. But these people are a small minority.

Most rugby followers are passionately interested in who's in this week's All Black team, and who is refereeing next week's test. But they couldn't care less about what went on in years past.

Today's feats are quickly consigned to history. I can see David Kirk raising the Webb Ellis Trophy at Eden Park as if it was today. In fact, it was 1987. So anyone under the age of about 23 has no real memory of that first World Cup, or of New Zealand being world rugby champions. The Springbok tour of 1981 and the huge protests that were associated with that tour, happened so long ago that you would need to be 30 to recall them clearly. Hell, most young people cannot remember a time when South Africa was excluded from the international sports arena.

For more than half a century, South Africa was the great New Zealand rugby rival. All Black-Springbok tests were seen as the ultimate by New Zealand fans. It is difficult to convey to today's rugby fans just what a Springbok test or tour meant. The shame of losing a series 4-0 to South Africa in 1949 was palpable, just as the series victory over the Springboks in 1956 caused national euphoria. We still like the All Blacks to win, but there isn't quite that national fervour any more, except possibly for World Cups.

South African tests don't have the needle they used to. In 1994, Peter Williams was doing what is known as a vox pop for Television New Zealand before the South Africa test in Dunedin. He was asking people at Carisbrook which team was New Zealand's greatest rival. The answers were interesting: younger fans named Australia, but older people went for South Africa. People under the age of 30 have never known a time when South Africa was New Zealand's greatest rugby rival. It shows how quickly tradition can be lost.

THE IMPORTANCE OF TRADITION

We should not be blasé about tradition. It is really appreciated only by those with an interest in history.

We live in an increasingly instantaneous age. A century ago, it took all night for a telegraphic message to be relayed from Britain so that rugby followers could find out the results of the latest Originals tour match. It took six or seven weeks before detailed match reports arrived back home, via ship. Now we have satellite television coverage and we have the Internet.

Though I have only anecdotal proof, I firmly believe top players today have less interest in former stars than they used to. Wilson Whineray, arguably New Zealand's finest rugby captain, related to me how he was called in to address the New Zealand Colts team before a big match in 2001. "I got into the room and looked around and thought, 'These fellows wouldn't have a clue who I am. I'm just some old bugger who retired about 20 years before they were born.' They were very polite and listened to what I had to say, but I don't know if they related to me."

When Bob Scott was touring Britain in 1953–54 with Bob Stuart's All Blacks, he was about to run out of the dressing room to act as a touch judge for one touring match (yes, in those days, the All Blacks provided their own linesmen for most matches), when an elderly gentleman caught his attention. Scott stopped and shook his hand and on chatting for a moment, discovered it was Charlie Seeling.

Seeling was a wonderful All Black, the forward star of the 1905 Originals. He'd moved to England a few years later and forged a lasting reputation as a rugby league player. His name was remembered in New Zealand for a few years, but then new stars came along, the most notable of them being Maurice Brownlie, the wonderful Invincibles forward.

Yet there was Scott, instantly recognising Seeling's name, and wanting to stop and talk to him. "It was such a pity," says Scott. "I was really in a hurry because the game was about to start. I'd have loved to have talked to him for longer."

Would today's All Blacks recognise a 70-year-old former star who had hardly been mentioned in his home country for more than 40 years? I doubt it. I am reminded of Walter Hadlee's habit as a teenager of reading all he could of cricket history, from *Wisden* almanacks to any biographies he could get his hands on. Hadlee toured England as a 21-year-old in 1937 and attended the 150th jubilee dinner of the MCC at Lord's. He sat next to distinguished former players such as Pelham Warner and Stanley Jackson and was able to talk easily with them about games they had played a half-century earlier. On the way home, while playing a match in Australia, he met Tom Garrett, who played in cricket's first test match, in 1877.

"I have often thought what a waste it would have been to have met those sorts of people and not known about them and their eras," Hadlee once told me.

Do today's sports stars show that sort of interest in history? I don't think so.

"They talk so much about money now," says Fred Allen, "The people who run the game aren't rugby people. They don't realise that 65 to 70 per cent of it is team spirit and the rest is fundamentals. When I was a youngster I appreciated All Black history and tradition. I idolised Charlie Oliver and Jack Sullivan and Maurice Brownlie and George Nepia and the rest of them. It's unreal that a kid like Lomu could get into the All Blacks and not know who Meads was.

"Once tradition goes, you're on the slide. The players today are so busy being selfish, not putting time into clubs. It's become a very selfish game and it saddens me. I guess I've spoken more than 500 times to various rugby gatherings and I have never accepted money for a talk. My reward was playing for the All Blacks. I don't think the fellows today think that way."

Former All Black lock Andy Haden: "The 1905 team sometimes walked from matches to their hotel carrying everything on their backs. It was bloody hard for them. They played when they were injured; they played too often. They really struggled and yet they had such pride in representing their country, in being All Blacks, that they turned in remarkable performances. In my time in the All Blacks, we felt obligated to honour the start that 1905 team had given us and to honour all the players who had trodden the All Black path in the intervening years. We were playing for the tradition of the team that we were representing. Is that the same feeling now? I don't think that part of it represents what it used to."

You might say all this doesn't matter. The All Blacks are in more demand than ever. Sponsors like adidas are happy to pay hundreds of millions of dollars to be associated with them. They still fill grounds for most test matches.

But this is the short-term view. Today's generation have grown up with the Warriors and the All Blacks. Many wouldn't have a clue which came first, and they wouldn't care. Who knows? One day soccer's Kingz may fall into the same category.

Young sports followers today are drawn by a team's results. If the All Blacks are winning, that's fine. They'll remain in huge demand. But if their results falter, allegiances will quickly be switched.

Coaches have been quick to seize on the importance of tradition. In 1987, Brian Lochore and his co-selectors spoke about how the All Blacks that year were playing for every player who had ever pulled on the All Black jersey when they took the field for the inaugural World Cup. Having spoken to several of the players in that World Cup campaign about this subject, I know that was a very effective motivational ploy.

All Blacks coaches generally make a point of emphasising tradition.

Laurie Mains clearly cherished the All Black jersey and left his players in no doubt that they were honoured to be following in the footsteps of some of the legendary names of the past. Wayne Smith was another who went out of his way to stress tradition. At the end of 2000 Smith took the All Blacks to France and he and manager Andrew Martin went to considerable lengths to organise for the team to visit the grave of Originals captain Dave Gallaher, who died of wounds received in the battle at Passchendaele and is buried in the Nine Elms cemetery in Poperinghe. The visit apparently had a deep effect on many members of the team. "It's important," Smith said to me before the team left. "You keep hammering the tradition side of things and gradually the message gets through. Hopefully the message is then passed on to the next group who come into the All Blacks."

There is nothing new in this. Cliff Porter's 1924 Invincibles also visited Gallaher's grave. But when they did so, early in 1925, the First World War was only a few years past. It was to Smith's credit that all these years later he made sure his players knew who Gallaher was, his role in All Black history, and the fact that he'd given his life fighting for his country.

WHO ARE THE GUARDIANS OF OUR GAME?

I had another snapshot of the traditions of rugby in 2001 when Don Clarke returned to New Zealand from South Africa, where he had lived for 25 years, to attend a luncheon in his honour at Eden Park. The luncheon, the brainchild of the indefatigable Pat Walsh, grew like topsy; the more so when the news emerged that Clarke had been diagnosed with cancer and was battling for his life.

The West Stand hospitality room at Eden Park was full that day. There were All Blacks in every direction. All but one or two of Clarke's living former team-mates attended. They paid their own way and made it their business to be at Eden Park to honour their famous fullback and be part of such a special occasion. I'm not sure official invitations were even issued. Some heard about the luncheon only days before, but everyone got there.

It was a magical occasion for those who knew their All Black history. To see Tiny White proudly wearing his All Black blazer of 50 years earlier. Wilson Whineray and Brian Lochore, two great All Black captains, deep in conversation. Kevin Skinner, Fred Allen, Bob Scott, Ross Brown, Nev MacEwan, Ron Horsley, John Graham, Waka Nathan and the rest of them.

What was interesting to me, as I looked around a room that contained more than 70 of these great rugby figures, was that there was almost no-one from the current All Black set-up. No players and none of the leading team management. The All Blacks were in Auckland at the time, preparing for a toot on the Saturday. They had to eat somewhere and I'd have thought an afternoon mixing with the likes of Nathan, White, Skinner and company would have proved inspiring. But they were nowhere in sight.

Many old All Blacks I spoke to that day described it as one of the most thrilling days of their lives. It was a chance to pay tribute to Camel (the public knew Clarke as the Boot, but his team-mates called him Camel), and to renew friendships that will never die.

Being an All Black was a lot simpler in their day. They played club and rep rugby and if they were good enough they were chosen to represent New Zealand. They heard their name announced on the wireless, or perhaps they were in attendance in the old social room at Athletic Park after the trial games. A day or two later they might receive written notification from the New Zealand union.

Nowadays things are more complicated and other issues get in the way. I believe that they all want to make the All Blacks just as passionately as did their predecessors, at least at the start. But other factors have to be considered. All Blacks today have agents acting for them. There are contract negotiations. Play for pay.

Would today's All Blacks converge en masse in 40 years' time to honour one of their company? Perhaps, but they'd want to know who was paying the hotel bills, who was providing the air tickets and who was shouting the food and booze.

Tradition is the biggest single factor the All Blacks have going for them. I'm constantly amazed how under-rated it is by today's marketing and media whiz kids.

Lindsay Knight tells the story of a conversation he had in 1996 with an employee of the Auckland union, one of the new wave of professional rugby administrators. During the course of their conversation, Knight mentioned the name Fred Allen. He was staggered when the Auckland official didn't have a clue who he was talking about.

Fred Allen is one of Auckland rugby's greatest sons. He was an Auckland representative and captain, an All Black captain, the coach of the champion Auckland Ranfurly Shield team of the early 1960s and later an unbeaten All Black coach. He is a giant of New Zealand rugby and is a proud Aucklander. This Auckland official had never heard of him.

A few years ago, Ray Harper, a Rugby Union councillor for 12 years, and a manager of All Black teams in the 1980s, travelled north from Invercargill to attend to some business in Wellington. It was revealing that when he paid a social visit to the Rugby Union offices one day, he was not recognised or remembered by one person.

As Lin Colling told the *Otago Daily Times* in 2001: "I'm afraid a lot of the people who are administering the game have come from outside the rugby heritage and culture. To them it is just a job and not a passion. They do it for two or three years and then move on to another job. What they are leaving behind is of no importance to them. It is just a stepping-stone on a career path.

"Someone has to accept the responsibility to become guardians of our game. Unless we speak out and make our points heard, then rugby may well be in crisis. We have to make sure we have a balance between the corporate culture that has come into the game and the rugby heritage and culture that used to be in the game."

Another way to judge how much tradition is or isn't revered is to look at the way former stars are treated. I've seen former All Blacks lining up to buy tickets to get into test matches. When a union does decide to give such players free entry, they are often given such poor seating that they prefer to stay at home.

Yet these former stars are great advertisements for the game. Before major boxing bouts, former champions are called to the ring and introduced to the crowd. At New Zealand rugby tests, our former champions are either excluded or shunted to the far end of the ground. What does that tell you about the way we revere our rugby history?

We overlook our history and tradition at our peril.

chapter ELEVEN

STYLE

HAS RUGBY IMPROVED?

Is rugby more attractive these days? It should be. Players today are bigger (a reflection of the general growth of people, and also of the body-building work many players do in the gym) and the forwards are much more skilled.

One of the biggest changes over the past decade or so has been the huge improvement in the ability of the forwards, and not just in traditional areas such as rucking, mauling and scrummaging, but also in running, kicking and passing. There was a time when big, rotund forwards were expected to push at scrum-time, drive in rucks and mauls and generally rumble about the paddock. They were not expected to take part in sweeping passing movements, and if by some chance the ball came to them in open play, there was no thought of launching a counter-attack. They would unload it as quickly as possible to one of the backs.

The modern game is played at a much faster pace and mistakes are no longer tolerated. Whereas 30 years ago, it was excusable even for backs to drop a pass, or miss-kick a ball, today every error is noted and examined later. I'm dubious that even the best backs now attack any better than those of previous eras, but their defence is definitely surer and more organised.

Bob Scott, one of the legends of All Black rugby, is in no doubt the players do things now that their counterparts 50 years ago could never have contemplated. "The players are very fit and athletic. We could never have played at the sort of pace they do. The work-rate of forwards now is remarkable. But it doesn't make them better players. I don't see any subtlety any more, with players devising clever ways to create space. There is almost total emphasis on retaining possession. I talk to a lot of former All Blacks and we all feel the same. We admire the physical skills of the players, but don't think the rugby they are playing is very intelligent or creative."

Until 1967, the kick-into-touch rule operated, meaning players could kick into touch on the full from anywhere. This led to a safety-first brand of rugby that hindered backline play. It was amazing that someone like Ron Jarden, playing in the 1950s, could score 145 tries in just 134 first class matches. Or that Bert Cooke, playing in the centres in the 1920s, could score 121 tries in 131 matches. What players they must have been!

In their time, matches often had such final scores as 3-0, 5-0 and 6-3. Scoreless draws were not uncommon. Wilson Whineray's New Zealand side drew 0-0 with Scotland on their 1963–64 tour of Britain and France, a result that prevented them becoming the first All Black team to score a Grand Slam of victories over the Home Nations.

Penalty kicks at goal were rare. In the 1949 New Zealand-South Africa series, the Springboks won the four tests 15-11, 12-6, 9-3 and 11-8. All Black kicker Bob Scott didn't have the best of series with his goal-kicking boot, but didn't get many shots at goal, either. As he says: "Every kick was an absolute pressure kick, because you knew you weren't going to get many chances."

The situation is totally different today. In an effort to encourage more open, expansive rugby, the game's law-makers have increased the value of a try from three points to four (in 1972) and then to five (in 1992). Except for penalty situations, kicking into touch on the full is permitted only from inside a player's 22.

There is no doubt the changes have meant much higher scoring. In 1970 and 1971, the All Blacks played a total of eight tests. In those they totalled 72 points at an average of nine points per test. In 2001 the All Blacks played 10 tests and totalled 323 points at 32.3 points per test. The last time the All Blacks failed to score in any match was way back in 1978, when Munster beat New Zealand 12-0 at Limerick.

But higher points don't always indicate more entertaining football. There are dozens of kicks at goal each game now. Andrew Mehrtens has seven times kicked at least six penalties in a test match. Grant Fox did so four times. So that's a lot of time wasted watching meticulous kickers line up their place-kicks. Why all the penalties? Well, it's certainly not because modern players are bigger cheats than their predecessors. The rulebook 100 years ago consisted of just a few pages. These days it is of encyclopedic proportions. In fact, the rulebook is so intimidating, and the rules have become so complicated, that many would-be amateur coaches are scared away. They'd rather try to fly an aeroplane.

Another contributing factor in the larger number of kicks at goal in the modern era is that with much better drainage of fields, the use of kicking tees, and the replacement of leather rugby balls with plastic ones, conditions are much more suited to place-kicking. What once might not have been a kickable target is now too enticing to ignore.

It's tries spectators like to see and there are generally lots of them these days, at all levels, from club to test. The Super 12, especially in its first few dizzy years, was full of helter-skelter rugby and tries by the truckload. In 2002, the Reds beat the Stormers by a score of 49-46. If a last-minute Stormers' penalty had been kicked, this would have been the highest draw in first class history. Also in 2002, the Crusaders scored 96 points against the Waratahs, astounding considering the Waratahs were placed second on the Super 12 table. Test rugby is a little grimmer, but still, generally even the tightest tests between Australia, South Africa and New Zealand produce high scores, sometimes with four, five or more tries.

So there's plenty there for the spectator to see. Why then does it sometimes seem a little repetitive? Talking about the Super 12, even as passionate a rugby follower as Bob Scott says: "I get a bit bored with it sometimes and go to bed. There are lots of points, but that doesn't always mean the rugby is interesting. Three penalties in the first three minutes doesn't make for interesting rugby to me."

The number of infringements these days is extremely high. In one Super 12 match I surveyed in 2002, the average amount of time between blows on the referee's whistle was 11 seconds. A rugby reporter way back in 1905 described one display of officiating during the Originals' tour of Britain as being like a "whistling symphony". Goodness knows what he'd make of the goings-on today. Not only does the referee blow his whistle incessantly, but he seems to never stop talking, either. He is constantly warning players against off-side, or coaching them on how to scrum properly, or telling players to release the ball. It's a regular talk-fest.

With all the talking and whistling, there is on average only about 19 or 20 minutes of rugby action in each 80-minute game. The rest of it is all down-time. Setting and re-setting scrums, forming lineouts, waiting while kickers line up their shots at goal.

THE VARIOUS PHASES OF RUGBY

What about the quality of the action that is taking place? The game has gone in phases over the years. In the late 1980s and into the early 1990s, Auckland, and to a slightly lesser extent the All Blacks, had such a dominant scrum that it intimidated most opposition. Zinzan Brooke, the supertalented No 8, scored dozens of pushover tries, controlling the ball with his feet while the scrum moved relentlessly forward, until he could fall on the ball and score.

We don't see pushovers like that now. Scrums are not set on a defending goal-line any more, but back on the five-metre mark, which somewhat cuts out the option. Maybe scrums no longer dominate to such a marked degree, or maybe there aren't players with Brooke's skills, or maybe it's a combination of all these factors.

Then there was the maul phase, when teams would march their opposition back during seemingly never-ending mauls. Players would stay on their feet and keep the maul going. Some tries were scored from mauls that began at halfway. What were opposition to do? They weren't allowed to kill the ball, but could not stop the maul.

Rugby's legislators brought in rules to lessen the influence of the maul, but these created other problems. The use-it-or-lose-it rule was introduced. If a maul wasn't moving forward, the ball had to be cleared. This severely lessened the importance and number of mauls, but it meant forwards began spending much more of their time out in the backline, cluttering up what might have been flowing backline movements. The game began to resemble rugby league, with very few players committed to rucks and mauls and everyone strung out across the field. It became critical to retain possession of the ball and sometimes there would be 12, 15 or more phases of play. It was rugby league, alright, except that there was no limit to the number of times the ball could be played.

This became very boring. Some teams became adept at this style. The ACT Brumbies, marshalled by halfback George Gregan, had it down to a fine art, retaining possession for phase after phase until finally a defence cracked. But it wasn't terribly interesting to watch. Gradually the entertainment factor in the Super 12 decreased. It became a defence-oriented, rather than an attack-oriented, competition. Teams copied the Brumbies' style, placing the emphasis almost totally on playing error-free rugby and retaining possession. Very seldom would teams playing this way try grubber kicks or up-and-unders . . . holding on to the ball was paramount.

The Brumbies and teams that imitated their style began to encounter well-organised defences spaced across the field, intent on repelling each little break until finally an infringement occurred and possession was lost. The Crusaders won the 2000 Super 12 final 20-19 in just this fashion. The Brumbies absolutely dominated possession, but the Crusaders, knowing exactly what they would be facing, defended with commitment and concentration and won against the odds. It was a fascinating spectacle the first time. But by 2002, when each team set out to counter the Brumbies the same way, it had become all too predictable.

Those who liked to see the ball spun through the backline for the wingers and the fullback, running into the line, to score, were often sorely disappointed. The second-five and centre stopped worrying about distribution and became ever more intent on charging back into the forwards. The game was all about-face — the forwards were out in the backs, and the backs were in where you would expect normally to find forwards.

So the rule-makers had another rethink. For 2002 they took steps to re-emphasise the maul, hoping to get rid of at least some of the forwards from the backline by making them commit to the sort of work forwards have traditionally done.

Andy Leslie is one of many former players who feels the game has become too physical. "There are very big hits now," says Leslie, "but we don't see enough good back play. The defences are good, but the thing I don't like is the total emphasis on the physical side."

John Hart describes modern rugby as "a physical game of chess", and says that's at least partly due to the Polynesian influence. "The physicality of rugby has become much more dominant," says Hart. "Unfortunately, there seems to be a co-relation between that physicality and a lack of thinking. The game is so physical now that the shelf life of top players is considerably shortened. Coaches have a responsibility to try to protect their players. It's so different now from the game we saw 30 years ago.

"One of my big regrets as All Black coach was that I introduced a heavy physical component to training. I tried to get training to mirror the matches. But it's too hard on the players. It kills them physically. They are playing all these internationals — Super 12 and tests — and then being hammered in training, too. It's hard to describe how physical the game is now. It's brutal."

The overpoweringly physical nature of top rugby today means there are many more injuries than previously and that many of them are very severe. They take out players for the season, and threaten careers. These injuries lead to one of the great posers facing coaches these days: what to do about injured players? I must say I think coaches fail miserably in this regard.

The temptation for a coach, who is desperate for results, perhaps to save his own neck, is to risk a player who is recovering from an injury. For most coaches 80 per cent fitness is good enough when the player is critical. Through the 2001 Super 12 season, Jeremy Stanley was bedevilled by a knee injury. He played in 10 of the Blues' 11 matches, but was clearly hampered, often not finishing the games. A coach thinking of Stanley's future might have rested him and allowed the knee to come right. Blues coach Frank Oliver watched his team lose match after match and kept trying to get the most out of Stanley.

In 2002, Wellington (and All Black) lock Dion Waller hurt his calf muscle against the Waratahs. It was clear he was handicapped, but the Hurricanes had to beat the Waratahs to stay in the hunt for a top four place. Waller returned to the fray after being treated. He struggled badly. The following week, though still not right, Waller turned out against the Crusaders. This was not good for Waller's fitness or his chances of impressing the All Black selectors, but it suited coach Graham Mourie's purposes, for he needed his best team on the park. Even an injured Waller was a better bet than the next best lock. What happened? Perhaps favouring his calf, Waller injured his hamstring and had to leave the field anyway. It wasn't the best of Super 12 campaigns for Waller because earlier on he'd broken his hand. He played while that injury was mending, too.

Players will almost always play when pressed to do so. They feel they are letting down their team if they don't. The responsibility is with the coaches to ensure they place the players' health first. In the professional era, where coaches can get sacked and lose large pay packets, it must be hard for them to keep things in perspective. Yet these days, with rugby such a torrid physical contest, there is more need than ever for the emphasis to be placed on rest and recuperation.

There are various reasons, quite apart from playing risk-free rugby, why teams are able to retain possession for such long periods today. There are virtually no tightheads. Whereas once a hooker like Has Catley might pick up seven tightheads in a match, now many hookers go through a season without winning one strike against the head. The scrummaging is so efficient that most hookers don't even bother striking on the opposition put-in.

Lineouts, too, have become far more predictable. Since lifting in the lineouts was legalised in the mid-1990s, teams have been much more likely to win their lineouts on their own throw-in. It doesn't mean lineouts are never won against the throw — no top team has had more trouble in this regard in recent years than the All Blacks — but if a hooker is adept at throwing in, and the lineouts are well planned, the chances of teams winning their own lineout throw-ins are very high.

THE EMPHASIS ON DEFENCE

A lot of work and planning goes into defence and cracking it is not easy. It is indicative of the reliance some teams place on defence that rugby league coaches have even been drafted in to help in this area. Auckland players have had the benefit of league star Mark Graham's knowledge about defence and tackling, and in Australia, there is a regular interchange of ideas between league and union coaches.

Opposing defences seem to be almost on top of the attackers, pushing the off-side rule to its limits. Rugby is in essence a simple game: 14 players striving to create a metre of space for the 15th, as Charlie Saxton used to say. But with the rules today, and the more scientific approach to such things as defence formations, that is no easy thing.

It's possible to take science too far, though. Over the past three or four seasons, rugby analysts, often based at Massey University, have been employed increasingly heavily. They come up with amazingly detailed statistics, having studied video replays of various rep games ad nauseam. Coaches place varying degrees of faith in these statistics, but the overwhelming impression is that rugby is becoming a game of numbers. Such assets as flair and instinct are not valued by the analysts, and, increasingly less by coaches.

A good rugby observer, perhaps a former player, will watch a game and know who has played well. Just as a cricket coach can watch a batsman in the nets for three minutes and pick out his strong points and faults, so a prop can watch 20 scrums and point out which players are weak, who is outstanding, and so on. He doesn't need statistical data. An astute coach, too, knows a good player. Imagine Fred Allen or Carwyn James poring over page after page of statistical data before a training session!

Yet the science and analysis of rugby is now becoming so dominant that it is giving boring, by-the-book coaches a reason to stop their players expressing themselves naturally on the field. A charm of rugby is being lost. According to Fred Allen, "There's too much talk about videos and analysts and not enough work being done on the field."

Former players have watched with bemusement as law-makers have made quite dramatic alterations to the rules each year, only to have to change them back a year or two later when other, unforeseen, problems arise. Andy Haden says that it has been obvious some changes haven't worked. "What amazes me is that there never seems to be any repercussions for those who keep coming up with these rules. Where's the accountability? They make mistakes, stuff up the game, and are still there next year to have another go, and probably to stuff it up again. I'm all for change, if it improves things, but some of these blokes seem to want to change things just so they can say they did something."

The scores are higher these days, partly because there are now five points awarded for a try (which makes a mockery of such things as points-scoring records), but I question whether rugby is as entertaining as it was in the late 1980s. Think back to the 1987 World Cup. Sure there were some inflated scorelines, such as when New Zealand dismantled Italy 70-6, Argentina 46-15 and Wales 49-6. But there were lots of matches where there was not a torrent of points. And the rugby was entertaining. The All Blacks would flip the ball out to centre Joe Stanley, who would wait for his moment, then pass to John Gallagher steaming in from fullback, or wingers John Kirwan and Craig Green. There were lots of tries by the forwards, too, notably Alan Whetton and Michael Jones, but they were more orthodox forwards tries, not the result of hookers or props swanning out on the wing.

It's sad to say, but there may not be a place in rugby today for such a multi-talented centre as Bruce Robertson. Even Stanley might struggle. The demand these days is for centres like Frank Bunce and Tana Umaga, big tacklers and players who will run back at the opposition. Recent All Black midfielders like Alama Ieremia and Pita Alatini have been chosen not because of the way they set up play for those outside, but for their ability and willingness to charge back into the hurly-burly of opposing forwards.

Umaga, the All Black centre through 2001 and 2002, can run like the wind, as he showed during his time on the wing, but he has bulked up and is now what might be called a power centre. That's all well and good, but it does mean that exciting runners like Christian Cullen, Jeff Wilson and Jonah Lomu haven't been given the amount of possession or space they should have.

The game has become much more physically demanding, a series of big hits. There is a certain attraction in watching this sort of rugby for a short time, but after a while you do yearn for more creativity and flair. It's a bit like watching a heavyweight boxer. You might admire the fearsome power of George Foreman or Mike Tyson, but after a while the artistry and all-round skills of a young Muhammad Ali are more compelling.

So I can understand it when Bob Scott says he sometimes heads off to bed during the Super 12, or when Colin Meads says he finds match after match of Super 12 a bit boring. Even commentator Keith Quinn, whose love of rugby is unquestioned, says Super 12 matches become "like wallpaper". Quinn says that administrators have done all they can, introducing night rugby, Sunday rugby, early games, late games, but that in the end there is just so much rugby that people cannot watch it all. It's not that they don't love their rugby, but the style is a bit predictable. And there's too much of it.

THE GROWTH OF THE ALL BLACKS

The All Blacks have grown physically, even more so than the general population.

Compare the sizes of the famous 1924–25 Invincibles with those of the team Anton Oliver led to Ireland, Scotland and Argentina at the end of 2001:

1924–25 INVINCIBLES

	AGE	HEIGHT	WEIGHT
George Nepia	19	1.75m	82.9kg
Handley Brown	19	1.77m	72.9kg
Gus Hart	26	1.69m	62.5kg
Freddie Lucas	22	1.78m	65.2kg
Alan Robilliard	20	1.78m	73.4kg
Jack Steel	24	1.78m	79.2kg
Snowy Svenson	25	1.70m	68.8kg
Ces Badeley	27	1.70m	67.4kg
Bert Cooke	22	1.75m	59.7kg
Neil McGregor	22	1.70m	66.1kg
Mark Nicholls	22	1.77m	69.7kg
Lui Paewai	19	1.74m	73.3kg
Bill Dalley	22	1.63m	64.3kg
Jimmy Mill	24	1.70m	68.8kg
—			
Jim Parker	27	1.83m	79.2kg
Cliff Porter	24	1.72m	79.7kg
Cyril Brownlie	27	1.90m	95.1kg
Maurice Brownlie	26	1.83m	88.3kg
Les Cupples	26	1.89m	87.8kg
Quentin Donald	24	1.78m	78.8kg
Ian Harvey	21	1.86m	92.4kg
Bill Irvine	25	1.71m	81.5kg
Read Masters	23	1.81m	88.7kg
Brian McCleary	27	1.75m	82.9kg

Abe Munro	27	1.75m	75.2kg
Jock Richardson	25	1.85m	91.1kg
Ron Stewart	20	1.85m	88.7kg
Alf West	30	1.85m	87.8kg
Son White	30	1.79m	78.8kg
Backs (average)	22	1.73m	69.5kg
Forwards (average)	25	1.81m	85.0kg
Team (average)	23	1.77m	77.5kg

2001

Ben Blair	22	1.74m	83kg
Leon MacDonald	23	1.81m	96kg
Doug Howlett	23	1.85m	92kg
Jonah Lomu	26	1.96m	119kg
Nathan Mauger	23	1.83m	98kg
Caleb Ralph	24	1.89m	91kg
Roger Randle	27	1.90m	100kg
Tana Umaga	28	1.87m	101kg
Pita Alatini	25	1.79m	90kg
David Hill	23	1.88m	94kg
Aaron Mauger	20	1.82m	92kg
Andrew Mehrtens	28	1.78m	89kg
Byron Kelleher	24	1.75m	94kg
Mark Robinson	26	1.79m	90kg
Jason Spice	26	1.78m	80kg
—			
Jerry Collins	21	1.90m	103kg
Marty Holah	25	1.84m	98kg
Richard McCaw	20	1.90m	101kg
Paul Miller	24	1.92m	120kg
Scott Robertson	27	1.90m	109kg
Reuben Thorne	26	1.92m	107kg
Chris Jack	25	2.02m	115kg
Simon Maling	26	1.97m	110kg
Norman Maxwell	25	1.98m	106kg
Dion Waller	27	1.98m	108kg
Greg Feek	26	1.85m	112kg
Dave Hewett	30	1.91m	116kg

Kees Meeuws	27	1.83m	121kg
Greg Somerville	23	1.86m	114kg
Anton Oliver	26	1.85m	112kg
Tom Willis	22	1.83m	103kg
Backs (average)	24	1.83m	93.9kg
Forwards (average)	25	1.90m	109.6kg
Team (average)	24	1.86m	102.0kg

EVOLUTION OF POINTS SCORING

1884	Try 1, conversion 2, other goals 3
1892	Try 2, conversion 3, penalty goal 3, dropped goal 4
1894	Try 3, conversion 2, penalty goal 3, dropped goal and goal from a mark 4
1905	Value of a goal from a mark reduced to 3
1948	Value of a dropped goal reduced to 3
1972	Value of a try increased to 4
1992	Value of a try increased to 5

chapter TWELVE
THE **EXPANDING** GAME

WOMEN

The most exciting trend in New Zealand rugby over the past 15 years has been the increase in women's rugby. Back in 1988, New Zealand Rugby Union councillor JJ Stewart described the union as being "favourably disposed" to women playing rugby. He was replying to a letter from Vicky Dombroski, who went on to coach and then manage the New Zealand women's team. Two years later, the JJ Stewart Trophy (the women's equivalent of the Ranfurly Shield) was donated. An unofficial New Zealand side played and beat the California Grizzlies and it became apparent the time had arrived for New Zealand women's rugby to develop an international programme.

One of the early pioneers of New Zealand women's rugby was Lawrie O'Reilly, who coached a Canterbury University women's team on a world tour in 1988 and in 1991 coached the New Zealand women who played in the inaugural women's World Cup, paying their own way to the tournament and attending without official NZRFU blessing. The women beat Canada and Wales, and lost 7-0 in the semi-final to eventual champions the United States. Perhaps the biggest name to emerge from that pioneering New Zealand team was Anna Richards, who was still a pivotal member of the national team as first five-eighth in 2002 when it won its second consecutive World Cup crown.

Women's rugby made steady progress over the next few years until in 1996 New Zealand attended the Canada Cup. They thrashed Australia, Canada, the United States and France and flying winger Vanessa Cootes scored 18 tries in three matches, earning herself a professional contract in France.

The rising impact of women's rugby was revealed in 1998 when coach Darryl Suasua's Black Ferns, as they had become known, won the World Cup, beating England 44-11 in the semi-finals and the United States 44-12 in the final. Cootes scored five tries in the final and centre Annaleah Rush was named player of the tournament. Other stars of that team included hooker Farah Palmer and halfback Monique Hirovanaa.

Now, for those close enough to realise, the national women's team had stars to match All Blacks Jonah Lomu, Andrew Mehrtens, Josh Kronfeld and Jeff Wilson. Former New Zealand netball rep Louisa Wall made a successful switch to rugby and not only boosted the Black Ferns, but gained the side increased exposure.

Over the next few years the New Zealanders were unbeatable, winning the Canada Cup again in 2000 and scoring a succession of big test wins. It wasn't until England won the second test of a two-match series 22-17 at North Harbour Stadium in 2001 that a 10-year, 24-test winning streak ended.

The women's National Provincial Championship began with 14 teams competing in 1999 and has now been enlarged to 22 teams, with a first division of six sides and a second-tier regional competition. The national women's sevens championship has been played since 1998 and New Zealand is now represented at international sevens tournaments, primarily in Asia.

The benefits of the increased amount of rugby were emphasised at the 16-team 2002 World Cup in Barcelona, when New Zealand beat Germany 117-0, Australia 36-3, France 30-0 and, in the final, England 29-9, to retain their world No 1 ranking.

It would be misleading to claim women's rugby is anything like a major sport. If men's rugby is only a minnow compared to soccer, basketball, athletics, golf, volleyball, tennis, swimming and so on, then women's rugby is microscopically small, as was illustrated by the empty stadium throughout the 2002 World Cup. The 2002 *New Zealand Rugby Almanack* comprised 368 pages, and of them 12 were devoted to women's rugby, which is probably a little generous in terms of participation and public interest. But, as the expression goes, "Out of small acorns . . ."

The expansion of the women's game in New Zealand has been a boon to the sport. There were 2800 female players in 1998 and that number had risen to about 7000 by 2002. This enables the New Zealand Rugby Union to claim that rugby union is almost holding its numbers, despite the fact that boys' and men's team numbers are falling depressingly quickly. And it has probably created a healthier social environment for rugby with entire families, and not just the males, now able to be involved.

The standard of play of the top women is outstanding. It will be interesting to see how New Zealand copes with the mass exodus of top names after the 2002 World Cup. Coach Suasua, who has been with the team since 1996, captain Palmer and up to half of the world champion squad of 26 were expected to retire. But, as with the All Blacks, there are always new stars emerging. Locks Monalisa Codling and Victoria Heighway, front rowers Halyn Va'aga and Casey Robertson, hooker Fiao'o Faamausili and backs Aroha Moore, Sandy Yates, Hannah Myers, who is the best goal-kicker in world women's rugby, Emma Jensen and Amiria Marsh are all stars of the future.

It's interesting that the issue of physically imposing Polynesian and Maori players dominating smaller Pakeha players is as relevant in women's as in men's rugby. Of the 26 players in the 2002 world champion squad, 11 were Maori, seven Polynesian and eight Pakeha. Coach Suasua said that Polynesian girls develop earlier and are therefore likely to gain representative honours earlier. "With Polynesian girls, other things, such as church and family, are very important, and you find that if they don't make teams fairly quickly, they are likely to give away the game to concentrate on other parts of their lives," said Suasua. "But there's no doubting they have a physical advantage.

"You don't see many Pakeha women playing club rugby in Auckland. Generally the Pakeha women who have come through into the New Zealand side have come from further south, where there aren't as many Polynesian and Maori women. Players like the Richards sisters, who were from Timaru and moved to Canterbury, Casey Robertson from Wyndham, Fiona King from Otago. They've taken to rugby, been able to develop their skills and then gone on to play at a higher level."

SEVENS

Without ever threatening the position of traditional 15-a-side rugby, sevens rugby has become an accepted part of the rugby landscape, to the extent where the New Zealand union contracts players and coaches specifically for sevens and where New Zealand has, over the past few years, become accepted as the best sevens team in the world.

Sevens has been played since the 1920s and in New Zealand a national sevens interprovincial championship has been held every year since 1975. As with the NPC, the traditionally major unions have dominated the national sevens tournament. Marlborough and Manawatu won the first five tournaments between them, but since then Auckland, Taranaki, Counties, North Harbour, Canterbury and Waikato have ruled. A New Zealand sevens team was chosen for one game in 1973, but it wasn't really until the mid-1980s that genuinely representative New Zealand sides were chosen.

For years, the Hong Kong sevens was regarded as the unofficial world championship, and even today that event is one of the most significant on the rugby calendar. But the sevens game has advanced internationally over the past decade. A sevens World Cup is held every fourth year. New Zealand failed to qualify for the semi-finals in 1993, lost in the semi-finals in 1997, and then won the world title at Mar del Plata, Argentina, in 2001. In addition, there is now an 11-event world sevens Grand Prix circuit that New Zealand has ruled over the past few years.

The circuit is heavily supported by the International Rugby Board as a way of introducing and fostering rugby in such countries as Chile, Japan, Malaysia, China and Dubai. It attracts only a modicum of interest back in New Zealand, but events draw large crowds, even in places like Buenos Aires, where rugby is far from the national sport. When the Grand Prix circuit stops off in Wellington in February, it is a big weekend for the capital.

Perhaps the biggest day in sevens history occurred at the 1998 Kuala Lumpur Commonwealth Games when New Zealand, bolstered by All Black recruits such as Lomu, Cullen and Joeli Vidiri, carried off the gold medal. The sevens tournament — the first at a Commonwealth Games — was massively popular and the New Zealanders' efforts were appreciated not only by the crowds at the stadium but by big television audiences throughout the world. The New Zealand sevens team continued the good work by retaining its Commonwealth Games title at Manchester in 2002, convincingly beating Fiji in the final.

New Zealand's good record in sevens is a reflection of the seriousness with which this version of the game is treated, and is also an indication of how ideally suited to sevens are the big, powerful Polynesian players who largely make up the New Zealand squad.

It must be said that sevens players are not the superstars of New Zealand rugby. They are generally players who have not attained Super 12 standard; indeed most of them are hoping that a series of good performances with the sevens side will lead to them being offered a big professional contract.

As the sevens game has become more specialised, there has become less of an immediate crossover of players. Sevens players tend to be exceedingly trim, with the emphasis on being fleet of foot. Traditional rugby rep players carry a bit more bulk because of the increased emphasis on defence. It is doubtful if the likes of Alex Wyllie, Wayne

Shelford and Todd Blackadder would make a national sevens team these days, yet all have represented New Zealand at that form of the game.

Sometimes a sevens player will emerge and display such obvious talent that it is only a matter of time before he becomes a star in the 15-a-side version. Jonah Lomu and Christian Cullen were two such cases in point for New Zealand. There are also sevens legends, players who might have gone as far as they are going to in the 15-a-side version and decide to concentrate more on sevens. Eric Rush, Karl Te Nana and Dallas Seymour are three such players. Long-serving New Zealand sevens coach Gordon Tietjens would be many people's choice as the best sevens coach in the world, though he showed his knowledge of rugby overall by continuing to coach Bay of Plenty with success in the National Provincial Championship.

Sevens rugby is another version of the professional game, and due attention must be paid it. But it still has only a marginal place in the set-up of New Zealand rugby. Very few New Zealand boys grow up hoping to be a New Zealand sevens representative. Test and Super 12 status is still the goal, and sevens rugby provides a diversion and, for some, a handy alternative way of progressing in rugby.

THE MEDIA

Because rugby has been New Zealand's national game for so long, there has always been a media presence involved in reporting it. But the way rugby has been reported has changed hugely over the years. Before the advent of the electronic media, there would be no more than a smattering of reporters covering a game, no matter how big. Their reports were basically print versions of a television screening. They relayed to readers what had happened throughout the 80 minutes. There was little or no attempt to get after-match quotes or to do colour pieces examining the personalities of various rugby stars.

Then, at the end of a tour, a senior rugby reporter would produce a tour book that was basically a series of match reports. These books were invariably snapped up — Terry McLean, the doyen of New Zealand rugby writers, wrote more than 20 tour books and every father got one for Christmas.

The advent of radio, and then television, took rugby to the masses and gave big games a much more immediate feel. Now rugby fans did not have to wait until the next day's newspaper to find out what had happened. A few commentators, such as radio's Winston McCarthy, Bob

Irvine, John Howson, John McBeth and Graham Moody established their reputations covering rugby. Television's best known New Zealand commentators have been Keith Quinn, who towers over everyone else in terms of longevity and professionalism, and Grant Nisbett.

Television helped invent the "personality journalists". Newspapers like to have former All Black stars writing (or having ghost-written) columns to attract readers. Radio and television use big-name experts for comments — people like Murray Mexted, Grant Fox, Chris Laidlaw and John Drake.

One must sympathise with top players who seem to be constantly hunted by an ever-growing media pack. Keith Quinn says that the demands on the players' time these days are massive compared to decades ago. "Even at the start of the professional era, which was only a few years ago, there wasn't the same amount of media chasing them. The number of media around an All Black team has trebled since 1995 and is exploding every year. Now there is the Internet, women's magazines, specialist sport and rugby magazines, newspapers, radio, television, including the subscriber networks . . . it never stops. On tour, adidas, the major All Black sponsor, tries to make sure the All Blacks are available to meet the public and sign autographs after training. I feel there is a lot of goodwill on the part of the players, but with the demands on their time, things do have to be managed."

What's interesting about the media is the impact on reporting the presence of the electronic media has made. With radio and television bringing followers a full description of the game, the written media have had to dig further for fresh stories. This means they have relied heavily on after-match comments of players and coaches, and have attempted to personalise their coverage with in-depth feature articles on rugby news-makers, be they players, coaches, referees or officials. They have also started to delve into players' personal lives, examining their off-the-field behaviour, their love life, their business life . . . anything that might draw readers. Nicole and Justin Marshall's decision to induce their baby so Marshall could guarantee being there for the birth, rather than playing in the Tri-Nations, was front-page news in *The Dominion Post*.

The most uncontrollable medium is talkback radio. Administrators, coaches and players hate talkback. It's the one element of the media that no amount of spin doctoring can rein in. There's no expert like a sports spectator. Your average rugby fan has loads of opinions and where better to express them than on air?

What it's meant is that rugby players have had to become more media savvy. They have had to learn how to handle big press conferences, what to say and what not to say. A couple of words, gruffly delivered, no longer suffice. Unless you're Sean Fitzpatrick, that is. His often-repeated "I give full credit to the opposition" became a trademark.

part FIVE

THE GREATEST THREAT

chapter THIRTEEN

RUGBY'S **SCHOOLS** CRISIS

THE COLLEGE DILEMMA

Nowhere is rugby under greater threat than in schools. This shows up most noticeably at secondary schools, and that has been my focus in examining the state of junior rugby. There was a trend for years that very young boys — of primary school age — often played soccer as their introduction to winter team sport, but that when they attended college they switched to rugby. While primary school soccer numbers have risen over the past decade, the real problem for rugby is that it isn't getting nearly as many boys swapping codes when they start college. It is, after all, college players who go on to play senior, and perhaps representative, rugby.

Primary school sport in New Zealand is generally very well organised, be it cricket, rugby, soccer or softball. Junior clubs are run by parents, who ensure teams have coaches and equipment, and are entered for the correct competitions. These junior officials work hard and are often very innovative.

For instance, weekend shopping has really hurt junior numbers, so officials are devising ways to get around the problem. Wellington junior rugby referee and administrator Mike Fairmaid says: "Parents have to work on Saturdays and are too busy to get their kids to sport and to supervise them, so the kids miss out." In response to that problem, Fairmaid has introduced a scheme for rugby in the area he administers to have some junior matches played on Friday evenings. "It depends on the availability of floodlit grounds, but the initial reaction has been very good."

Fairmaid's Friday night scheme has been adopted after the success of North Harbour's "fish and chip" rugby nights. North Harbour began playing some junior matches on Friday nights back in 2000 and the response has been overwhelmingly positive.

So the problem isn't at primary school. It is when the youngsters move on to college and leave the umbrella of their junior clubs that the crunch comes.

There was a time when the sports reputations of boys colleges basically revolved around their success at rugby, but those days are gone. Though it is all too easy to blame the New Zealand Rugby Union, the finger should be pointed first at the 27 provincial unions that have, collectively, allowed the situation to occur. The provincial unions are responsible for grassroots rugby and they have been very remiss in this area. A few are endeavouring to retrieve the situation now; a lot still don't seem to grasp how dire the position is and are not doing nearly enough.

Amazingly, the New Zealand Rugby Union has done no real research into school numbers . . . where rugby is still strong, where numbers are declining and why. Over the past year a little work has finally been undertaken in this area, but still nothing terribly substantial.

To get a feel for the situation, I surveyed some of New Zealand's major rugby schools. The results are frightening for rugby.

Auckland Grammar has been New Zealand's greatest rugby school. It has produced more All Blacks than any other college, 49 from Maurice Herrold in 1893 to Doug Howlett in 2000, and seven of those boys — Ces Badeley, Merv Corner, John Tanner, Wilson Whineray, Kel Tremain, Gary Whetton and Grant Fox — have gone on to captain New Zealand. But rugby at Auckland Grammar is under threat. Look at these statistics:

	ROLL	RUGBY TEAMS	SOCCER TEAMS
1940	874	15	0
1970	1264	17	11
1990	1885	26	20
2000	1977	17	32

Rugby has been well and truly eclipsed by soccer as the main winter game at Auckland Grammar, an unthinkable situation in the 1960s. The pattern is similar elsewhere in Auckland. Here are the figures for Takapuna Grammar:

	ROLL	RUGBY TEAMS	SOCCER TEAMS
1940	523	6	3
1970	1055	6	3
1990	1033	5	6
2000	1366	6	14

The Takapuna Grammar situation is affected by the fact that a significant number of girls are now playing football at the school, and that most of them are choosing soccer, but again the trend is clear.

Outside Auckland, too, college rugby is battling.

Wanganui Collegiate was once as staunch a backer of rugby as could be found in New Zealand. There was no soccer played in the school until the late 1970s, and then only for the fourth form and above. Hockey was the winter option. Look at the drop-off in rugby numbers:

	ROLL	RUGBY TEAMS	SOCCER TEAMS	HOCKEY TEAMS
1940	320	8	0	7
1970	480	17	0	7
1990	470	13	6	7
2000	355	8	4	5

Note: the roll figures include only boys. Girls were admitted to the school in the early 1990s.

Wellington College has produced more than 30 All Blacks, including captains Ginger and Mark Nicholls, Cliff Porter and Jack Griffiths. This is what the figures look like for Wellington College:

	ROLL	RUGBY TEAMS	SOCCER TEAMS
1940	656	16	0
1970	1073	15	5
1990	1115	14	14
2000	1258	16	19

Rugby has held its junior numbers better in the South Island, but still the signs are there. Christ's College was for decades so pro-rugby that soccer was not even offered as an option. But soccer has won a strong following over the past 30 years, during which time rugby has dipped markedly:

	ROLL	RUGBY TEAMS	SOCCER TEAMS
1940	342	9	0
1970	587	21	0
1990	568	14	6
2000	627	13	5

At Otago Boys, rugby is nearly holding on, as the roll declines, though the percentage of boys in the school playing soccer is increasing:

	ROLL	RUGBY TEAMS	SOCCER TEAMS
1970	1018	12	7
1990	1049	14	5
2000	673	13	5

The swing away from rugby, though a national trend, is far from standard, and is more noticeable in the urban centres, particularly in the North Island. Christchurch Boys is fielding four times as many soccer teams as it did in 1970, while rugby has risen by one-third. At Southland Boys, rugby remains dominant, though both rugby and soccer are dipping. At Palmerston North Boys, rugby has about kept pace with the increased roll and has surged over the past decade, while there has been a drop-off in soccer numbers:

	ROLL	RUGBY TEAMS	SOCCER TEAMS
1970	1088	17	8
1990	1202	18	16
2000	1467	22	14

Traditionally Te Aute College in southern Hawke's Bay has not offered soccer as a winter option. In 1990, there were nine rugby teams, which was very impressive for a school roll of 235. By 2000 the roll had dropped by 55 and the number of rugby teams had nearly halved. Soccer is still not really a factor at the school, though with some girls now on the roll, there is one team.

To make some sense of the figures, it is necessary to generalise. Rugby is struggling in many big city schools, where increasing numbers of boys find soccer a more attractive option. There are many reasons for the drift away from rugby, including the increasing urbanisation of New Zealand and the issue of "white flight".

The New Zealand union should be extremely concerned about junior rugby, not the quality, but the numbers. The quality is still very good, as is illustrated by the fact that New Zealand, boosted by a number of early-developing Polynesian boys, has over the past decade been the leading team in the world at under-19 and under-21 level. It's the decline in numbers that should be ringing alarm bells.

For decades it was assumed that rugby was far and away the most popular junior winter sport, though exact figures were never available. Therefore it was with shock that rugby fans received these figures from the Hillary Commission in March, 2001: there were 114,000 young New Zealanders playing soccer regularly, compared with 99,500 playing rugby. This was a significant swing around from the 1991 *Life in New Zealand* survey, published by the Hillary Commission, which showed that junior soccer and rugby numbers were equal. Both sports then had nine per cent participation at junior level.

The New Zealand Rugby Union's own figures are even more concerning. Brent Anderson, the union's community rugby officer, says that in 2001, there were 87,500 players of primary and secondary school age in New Zealand. He is unable to say how that figure compares with previous years because, amazingly for a body administering a professional code, the union has no figures from previous years with which to compare.

BLISSFUL IGNORANCE

In my dealings with various rugby officials at provincial and national level, there often seemed surprisingly little awareness of the plunging numbers. Some painted a curiously glowing picture of schoolboy rugby in their region.

The Auckland Rugby Union rugby development officer, Daniel Faleolo, said secondary school rugby in the Auckland area was in a very healthy state. "The number of secondary school rugby players is increasing all the time, and the rugby is very well organised," he said. "The quality of the junior rugby is strong, as is shown by the number of national age group representatives from Auckland, and the quantity of players is on the rise. We have 4500 kids playing secondary schools rugby. That's a lot."

One point that rugby officials sometimes omit to mention — and this applies to officials of senior and junior rugby throughout the country — is that figures can be misleading because over the past decade a small but important number of women's and girls' teams have been formed. These help boost — or at least hold — rugby's overall playing numbers, and often obscure the fact that boys' or men's rugby has suffered a significant decline in numbers.

Faleolo's rosy picture surprised me because teachers and club officials in Auckland I had spoken to without exception told a much bleaker story. I mentioned the Auckland Grammar and Takapuna Grammar figures and Faleolo said such schools were aberrations. "There are a few schools which for various reasons have had a dip in rugby but for every one of them, there are several where rugby is on the rise. What about King's College, Onehunga, Mt Albert Grammar? Auckland Grammar has a big soccer influence these days, but that situation is unusual."

I have been told by many people in Auckland — journalists, parents, school and club officials — that the increasing number of Polynesian players has pushed many white boys out of rugby, often into soccer. Faleolo said he didn't see white flight as a factor at all. "It's just not a major issue in secondary schools," he said. "Rugby is a big enough game that kids of one particular group would not drive away others.

"School teams are graded by weight and we have both weight and open age rep teams." Wouldn't that lead, logically, to Polynesian and Maori boys dominating the open weight age teams and white boys filling most of the weight-restricted rep teams? "No, not at all," said Faleolo. "There's a fairly even split in all the teams."

It's pleasing that Faleolo, who is responsible for Auckland junior rugby, is so positive, but I can only repeat that many Auckland schoolteachers I spoke to do not share his view. They feel secondary school rugby is not being administered as well as it was a decade ago, that the Auckland union does not offer enough coaching resources and that the increasing number of big Polynesian boys is pushing large numbers of white boys away, often into soccer.

The Wellington union's director of rugby development, Brian Cederwall, also felt things were going well at the junior level. "Rugby is on the incline at the moment, and there is a real high in pre-secondary school level, even though statistics show there are also a lot of soccer players," he says. "Rugby is holding its own quite well. Obviously in the modern age where there are all sorts of sports, and computers and other distractions, rugby has to fight for numbers, but I don't think the sport is in trouble. Cricket, by contrast, is in huge trouble at colleges. Teachers seem to have stopped being involved in cricket, whereas there are still a lot of teachers coaching rugby."

How dramatic does the situation need to become before these people, paid to monitor and improve the development of junior rugby, begin to worry?

Just think back to the *New Zealand Rugby World* cover story of October, 2001. It quoted figures from the Pakuranga Rugby Club in largely white, middle-class Auckland. Pakuranga fields more than 50 junior teams, yet, according to the story, lost 12 per cent of its juniors in 2000 and another 15 per cent in 2001.

I'd have thought that would have sent shock waves through the rugby community because one thing is for sure: Pakuranga is not alone. Asked for the New Zealand union's response to this problem, Anderson said a questionnaire was being sent, through provincial unions, to juniors who had not re-enrolled for rugby in 2002. Another questionnaire was to be sent to some junior rep rugby players.

Anderson, while conceding that any loss in numbers was undesirable, feels that the drop-off in young rugby players is the result of changes in society, such as youngsters wanting part-time employment to earn money, more single-parent families, more emphasis being placed on the scholastic side of school, children being more independent thinkers and deciding for themselves what sports they want to play, the decline of the rural population, weekend shopping and so on.

I suggested that perhaps clubs didn't liaise well enough with schools, but Anderson feels that is too general a criticism, and that some schools are extremely well looked after by clubs. "In the Waikato, generally the relationship between schools and clubs is good," he said. "Auckland is approaching this issue as well. Sometimes, it's an easy link — St Pat's boys go to Marist St Pat's, or Feilding College boys go naturally to Feilding Old Boys. But what about Wellington College in Wellington? Boys at that school could go equally to Poneke, Wellington, Old Boys-University or Oriental-Rongotai. The transition is not clear-cut."

Greg Kasper, who was the Pakuranga club Chairman until 2002, was in no doubt that a root cause of the exodus was white flight. I was surprised to find, when I questioned Brent Anderson on this issue, to get this reply: "There is anecdotal evidence that this issue is a concern. We don't have the data base information to make an absolute judgment, but certainly there are more Polynesians playing the game. The balance of numbers is swinging more towards the Polynesians."

The First XV no longer represents a random-looking smattering of boys from a college. If you look at the First XV of a major boys college nowadays, you will find the forwards are all either exceptionally tall — often in the region of 2m — and/or incredibly heavy — often more than 110kg. The backs will be built for speed, but will be robust. There are no puny specimens on the paddock, and the boys look older. In fact, some look like they have a wife and two kids back home.

RUGBY'S NOT THE ONLY GAME IN TOWN

What is undeniable is that rugby is no longer the only major winter sport on offer. Wellington College did not offer soccer as an option until 1946. Until the mid-1970s, every third-former at Wanganui Collegiate virtually had to play rugby. Nelson College had a similar rugby-only rule. My father attended St Pat's Town in Wellington in the 1940s and says that back then it required that the parents meet the rector before their son could be excused from rugby in favour of soccer. This mindset was replicated throughout the country.

Rugby, therefore, has had a brilliant feeder system of boys colleges whose emphasis on rugby has stretched back generations. Look at the list: Whangarei Boys, Takapuna Grammar, Rosmini College, Westlake Boys High, Auckland Grammar, Mount Albert Grammar, Kelston Boys, St Kentigern, Sacred Heart College, King's College, St Peter's College (Auckland), Wesley College, St Stephen's School (Bombay), St Paul's Collegiate (Hamilton), Hamilton Boys, Western Heights High, Tauranga Boys, Gisborne Boys, Napier Boys, St John's, Lindisfarne College, Hastings Boys, New Plymouth Boys, Te Aute College, Wanganui Collegiate, Hato Paora College, Palmerston North Boys, Wairarapa College, Rathkeale College, Upper Hutt College, Hutt Valley High, St Bernard's, St Patrick's Town and St Patrick's Silverstream, Wellington College, Marlborough Boys, Nelson College, St Bede's, Christ's College, Christchurch Boys, Waitaki Boys, Timaru Boys, Otago Boys and Southland Boys . . . each of these major schools has not only catered for hundreds of boys every year playing rugby, but has ensured that for decade after decade there were always vast numbers of boys leaving college with rugby firmly embedded as their No 1 sport.

All boys colleges were big on rugby, though as a rule of thumb, the private schools pushed the sport even more than the state schools.

Even with the natural drop-off by boys as they left college, there were still many thousands joining rugby clubs each year. The sport thrived. If boys didn't continue to play, more than likely they maintained their interest in the game because it had been drilled into them through their college years that rugby was the most important sport in New Zealand. Soccer, on the other hand, struggled. With colleges fielding only a smattering of teams, there wasn't nearly the talent pool and usually the best athletes were drawn to rugby.

A boy had to be deadly serious about playing soccer, perhaps through parental interest, to continue with the sport at college, when so much attention and so much kudos was focused on rugby. But those days are changing. Colleges still like to have a strong First XV and take pride in that team's performances. But rugby isn't the be-all and end-all as it once was.

Palmerston North Boys High has always been one of the great rugby colleges. It held the Moascar Cup, contested nationally by secondary schools, many times, sometimes for years on end. The school's identity was very much tied in with its rugby prowess. The scene has changed, though rugby is still a very important sport at the school. Dave Syms, himself a former representative player, a coach of many years' experience and now a Manawatu rugby administrator, says that whereas the First XV would once have been the overwhelmingly dominant sports team, now the school takes equal pride in the results of its top teams in all sports.

"As the principal at Palmerston North Boys, I know that if our school soccer team, or hockey team, or cricket team or any other team has a big win, they are given equal kudos in the school. That's a change. For a long time, the First XV was the only team in the school. Ian Colquhoun coached the team for 25 years and he had an outstanding team. In fact, when I was teaching at Auckland Grammar, I coached against Palmerston North Boys High teams. Those were always very big games. But times have moved on."

Syms points out that rugby at Palmerston North Boys High has not really faced two major problems some colleges have encountered — the drift from rugby to soccer, and the domination of Maori and Pacific Island boys at rugby.

"In some ways, it's not a typical boys college. Because there is a strong rural client base and there isn't a particularly high percentage of Maori and Pacific Island boys attending, rugby at the school has not come under threat the way it has in some other colleges. Palmerston North is a strong soccer area, and that's reflected in this school, but rugby has pretty much held its numbers."

However, said Syms, the school First XV struggles these days in some annual fixture matches against colleges with much bigger First XVs. "It's even more noticeable in the younger age grades, where one big strong Polynesian boy can virtually run the whole game," he says.

Palmerston North Boys, like most colleges, has also had to combat the lessening of interest of teachers in coaching sport. Syms feels that having more female teachers now probably doesn't help rugby. But, he says, a lot of schools cope by setting up clubs within their schools and having them run externally, using parents and importing professional coaches.

"Palmerston North Boys uses some Massey University boys who are doing sports management courses. They are put beside teachers to look after teams and are able to tap into their expertise. But there is also a rule at Palmerston North Boys that if you want to be a teacher, you must coach a sports team or take some other sort of extra-curricular activity, such as music or drama."

In my first year at St Patrick's College (Town) in 1970, we fielded 19 rugby teams and five soccer teams. Thirty years later, there were eight rugby teams and six soccer teams, this change despite the fact that the college has moved from the city to Kilbirnie, in Wellington's eastern suburbs, and a much greater percentage of the pupils are of Maori or Pacific Island origins.

When I was at St Pat's, the rugby teams were virtually all coached by teachers; the soccer teams mainly by parents. Most boys in the school knew who the members of the First XV were. Our whole school would attend the annual fixtures against Wellington College and St Pat's Silverstream. We'd do the haka during the game, cheer on our team and really cared who won. First XV players were school heroes and were generally prefects.

By contrast, the soccer team was like some sort of mysterious religious cult. Hardly any of us knew who was in the team, and no-one really cared. The players themselves went about their business, training and playing, while the rest of the school was oblivious to their activities. Pupils were never given time off to attend the soccer team's big fixtures, if there were any. The soccer players did not bring pride to the school, even if they were extremely good at their sport, as some of them were. That was because soccer was a minor game at St Pat's, a traditional boys school where rugby ruled.

Other colleges have mirrored this trend. At St Bede's College in Christchurch, soccer was not even introduced into the range of sports available until the 1960s, but has quickly taken hold. In 1970 the school fielded 26 rugby teams and three soccer teams. Now the number of rugby teams has nearly halved, to 14, and soccer is up to five teams, and climbing.

Wellington College principal Roger Moses says that these days rugby and soccer are about equally popular at his school. "For 2002 we have 22 soccer teams and 16 rugby teams. Maybe rugby has dropped slightly since I arrived here in the mid-1990s. You can't just look at soccer as the reason, though. Lots of winter sports are an option now. We field basketball, hockey, water polo, squash, underwater hockey teams...all sorts. Some boys do cross-country. Other boys are into such diverse sports as skateboarding, mountain biking, canoe polo and kayaking. Having fun is very important to the boys and there is a high proliferation of alternative sports.

"We have a strong rugby club and we push rugby as a major sport, but it's definitely not as dominant as it once was."

There was a snapshot of the diversity of sport on offer at the Halberg Awards dinner in 2002. The world champion New Zealand sevens rugby team was a finalist. But so were Melissa Moon (mountain running), Steve Gurney (endurance sport), Cameron Brown and Craig Watson (triathlon). These sorts of sports stars are the new role models.

Whereas for many years, the school's First XV matches were the focus of winter sport, the emphasis has changed more to a sports day. "We have an annual exchange with St Patrick's — alternating between Town and Silverstream each year," says Moses. "On that day the schools' first rugby and soccer teams meet and our boys can watch either. It's not all rugby now. The school First XV is still a big deal, but doesn't have quite the same importance it once did."

Moses makes his point by talking about the "quad" — the quadrangular rugby tournament contested each year by Wellington College, Nelson College, Wanganui Collegiate and Christ's College. "Old boys of the school always ask about the quad. In their day it was an all-important tournament. It still means a lot, but now you have to put it in the context of greater competition — there is a surfeit of sport available."

THE CHANGING FACE OF COLLEGE RUGBY

Wellington College provides a good example of what has become known as "the browning of rugby". "At the moment nearly 10 per cent of our pupils are either Maori or Polynesian," says Moses. "But our First XV is at least 50 per cent Maori or Polynesian, often more. Our open under-15 grade team, another very important rugby team in the school, is 75 percent Maori or Polynesian.

"There is no doubting that Polynesians, especially, mature early. They are often wonderful physical specimens. They are bigger, faster, stronger and more explosive. Their presence is definitely putting off some other, smaller kids. I use myself as an example. I was in the Auckland Grammar First XV as a flanker in 1972. I was 11 stone [70 kg]. Well, I wouldn't get a look in now. Our First XV front row in 2000 was heavier than the All Black front row. Our props were 130kg each!"

Invariably, he says, these big boys are brown-skinned, usually Tongan or Samoan. "A lot of white kids are being dissuaded from playing rugby. Some will continue to play in the restricted grades, but once they reach open grades, they will give away the game. That is obviously a big problem for rugby. The higher the grade you look at, the higher proportion you will see of Maori and Polynesian kids in those teams."

Flicking through the Wellington College yearbook for 2000, Moses notes that there was one Maori boy in the school soccer First XI and one in the cricket team, in contrast to the high proportion in the rugby First XV (and, by way of interest, also in the school dragon boating teams).

Moses feels the Maori and Polynesian influence has become an issue at Wellington College as the percentage of those boys attending increases. "If you go back 30 years, you would find nothing like 10 per cent of our roll made up of Polynesian and Maori boys. The percentage will keep increasing. Rugby is a game that really appeals to them. It is a team sport and is very physical."

There is another factor, too — money. It is not quite like the United States, where black boys from ghettos lift themselves from poverty by excelling at basketball, or football, or boxing, but the chance to earn big money is undoubtedly a lure. Moses: "I have no doubt the prospect of making a career out of rugby is enticing to many boys, and to their parents. It is a game they can play well, and they enjoy it. Now, with the chance to earn good money out of the game if they can progress, there is more incentive to stick with it more seriously."

The issue of not having enough teachers with an interest in coaching sport has hit Wellington College hard. In 1988 a rugby club was formed within the school. The club is run by parents and it is often parents who are responsible for organising, and/or coaching teams.

Moses echoes Dave Syms when he says there are more female teachers at boys schools these days and, not surprisingly, not a lot of them are very interested in coaching rugby. "Teachers generally don't see coaching sports teams after school as part of their job description. And there are fewer people interested in sport who go into teaching these days. If I go back to my time as an Auckland Grammar teacher, we had Dave Syms,

Stu Watt, John Graham, Graham Henry, and a few years later, John Mills, among others on the teaching staff. They were all rep rugby players or coaches. You don't get many of those sort of people teaching now, because they can make a career out of rugby, playing, then coaching. That drift away from teaching is definitely hurting rugby."

The situation was exacerbated in 2002 by the prolonged secondary school teacher strikes and the ban on extra-curricular activities, including coaching sports teams after school and at weekends. Some schools found the teachers less than enthusiastic about resuming coaching duties once the ban was finally lifted.

John Mills, a former All Black who taught at Christ's College from 1986–2000, says that once, teaching was a career that enabled men to play rep rugby. "These days you get very few rep footballers coming into teaching. It used to be seen as a Government-type state sector agency in which there was a trade-off between a lower level of remuneration and job security, plus the chance to play rep football. Would schools want to hire a rep rugby player as a teacher now, knowing how often he would be away? It's almost seen as a disadvantage for a school to have a rep player as a teacher because it means other staff are going to have to be called in to cover sometimes.

"It's a pity because players who have excelled in sport — any sport — add tremendously to a school. For instance, [netballer] Irene van Dyk was teaching in the Hutt Valley, and her presence would have been of great value to her school."

The solution of forming a rugby club within a school is not always ideal. The school runs the danger of losing touch with its teams as it hands over control to parents.

Until perhaps 20 years ago, the teachers basically coached the school teams. It was seen as a part of their responsibility, and they seemed to enjoy it. It wasn't only male teachers who did the coaching, either. In one and two-teacher country schools, the boys were generally coached by their teacher, even if she was a woman. It's debatable how much some of these teacher-coaches knew about the game, but they generally offered organisation, discipline and a degree of enthusiasm. Lucky boys — for they were all boys in those days — might also strike a teacher-coach who had played the game to a high level and could offer genuine expertise.

Teachers no longer see the coaching of rugby teams as part of their job description. There were signs that things were changing in the early 1980s. The Springbok tour that so divided the country in 1981 soured many teachers' views of rugby. Why devote any of their spare time to coaching a sport where the national body acts against the best interests of the country? That seemed to be a widely-held view. Perhaps some teachers, not brought up in the rugby-mad 1940s and '50s, were looking for a way out of being roped into coaching, and the Springbok tour, followed a few years later by the Cavaliers tour of South Africa, offered that opportunity.

Another reason why rugby numbers in colleges are dropping so much is that there is so much more commitment required these days by boys who want to play rugby seriously. The rugby season is much longer now, and not just at international or first class level. First XVs hold their trials in mid-March and the school season runs through until October. Whereas once a school might have had a dozen matches, now there are many more inter-school fixtures and a fuller and longer Saturday programme.

Not surprisingly, many boys look at the commitment required and decide not to bother. Many of them want to work to earn money, perhaps to buy a car. The best day available to them to work is Saturday, so rugby goes out the window. They might want to work after school, which makes it impossible to attend one or two practices a week.

When I think of college sport, I cannot get past Rotorua Boys High School, which has obviously promoted golf as a good sport. The school has boasted a string of outstanding prospects over the past few years, among them Sam Hunt, Eddie Lee and Jae An, who as a 13-year-old captured Tiger Woods' attention during the New Zealand Open at Paraparaumu in January, 2002. The thought of a school pushing golf as a major sport would not have occurred to anyone in the 1970s. Yet Rotorua Boys High now has a golf driving range. Ironically Rotorua Boys is still a very strong rugby force (as with its golf, many of its best rugby players are drawn from outside Rotorua). Its First XV, dominated by Maori and Pacific Island Boys, is one of the strongest in the country. But by placing an emphasis on golf, it has shown how important it is now for colleges to go beyond rugby. Now, big colleges delight in the sports success of their rowers, squash players, dragon boat racers, snooker players and tri-athletes, just as much as their rugby players.

AT LAST – THE UNIONS FIGHT BACK

Provincial rugby unions have been very slow to realise the threat their game is under, and to respond, though some are now taking up the challenge. Waikato is a good example of a union that is fighting back. In

2002, the Waikato Rugby Union launched a new initiative to try to halt the decline in the number of juniors attracted to rugby. Under a three-year management unit scheme, the union decided a teacher would be paid to dedicate at least two hours a week to developing the sport at each participating school.

Waikato union amateur rugby manager David Cooper said it was hoped the scheme would increase rugby participation rates in secondary schools to 20 per cent of the total school roll by 2004. By the start of 2002, that figure had dropped to just 10 per cent in Waikato. The development scheme was a response to a Deloittes survey that revealed there had been a 52 per cent drop-off in Waikato secondary school student rugby participation, compared with 1999. "Hamilton schools have fairly much held their rugby numbers," says Cooper, "but numbers have dropped off in places like Cambridge and Matamata, the more rural areas."

The goal of 20 per cent interests me. In 1973, Wellington's St Pat's (Town) school role was 644. The number of rugby players in the school was 312, so nearly 50 per cent of the boys played rugby. At Christ's College, the school roll in 1970 was 587 and 400 played rugby, so 68 per cent of the boys played rugby. Percentages were not vastly different in most other big boys schools. If that number has now dropped to 10 per cent, and the Waikato union feels it is being ambitious trying to raise it to 20 per cent again, you can see how massive the drop-off from rugby has been in just three decades.

Not all provincial unions have responded as well to the challenges rugby faces as Waikato. Roger Moses says that his school gets surprisingly little assistance from the Wellington union. "I don't think the Wellington union understands the situation," says Moses. "I have tried several times to get the union to send a top player to our prizegiving, and have got nowhere. It employs these players and could get one of them to come along, but doesn't. Wellington College has been a big feeder of rugby players into the system and I'm sure it would be worth the union's while to take every opportunity to push the game at college level. It is an example of where the Wellington union is missing out."

Cooper says administrators have been too slow responding to rugby's demands in the modern era. "It has taken some provincial unions far too long to realise that rugby is struggling. Unions have not been in touch with schools enough. Some school boards, too, have isolated themselves from their provincial unions. So we've had different groups working in isolation, instead of alongside each other."

He says he has seen soccer make significant inroads into rugby over the past few years, "especially in the five-to-10-year-olds, where safety is such an issue". One problem, says Cooper, has been persuading boys to return to rugby in the third form. "You can't have all the third formers in together. There's too much disparity in size."

Cooper cites recent examples of situations where some boys are clearly too heavy to play in teams of boys their own age. "There is an under-13 open weight tournament involving Auckland, North Harbour, Counties and Waikato. The average weight of the Auckland teams was 95kg and they fielded a 120kg prop. Our heaviest player was 94kg. You can't really have that situation. It means rugby won't be fun for the boys who are simply not big enough."

SO WHAT CAN BE DONE?

Cooper: "Provincial unions need to support grassroots rugby in schools by helping with programmes. The unions need to have forms of the game that make rugby more attractive — versions like 10-a-side. We must make rugby accessible and fun. Saturday work is now an issue. Maybe we need to look outside the square, by playing competition games on other days. There is also a lot more that clubs can do, and the provincial unions have to make clubs aware of their responsibility in promoting and fostering the game in schools. Overall, you would say unions must be much more hands-on. The situation is more critical in colleges than in primary schools."

Some people are fighting back. One of the busiest and most innovative thinkers on rugby has been Bryan Williams, whose influence has touched so many areas of the game — playing, coaching at school, NPC, Super 12 and international levels, administration from club to international. Williams realised rugby was up against what he calls "the PlayStation generation", watched the way the sport was declining in some colleges in Auckland and decided what was required was for youngsters to have a greater appreciation of rugby. He thought it would be a good idea if rugby was taught as a legitimate subject at college, just like art and music. Not just how to play the game. After all, he reasoned, rugby was now an industry, just like art and music. He started with his old college, Mt Albert Grammar, where the scheme has proved immensely popular.

Other colleges, such as Kelston Boys, Tangaroa and Tamaki, have picked up the idea and the concepts have flowed through to the Auckland Rugby Academy.

"The idea was to have a composite course," says Williams. "I have included some outdoor tuition of skills and drills and some classroom work on the history of the game, the culture of rugby, areas like sponsorship and management." As yet, there is no formal, New Zealand-approved qualification attached to the subject, but Williams is hopeful there might be one day soon and is working on that with the Auckland Rugby Union.

The way the course works, Mt Albert Grammar provides the classroom content and the Auckland Rugby Union runs the skills and drills side. Williams says the response in the three years his course has been running has been very heartening. "These kids are now coming through into the First XV and other senior teams in the college and we're starting to see a different attitude.

"It's come just at the right time for rugby, certainly at Mt Albert Grammar. When I was there in the 1960s, there were about 18 rugby teams. By 1999 that was down to eight or nine and was still declining. But now we're back up to 11 or 12. Soccer numbers have increased, so it's very nice to see rugby climbing back as well."

Williams feels that over the years the various unions have not realised how critical secondary school rugby is and have basically left it to the secondary schools to run the game themselves. "There is a lot of talk about forging closer relationships between clubs and schools, but the clubs are struggling, too. There are a lot of sports-related tertiary courses now and I think that some of these graduates need to be employed in the schools. There is room for a big improvement in this area, liaising with the provincial unions and the clubs, improving the coaching and organisation of schools rugby. The unions have really been out of touch with the school scene for years.

"It's been the same for a long time. Prior to secondary school the kids come through junior clubs. Then they are handed over to the colleges from the ages of 13–18, then there is a mad scramble to get them back again. But a lot of them are lost in that time. The organisation at colleges is the key. With female teachers now outnumbering male teachers, there is a chronic lack of coaches. If you don't have a coach and a manager, you won't have a team.

"We have also devised a gap year course type of thing, using school leavers to help to coach and organise rugby."

The Auckland Rugby Union is fortunate having someone of Williams' flair and foresight, and has picked up some of his ideas. For instance, the Pro Sport Career Programme (the official name for the gap year course) is run by Auckland Rugby and is a 48-week course. In 2002, its first year, it involved 12 school leavers. The New Zealand Qualification Authority course is run in conjunction with Mt Albert Grammar and has been developed after consultation with Skill NZ, the Community Employment Group and WINZ.

Williams says it's imperative that the provincial unions act more decisively to help schools because the days of teachers taking rugby teams are drawing to a close. "I don't blame the teachers. They're very busy these days, more busy than people realise. It's up to rugby people to come up with ideas and put them in place to help out."

THE TOUCHY SUBJECT OF RUGBY SCHOLARSHIPS

The college rugby scene has changed massively. In New Zealand, perhaps mirroring what has happened in the United States, some major boys colleges are apparently offering rugby scholarships to promising players, enticing them to the school to try to bolster the college's First XV. This is hard to prove, because though anecdotal evidence suggests this is undoubtedly happening, colleges often deny it. The attitude of the provincial unions towards these scholarships has been interesting. While officially frowning on it, I know some major unions that are secretly delighted to see their promising young rugby players lured to major rugby colleges where they will be better coached and placed in a more competitive environment.

It's a thorny question. John Hart says he would far rather see the amateur ethos flourish at school level. "Players are now being educated in attitudes of semi-professionalism far beyond their status," he says. "That's what offering a scholarship does. Being in the First XV is part of building spirit. Factors such as money should not be entering the equation at college level.

"If there is to be any money going from rugby into colleges, it should be going via clubs into the schools generally, to assist with administration and coaching, not buying players."

A classic case of colleges enticing boys on the score of rugby prowess occurred over many years in Dunedin, where Otago Boys and King's High were the two big rugby colleges. Otago Boys would tend to target the boys from the country and Kings concentrated more on ensuring boys from Dunedin enrolled there. So it became almost a Town v County match when the two colleges clashed at rugby. There was a huge amount of prestige at stake in that match, and the result influenced the schools' rolls.

It is not difficult to imagine boys (and their parents), when considering which secondary school to attend, reflecting on the First XV results. If the boys fancied themselves at rugby and were looking at making progress in the sport, being noticed by representative selectors and so on, then naturally the school with the superior First XV would be attractive. In Dunedin, where the population is not huge, the two secondary schools towered above all other opposition, so the pressure on them in that annual First XV fixture was immense.

Player recruitment, though officially frowned upon, has been going on all over the country. Some people are more up-front about it. In 1987, Keith Laws, principal of Scots College, a private boys school in Wellington, began deliberately recruiting players and had special success in luring talented Fijian players to his school, to bolster the First XV, which he was coaching.

"Scots had traditionally been rugby minnows, and the recruitment scheme made such a difference that we began to be a real rugby power, even sharing the premier title. The board ratified the scheme and I never had people tell me to my face that they disagreed with what we were doing, though I dare say there was some talking behind my back.

"We advertised in the local newspapers, offering full scholarships — fees and board. The boys had to be able to play two sports and we had to feel they would benefit from their time at Scots. One of the first boys we recruited was Jason O'Halloran's brother. He came to us from Hutt Valley High School. He was a good fullback, a fine goal-kicker, and a cricketer as well.

"Then we developed a connection with Fiji. I had coached the Wanganui Tech First XV, whose captain, Tuki Tu'uakitau, had moved back to Fiji. We'd stayed in touch. So Tuki was my original contact in the schools in Suva. I'd go over there to see if they had any boys who would gain from scholarships. We were careful to ensure they were at Scots not just for the sport.

"That worked each year until the Fijian coup in 1991. One of our most well-known recruitments, though certainly not the only successful one, was Bill Cavubati. He was about 20 stone when he arrived at Scots, and he teamed up with another prop we'd got from Fiji, of about the same weight. Nobody could move our scrums. Until then, we'd found ourselves overpowered by school teams with very big players. If you don't have the size, you won't be able to compete. Bill was with us two years and gave us good service. In the summer he did athletics — he was a shot putter."

Cavubati went on to represent Wellington's provincial side for five seasons and played 55 games for the union.

Laws said the Scots scholarships were not offered in a devious way. "We were totally open about them. We never went and poached players. Boys applied to us for the scholarships. I always thought the scheme was a good idea. It helped our sports teams and it gave the boys a good all-round education. A lot of the Fijian boys have gone home and made a real contribution to Fijian society."

Recruitment happens all over the country. Rotorua Boys High seems to attract many fine players from out of town. In Auckland and Christchurch, several private schools have chosen to build up their First XVs by offering scholarships. There are suggestions that Auckland Grammar, fighting hard to keep its rugby status, has drafted in the odd beefy teenager from Samoa, offering them accommodation at the boarding establishment.

With rugby now offering serious money to players who make the top level, the reasons boys are playing the game have altered. I'm not saying that pride in the school, team spirit and enjoyment of the game have vanished, but the opportunity to land a place in the local rugby academy, with the promise of an NPC or Super 12 contract, is most enticing.

The money factor enters rugby very young these days. In late 2001, one major province ran a camp for promising young players of the 12-14 age-group. The camp was meant to increase the boys' interest in rugby, as well as their skills. Speakers included several former All Blacks and some leading coaches from the area. What disappointed some parents was how much time was spent telling the boys how much they might be able to earn from the game if they continued with it. There was more talk about the opportunities to get big sponsorship deals and big pay packets than there was of the others benefits of rugby, such as fostering team spirit, and ball skills. It was an interesting insight into the way today's administrators, or at least some of them, think.

THE EFFECTS OF ZONING

Zoning has also had an effect on school rugby. For an example of this, we need look no further than Auckland Grammar. Before zoning was tightened in 2000, meaning colleges had to accept all students living within their geographic zone, colleges could be very picky about which pupils they took. During the 1980s, when Dave Syms coached the Auckland Grammar First XV, he had just one player who lived within the zone. Not any more. In fact, the signs are that zoning is massively undermining rugby at Auckland Grammar. The third form intake at Auckland Grammar in 2002 was about 40 per cent Asian. It would be logical to assume that few of these students are especially interested in playing rugby. If this trend continues and in five years' time nearly 40 per cent of Auckland Grammar students are of Asian extraction, it will obviously hugely reduce the number of rugby players and the strength of the school's teams.

Linked to this factor is the increased number of overseas students now studying in New Zealand. Overseas students, once extremely rare, are making up an increasing percentage of college rolls, and few of them arrive in New Zealand with much interest in rugby. Whether they are foreign exchange students, perhaps from Switzerland, Germany or Austria, or, more likely, foreign students from the likes of China, South Korea, Taiwan, Malaysia, Thailand, Hong Kong, the Philippines, Vietnam or Indonesia paying inflated fees to study in New Zealand, few have even a passing interest in rugby. With colleges actively seeking foreign students to provide extra income — even to the extent of sending recruiters to Asia to spread the good word about a college — it is difficult to see how the trend of declining playing numbers can be arrested.

The makeup of the New Zealand secondary school population is changing. Some in rugby are responding better than others. For instance, Bryan Williams adopts the attitude that teenagers who live in New Zealand and attend New Zealand colleges should do all they can to learn and embrace traditional New Zealand interests. One of them is rugby. So Williams runs a rugby course specifically targeted at Somali students. It's difficult to envisage many Somalis packing down for the All Blacks, but Williams feels he might at least introduce them to rugby and interest them in New Zealand's national game. He feels the same thing should be done for other races.

Rugby administrators have only themselves to blame for finding the game in such a precarious situation in schools. The signs have been there for years. In 1970, the *Sports Post* ran a story pointing out how quickly soccer was growing at rugby's expense. If soccer had been better organised since then, and if the All Whites had performed consistently better (for they are the sport's shop window), there would have been an even more significant drift from rugby to soccer.

HAVE THE WARNINGS BEEN HEEDED?

There have been some positives for rugby over the past decade. The massive rise in the popularity of touch rugby has at least kept thousands of New Zealanders involved with football, even if it is a bastardised version of rugby. It's the same with sevens rugby. While sevens is not everyone's cup of tea, it is another strand of the game, and it does attract not only players, but also a large number of spectators. They watch the world sevens circuit on television, partly because New Zealand traditionally does well in that event. And they turn up to watch sevens in New Zealand, whether it is the regional and national sevens events, or the international sevens tournament that is held in Wellington's stadium each February. You would imagine that both touch and sevens would be of particular appeal to younger players.

Women's rugby has expanded dramatically in New Zealand since the first women's World Cup was played in 1991, and the emphasis on women has clearly helped New Zealand rugby generally. It has brought teenaged girls into the game as players and also as followers of the sport. Many girls colleges now field at least a couple of rugby teams. This number pales alongside perhaps 35 netball teams, but it is still a significant boost for rugby and certainly helps inflate rugby's numbers nationally.

But even with the influx of new players through touch, sevens and girls' rugby, the downward trend is undeniable. In 1992 Arthur Reeve, that indefatigable supporter of schoolboy rugby, wrote *The Cradle of Rugby*, a history of rugby in New Zealand schools. Reeve, a Wellington freelance journalist, had covered schoolboy rugby since 1958 and until his death in 2002 was the acknowledged expert on that area of the game in New Zealand. His chapter entitled "The Future" was superb, and is all the more chilling as we read it 10 years later, during which time rugby has gone professional. Here is what highly-successful Palmerston North Boys High First XV coach Ian Colquhoun had to say about schools rugby a decade ago:

"I believe rugby is in crisis. The hype of the World Cup, that the All Blacks are world strong, hides the problems the game must eventually face up to. Television has stolen the attendances. Patrons who once attended club games and representative games as of habit and who, 20 years ago, only read or listened to tests, now demand only the tops. Rugby's reply has been new representative tournaments — the dollar, very important, is a short-term approach. Support for representative rugby has fallen away, club competition is diminished beyond recognition and the numbers of school teams playing, although rolls have increased, have dropped. It is not sufficient to select the elite. The bigger the base, the better the game. The majority of those who play rugby don't reach senior rugby, but they and their families are potential life-long supporters.

"The New Zealand Rugby Football Union and provincial unions must re-promote the base of rugby. Schools feed clubs — that is the base. Rebuild the game in schools, emphasise fun in participating."

What a pity those wise words from one of the giants of New Zealand schoolboy rugby coaching were ignored.

NEW ZEALAND SCHOOLBOY REPS WHO HAVE GONE ON TO BECOME ALL BLACKS:

Pita Alatini (King's College)
Steve Bachop (Hagley High)
Andrew Blowers (Mt Albert Grammar)
Mike Brewer (Pukekohe High)
Robin Brooke (Mahurangi College)
Mark Brooke-Cowden (Mt Albert Grammar)
Olo Brown (Mt Albert Grammar)
Adrian Cashmore (Tauranga Boys)
Jerry Collins (St Pat's Silverstream)
Mark Cooksley (Manurewa High)
Greg Cooper (St John's, Hastings)
Matthew Cooper (St John's, Hastings)
Ron Cribb (Massey High)
Christian Cullen (Kapiti College)
Chresten Davis (Morrinsville College)
Marc Ellis (Wellington College)
Mark Finlay (Palmerston North Boys)
Sean Fitzpatrick (Sacred Heart College)
Grant Fox (Auckland Grammar)
Daryl Gibson (Christchurch Boys)
Jasin Goldsmith (Forest View High)
Rob Gordon (Te Awamutu College)
Steve Gordon (Te Awamutu College)
Carl Hayman (King's High)
Paul Henderson (Southland Boys)
Jason Hewett (Kelston Boys High / Freyberg High)
Carl Hoeft (Te Aroha College)
Doug Howlett (Auckland Grammar)
Laurence Hullena (Wairarapa College)
Craig Innes (Sacred Heart College)
Jamie Joseph (Church College)

Dean Kenny (Palmerston North Boys)
Pat Lam (St Peter's College)
Walter Little (Hato Petera College)
Jonah Lomu (Wesley College)
Leon MacDonald (Marlborough Boys)
Isitola Maka (Sacred Heart College)
Simon Mannix (St Pat's Silverstream)
Tabai Matson (Christ's College)
Aaron Mauger (Christchurch Boys)
Norm Maxwell (Whangarei Boys)
Dylan Mika (St Peter's College)
Paul Miller (King's High)
Todd Miller (Kamo)
Anton Oliver (Marlborough Boys)
Jon Preston (St Bede's)
Caleb Ralph (Western Heights High)
Mark Ranby (Freyberg High School)
Taine Randell (Lindisfarne)
Matthew Ridge (Auckland Grammar)
Charles Riechelmann (Auckland Grammar)
Xavier Rush (Sacred Heart College)
Dallas Seymour (St Stephen's School)
Gordon Slater (New Plymouth Boys High)
Carlos Spencer (Waiopehu College)
Jeremy Stanley (Auckland Grammar)
Steve Surridge (St Kentigern)
Filo Tiatia (Wellington College)
John Timu (Lindisfarne College)
Inga Tuigamala (Kelston High School)
Richard Turner (Napier Boys High School)
Craig Wickes (Palmerston North Boys)
Royce Willis (Tauranga Boys)
Tom Willis (King's High)
Jeff Wilson (Cargill High School)

Only a select few players have made the New Zealand Schoolboys team in three consecutive years. They are:

John Afoa (St Kentigern) 2000–02
Ben Atiga (Auckland Grammar) 1999–2002
Steve Bachop (Hagley High) 1983–85

Matthew Carrington (King's College) 1993–95
Tumai Edwards (King's College) 1996–98
Rhys Ellison (Hamilton Boys) 1982–85
Rob Gordon (Te Awamutu College) 1982–84
Todd Miller (Kamo High) 1990–92
Eugene Morgan (Gisborne Boys) 1993–95
Charles Riechelmann (Auckland Grammar) 1989–91
Joe Rokocoko (St Kentigern) 2000–02
Matthew Stone (St Bede's) 1983–85
Ray Tuivaiti (Kelston Boys) 2000–02
Royce Willis (Tauranga Boys) 1992–94
Note: Albert Hawea (Te Aute/Rathkeale) was selected in 1978 and 1981.
Mackie Herewini (St Stephen's) was selected in 1980 and 1982.
Sione Kepu (Wesley College) was selected in 1997 and 1999

Of these 17 boys, evidently all absolutely outstanding secondary school rugby
players, only five became All Blacks. There's a lesson there for those who are too
swayed by talent that flowers young.

THE HISTORY OF SECONDARY SCHOOLS RUGBY

That rugby should now find itself in a situation where it has been supplanted at
college level by soccer is all the more astounding when we consider how integral to
the fabric of the country rugby, especially school rugby, has been.

Just six years after the introduction of rugby to New Zealand, the first inter-
collegiate match was played, between Nelson College and Wellington College, at
the Basin Reserve on June 20, 1876. Nelson College took to rugby because of the
influence of the schoolmaster, Charles John Monro, often cited as the father of
New Zealand rugby. Nelson fielded only 13 players, of whom one was a teacher, J
P Firth. Perhaps not surprisingly, the home team won 14-0, but in a return match,
Nelson triumphed 7-2.

Firth's name pops up again in 1878 when he refereed the corresponding college
fixture and amazed players and spectators alike when a Wellington player made a
break. Firth forgot his refereeing duties and tackled the player to prevent a try
being scored. He apologised profusely and awarded a penalty to Wellington. The
match was drawn 3-3. The incident did not have any long-term effects on Firth's
standing, for in 1881 he was welcomed to the staff of Wellington College, where
he distinguished himself greatly.

While Wellington and Nelson colleges can claim the first inter-college match, Otago Boys High School was active in rugby even earlier, and in 1871, a school team played Otago University at the Southern Recreation Ground in Dunedin. In 1872 the Union Rugby Club was formed for old boys of Otago Boys High School.

Wellington College and Nelson College have continued to meet regularly. Other regular school fixtures grew, such as the Christ's College v Otago Boys High game, which began in 1883. Timaru Boys and Waitaki Boys first met in 1884. In 1885, Wellington College and St Pat's (Town) began their annual rivalry, with a 5-0 win to Wellington College that first year. In 1892 Christchurch Boys High and Christ's College began what has become an annual and much-awaited clash.

By 1890, college tournaments were being played. For instance, Wellington College, Christ's College and Wanganui Collegiate first played a tournament in 1890. The format was expanded to a quadrangular event when Nelson College joined in 1925.

Auckland was a little slower than other parts of the country in getting college rugby on to an organised footing. The annual Auckland Grammar-King's College game dates back to 1897, when King's caused a shock by beating Grammar 4-3. King's and Sacred Heart first played in 1904 when the two games that year were both won by Sacred Heart.

Outside the main centres, traditional rugby colleges got into action surprisingly early. Wanganui Collegiate and Te Aute College first met in 1897. Napier Boys High School opened in 1899 and Palmerston North Boys in 1904. They had their first rugby encounter that year, Napier winning 16-0. These schools still meet for the Polson Banner. In 1905 the Waitaki Boys-Otago Boys game started, Waitaki winning 20-0. Waitaki, from Oamaru, had much the better of the early contests. Southland Boys played its first game in 1902, against Otago Boys, and first played Waitaki in 1908. Timaru Boys first played Southland Boys in 1913, and began its rugby rivalry with St Andrew's in 1929. Otago Boys and Christchurch Boys first played in 1913.

Other fine rugby colleges sprang up. Dannevirke High School was founded in 1903 and within five years had established a strong rugby reputation, being unbeaten in 1908. As a result, it was asked to play Palmerston North Boys High as the curtain-raiser to the international between Anglo-Welsh and Manawatu-Horowhenua that year. Dannevirke was probably the first co-ed school to make such an impact on rugby. Even 35 years later, it was still a major rugby school and in 1946 Dannevirke and Hutt Valley High played a memorable curtain-raiser at Athletic Park to the Kiwis v Wellington match.

At the end of the First World War, with rugby absolutely the dominant sport among secondary schools, the Moascar Cup was presented to the New Zealand union by Lt Col E J Hulbert, the commanding officer of the New Zealand Mounted

Rifles, which had won the trophy playing services rugby in Egypt. This trophy was put up for competition among secondary schools. After Island elimination contests, Palmerston North Boys High and Christchurch Boys High met in the first final, in 1920, played at Athletic Park in appalling conditions. There was no score at fulltime, so five minutes' extra each way was called for. It was agreed that if the scores were still deadlocked, the team that touched the ball down first behind its line would lose. The southerners won by a disputed kick into touch by Palmerston North Boys. The referee counted that kick as a force down, so Christchurch Boys thus became the first holders of the Moascar Cup, their winning margin being an unrugby-like 1-0.

After 1922, the Moascar Cup format changed and became a challenge cup. It's now played for when a holder meets a traditional rival either at home or away, though special challenges may be lodged. Moascar Cup matches have often been fierce encounters, played with an intensity that rivals international rugby. For most of its history, the Moascar Cup, while the most prestigious schools trophy in New Zealand, has been primarily a contest among North Island schools, though in the early 1990s the rules were amended to make acceptance of at least one challenge from the other island compulsory if received.

In the first 30 or 40 years of the 20th century, big college matches drew crowds of many thousands. The games were previewed in newspapers and comprehensively reported. Interest in First XV college rugby has waned in recent times, though there are still some, such as the Auckland Grammar v King's College match, that will attract crowds of more than 4000, mainly old boys.

In these days where transport presents little difficulty, it is important to realise how hard it once was for college teams to meet. Schools had to be very committed to engage in inter-college battles. For instance, early Te Aute-Wanganui Collegiate games were played in Palmerton North. Even then the Te Aute boys were away from school for three days. This makes Te Aute's effort in 1904 all the more incredible. That year, Te Aute broke new ground by venturing to Australia, where the team was unbeaten in five games.

Schoolboy rugby became an important part of New Zealand rugby history when on June 28, 1967, the first televised rugby match in New Zealand took place at Athletic Park. It featured the annual St Pat's (Town) v Wellington College match, St Pat's winning 9-8. They were early days for television. *Evening Post* sports editor Gabriel David said the commentary "was something like sitting in the main stand at Athletic Park and being irritated by a fellow up the row who had refused to turn down his transistor".

Surprisingly, in view of the hold rugby had on New Zealand through most of the 20th century, New Zealand was the last of the major rugby-playing countries to play school football at international level. A New Zealand Secondary Schools Rugby

Council was finally formed in 1976 and in 1978, a New Zealand schoolboy team played Australia at Eden Park. The New Zealand team, coached by former rep loose forward Don Riesterer and captained by Miles Valentine of Auckland Grammar, won 7-6. Though it was called a national team, the New Zealand boys were nearly all from the northern part of the country with a few southern players with big reputations added to the mix. Perhaps not surprisingly, none of the 1978 group went on to become All Blacks.

Craig Wickes of Palmerston North Boys High, was a 1979 New Zealand schoolboy rep (in a team that lost 23-4 to England at Pukekohe), and became the youngest-ever All Black (an honour now claimed by Jonah Lomu). Generally, however, the conversion rate of schoolboy national reps into All Blacks was surprisingly low until the 1990s. Then, as the art of selecting national schools teams became more refined, the number of future All Blacks in such teams increased dramatically. (Interestingly, there is not nearly the same successful conversion rate among other national representative teams, such as under-21.)

The New Zealand schoolboy selectors struck the jackpot in 1986, when four of the Baby Blacks team that took on France had been national schoolboys reps — Mike Brewer (Pukekohe High School), Mark Brooke-Cowden (Mt Albert Grammar), Sean Fitzpatrick (Sacred Heart College) and Greg Cooper (St John's, Hastings).

By 1995, the influence of the secondary schools team was becoming more obvious and 10 of Laurie Mains' team at the World Cup that year had represented New Zealand secondary schools. They were: Brewer, Robin Brooke (Mahurangi College), Olo Brown (Mt Albert Grammar), Marc Ellis (Wellington College), Fitzpatrick, Paul Henderson (Southland Boys), Jamie Joseph (Church College), Walter Little (Hato Petera College), Jonah Lomu (Wesley College) and Jeff Wilson (Cargill High).

Even so, it is amazing how many boys are considered outstanding prospects at secondary school and never progress even to senior representative level. For every Alex Wyllie, Grant Batty, Ian Kirkpatrick, Grahame Thorne, Joe Karam, Chris Laidlaw or Grant Fox, schoolboy prodigies who became famous All Blacks, there are dozens whose careers trail off disappointingly.

chapterFOURTEEN
THE **CHALLENGE**

LOOKING TO THE FUTURE

I have purposely left the chapter on schools rugby until the end of this book. As we look to the future, it's the issue of school rugby — particularly secondary school — that has to be addressed first. It's a simple fact: if New Zealand can't produce schoolboys playing rugby, it will cease to be a factor in world rugby. That is the last, and most important, message contained in this book.

School rugby isn't a particularly sexy subject. There's no particular kudos for a politician entering a schoolboys' dressing room and being photographed with the winning captain. It's not like the photo opportunity available when sidling up to a World Cup-winning captain.

Funding agencies, when they run their glitzy dinners, like to have plenty of superstars present. It means they'll get buckets of publicity and, besides, all that reflected glory is good for the ego. There's not quite the same feeling of mixing with the stars when the room is full of schoolboys. Those same funding agencies love to boast about how they helped this world champion and that gold medallist. It doesn't have quite the same ring when they talk of assisting a school team or sport.

The annual Halberg Awards honour our champions — Danyon Loader, Rob Waddell, the Evers-Swindell twins, the America's Cup yachties, Beatrice Faumuina. They also honour administrators who have given long service, people of the stature of Arthur Lydiard, Ces Blazey and Walter Hadlee. No schoolboys on show.

That's all fine. We need to honour our champions. They deserve it. They have taken on the best and won and, anyhow, they provide others with inspiration. So I don't have a problem with that. In fact, I love the fact that New Zealand has a Sports Hall of Fame full of achievers in sports as diverse as snooker and shearing, cricket and mountaineering.

But the point here, and I can't emphasise it strongly enough, is that, at least as far as rugby is concerned, the supply of champions will dry up if something isn't done urgently to turn around the alarming trend now apparent in secondary schools.

It's to the New Zealand Rugby Union's shame that it has no reliable figures available tracing the numbers of college rugby players and teams through the years. The work required to gather such information has never been done, which in itself speaks volumes for the Rugby Union's cock-eyed priorities. I hope what's provided in this chapter provides food for thought for all those administrators who think things are fine, and who seem to assume that there is some sort of school rugby production line that will never break down.

The message must be hammered home to those rugby officials: your sport is no longer No 1 at college. Soccer has taken over. Your playing numbers are dropping dramatically.

Many rugby administrators, provincial and national, seem to live in splendid isolation. There is still an All Black team. We do well in the Super 12. Everything must be okay. Get with it. Go and ask some of the principals at the big boys colleges and you'll get a different picture.

College rugby has been left to flounder. It was all right when it was the only game in town, until perhaps the 1960s or '70s. But the rules have changed. Boys now have a much wider choice, and many of them are not choosing rugby.

Because of all the factors that are so quickly trotted out — the increasing number of female teachers, the seven-day working week, the greater commitment required to play a season of rugby, the browning of the game in this country — rugby is losing its pre-eminent position. A First XV clash is still a big deal, but it's not the be-all and end-all it once was.

Rugby administrators have a choice. They can stick their heads even further in the sand and pretend everything is fine. They can shrug their shoulders, acknowledge the problem and say there's nothing to be done. Or they can fight back.

It's not going to be easy, because rugby has slipped further and more quickly than most people realise. To turn things around will require commitment, innovation and money.

There are problems in New Zealand rugby at every level. But if we start at the most important — junior — the answers are obvious. Colleges need more help. The provincial unions must ensure that colleges are being supplied with the rugby coaching expertise necessary. To do so they will need their clubs to be strong. So there's a challenge. Help the clubs, with an eye to them liaising better with schools.

The college-club link is critical. If clubs are struggling so much they have no ability to assist schools, things are bleak. Schools will not be able to feed clubs with young players if they can't induce college boys to play rugby. Provincial unions are granted a massive amount of money these days by the New Zealand Rugby Union. The challenge for the provincial unions is to ensure this money is used as wisely as possible.

The priority must be to do everything possible to foster college rugby, in the knowledge that clubs will benefit.

Rugby is not an easy game to coach. It's vastly more complex than soccer. Rugby administrators must produce more coaches and get them into schools.

There are many other challenges for rugby up the line. The National Provincial Championship is not the competition it once was because the advent of professional rugby has turned it into a competition for the haves and the have-nots. What fun is a competition in which only half the starters have a realistic chance of winning?

The Super 12 is thrilling, giving us a delectable mixture of international and provincial rugby. But it is sucking the life out of New Zealand rugby, hurting the NPC, hurting the All Blacks. It is time the New Zealand Rugby Union decided what was most important, the All Blacks and domestic rugby, or the Super 12. Australia loves the Super 12, but let's think about our own game.

Then there's the All Blacks. The very name of the team inspires admiration and respect. Yet, are we living in a fool's paradise? The All Blacks haven't won the World Cup since 1987. They were fourth in 1999. They haven't held the Bledisloe Cup since 1997. They are not viewed by the rest of the world as unbeatable. We cannot smile smugly and say that it doesn't matter what else is wrong with the country, at least the All Blacks will win.

There are some exciting things happening in New Zealand rugby. The top female players are brilliant. So are our sevens players. But let's face it: what good is it really if women's and sevens rugby thrives and the rest of the game is withering? It's like seeing a person in hospital dying of cancer, but with beautifully-painted fingernails.

In researching this book, I have been very impressed with the willingness and desire of so many people to serve rugby. There are the former players like Lin Colling, Andy Leslie, Bryan Williams and Colin Meads, who would do anything they could to help the game they have always loved. There are club officials, the unpaid servants of the game, who work ceaselessly. They care desperately for their club. There are school team coaches — a dwindling number, admittedly — who love nothing more than helping a group of keen young boys improve their games.

That's always been a strength of New Zealand rugby — the huge core of rugby support. But it's coming apart at the seams.

The New Zealand Rugby Union has taken its eye off the ball. It has been very concerned with the game at the top level, where it is most visible, and forgotten about the foundations of New Zealand rugby.

And we're about to pay the price.

POSTSCRIPT

This book ends on a positive note.

I was greatly encouraged by events in Wellington on September 18, 2002. On that day, a new New Zealand Rugby Union board was installed and, within a few hours, Jock Hobbs had been elected its Chairman. As I write this, the board is not quite complete — two independent members are to be elected by postal vote. But the signs are, unarguably, heartening.

Of the old board, Chairman Murray McCaw has gone. He had initially wanted to stand down only as Chairman, before the reality of the situation was made clear to him. The New Zealand rugby community largely blamed McCaw for the shambolic goings-on in 2002. Incredibly, he seemed the last to realise it.

Rob Fisher, former board Chairman, IRB vice-chairman and Rugby World Cup director, chose not to stand again. Similarly it took Fisher an inordinately long time to realise how unacceptable he had become to New Zealand rugby. He took over from McCaw as Chairman, and then said he would not be available for the new board. It was some months — September 14, in fact — before he actually resigned his IRB role.

Craig Norgate decided not to seek re-election. This was also good decision. The Fonterra chief is busy enough in his normal business life and did not bring the required knowledge to the Rugby Union board.

Of the rest, Maori representative Paul Quinn and Northland's Warwick Syers survived. This was fair enough. Both were voted onto the board in April 2002 — after the World Cup hosting debacle. They could hardly be held accountable.

What was amazing though, was that others continued to try to hold on. Tim Gresson, for 11 years a Rugby Union councillor or board member, and one of New Zealand's two representatives on the IRB, fought hard to keep his position. Gresson was the man who made the crucial presentation to the IRB meeting in Dublin that threw out New Zealand's desperate bid to be reinstated as a World Cup sub-host. Some of those present were far from impressed by Gresson's effort. But the Timaru Crown Solicitor still wanted to keep his board membership. He was axed.

John Spicer, of Otago, the old board's deputy-chairman, also made a bid for re-election. At 67 years of age, he felt he still had plenty to offer. Again, though, it was obvious he was hopelessly compromised. He had been deputy-chairman of an inept, under-performing board whose decisions and actions had led to the international ridicule of New

Zealand rugby. Spicer was axed. Both Gresson and Spicer were gracious in defeat, stressing the need to support the new board.

Steve Lunn, of Hawke's Bay, also tried to hold on, unable apparently to read the signs. I am still bemused by his comment on the day of the vote: "There has been enough of the Rugby Union being blamed for things that often aren't its fault. One almost expects George W Bush to blame his problems on the New Zealand Rugby Union." Lunn playing the role of a victim wasn't a good look. He was axed.

One independent director, Chris Liddell, was considering trying for re-selection in the postal vote. However, he was part of a poor board and there are people about who can offer the New Zealand Rugby Union much more. For a start, former All Blacks Andy Haden, Bryan Williams, Andy Dalton and David Kirk — all successful businessmen — have a vast amount more rugby knowledge. Kirk, because he lives in Sydney, would also offer a crucial link with Australia.

The new board (with the two independents to come) comprises:

Jock Hobbs, 42, Wellington. Former All Black captain, former member of the New Zealand Rugby Union council, Chief Executive of Strategic Investment Group. I have written a lot about Hobbs already in this book. It says much for the people doing the voting that he was in the New Zealand rugby wilderness from 1996-2002, despite all his efforts on behalf of the game in this country.

Mike Eagles, 55, Christchurch. Chairman of the Canterbury Rugby Union and the Crusaders board since 1996. Represented Canterbury B as a player. A partner and director in an electrical company. He has plenty to say and most of it makes good sense. Eagles said he would step down as Crusaders franchise chairman, but remain the Canterbury union chairman.

Ivan Haines, 53, Cambridge. Chairman of the King Country Rugby Union and the Chiefs board. Haines is a long-time member of the Waitete club, and that link to the iconic Colin Meads can't have done him any harm in the voting. He has been involved in businesses covering motels, construction and catering.

Graham Mourie, 49, Wellington. Regarded as one of New Zealand's finest All Black captains. Former coach of Wellington and the Hurricanes. Was involved with the West Nally company that promoted the first rugby World Cup. "The future does not happen, it is created," warned Mourie, during his short speech to the assembled delegates in Wellington. "If we don't have a base in 15 to 20 years' time, we won't have a game."

Mark Peters, 53, Blenheim. Chairman of the Marlborough Rugby Union from 1995–2001, and a former member of various New Zealand union sub-committees. A chartered accountant. Forthright and clear-thinking.

Paul Quinn, 50, Wellington. A former New Zealand Maori and Wellington captain. A member of the Wellington Rugby Union board since 1997. A senior manager in the Maori Development Ministry, Te Puni Kokiri.

Warwick Syers, 55, Whangarei. Northland Rugby Union chairman for the past four years, a current member of the Blues board. Refereed for some years after he stopped playing rugby. An accountant.

The voting caused some grumbles in Auckland and Otago because neither major union is represented on the new board. But otherwise it has been greeted with approval by New Zealand rugby followers who were desperate to start again after the previous board's problems.

Hobbs and Mourie, the two All Blacks elected on September 18, have always been their own people. Mourie declined to lie and said openly he was taking money for writing his autobiography, *Graham Mourie: Captain*. He was banned from rugby for most of the 1980s as a result. Hobbs incurred the wrath of many New Zealanders by touring South Africa with the rebel Cavaliers in 1986. The New Zealand union suspended him briefly on his return.

The Rugby Union was extremely fortunate to have Hobbs available. He proved himself a lot bigger person than those who shafted him in 1996, when the New Zealand union's council was being replaced by a board. Within hours of being elected, Hobbs was appointed one of New Zealand's two IRB members, a decision so sensible that you wonder why the previous board did not insist on having its chairman on the IRB.

New Zealand's other IRB man will be the new New Zealand Rugby Union Chief Executive, which again makes sense. Hobbs said getting the right man for this job was a priority. "This is the most important position in the whole set-up," he told me. "It requires an absolutely top-class businessman with the ability to turn his talents to running New Zealand rugby. We have to canvass the whole country, and abroad, to make sure we get the right person." That person will have to run New Zealand rugby like a business, but love it like a sport.

Hobbs said he wanted the New Zealand Rugby Union to be pyramid-like, where the values would be about the team rather than self-interest. Hard work and transparency had to be offered and a winning attitude regained, although it should be winning with humility. It seems simple enough, yet New Zealand rugby has strayed off-course in recent years.

As I say, I have a lot of faith in people like Hobbs and Mourie, whose places in the history of New Zealand rugby are already secure. They do not need to boast that they are members of the New Zealand board to increase their stature in rugby circles. As former All Black captains, they belong to one of the most elite groups in New Zealand sport. Their motives for being on the board cannot be questioned.

I also like Hobbs' attitude to how the board should work. He wants the board to act in a governance role, rather than as a body that devises policy. That will be a change from what has happened over the past few years. Senior staff at the New Zealand Rugby Union will be charged with formulating and developing policy. They had better be good enough. I would be surprised if there are not some changes at the top level of the New Zealand union staff early in 2003.

As can be seen from the contents of this book, Hobbs and his board – plus the new Chief Executive – face some huge problems. They have been glossed over by rugby officials painting a ridiculously glowing, if false, picture. New Zealand rugby is in big trouble in several areas.

It was telling that through September-October, which is the heart of the National Provincial Championship segment of the season, the most talked-about football team in the country was rugby league's New Zealand Warriors, as they marched triumphantly to the NRL Grand Final, where they lost valiantly to the Sydney Roosters 30-8, watched on television by more than one million people back home. Rugby union no longer rules as of right in New Zealand. It has to earn its position, as it never had to 100, 50, even 25 years ago.

The percentage of rugby players at college level is declining, as other sports become more acceptable and attractive options. Club rugby is in a terrible state. In all New Zealand's main towns, famous old clubs have either died or are in dire straits. The position is, if anything, even more serious in many rural areas.

At representative level, some matters need to be addressed urgently. Are the All Blacks going to continue to play "second-rate" tests? Or, to put it another way, are test caps going to continue to be gifted to players who don't merit them? Will New Zealand's rugby administrators concede that too much is being expected of New Zealand's leading players?

Just look at the performance of Canterbury in the early rounds of the 2002 NPC. After going through the Super 12 unbeaten as the Crusaders, and then making up virtually the entire All Black team, Canterbury's finest had little to offer in the early rounds of the NPC. Top players either took time off for rest and recuperation, or played well below their best.

What is to be the New Zealand union's attitude to the Super 12, the competition that seems to help Australia as much as it hurts New Zealand? Tied in with that, what provision will the New Zealand union make in the lead-up to 2005, when the half-billion dollar contract with News Limited expires?

Does the New Zealand union want to make the NPC a top-shelf competition, or does it want it to become even more a case of haves and have-nots? In the 2002 NPC, Canterbury was able to call on 25 professional players, Otago 24, Waikato 20, Wellington 18, Auckland 16, North Harbour and Northland 10, Taranaki 9, Bay of Plenty 3, Southland 1. How can such a lop-sided first division competition be good for New Zealand rugby?

There are other issues that need to be acknowledged. Though it is not politically correct to say so, there is a problem in New Zealand rugby with the increasing dominance of Polynesian (especially) and Maori players. Their size, compared to the average Pakeha of the same age, gives them such an advantage that it is pushing many who would normally play rugby to other sports. The problem has been addressed partially, with the introduction in some areas of weight-age rugby, but still many clubs and areas report a drift away from rugby. Much more work is needed in this area.

Tied in with this issue is the changing face of New Zealand. The ethnic makeup of New Zealand is altering quickly. Will the New Zealand union make any attempt to respond? It has not done so to any noticeable extent yet.

Player retention is another area of concern. During 2001, there were 121 representative New Zealand players plying their wares overseas. They were playing in Argentina, Australia, Canada, the Cook Islands, Croatia, Denmark, England, Fiji, France, Germany, Holland, Hong Kong, Ireland, Italy, Japan, Papua New Guinea, Samoa, Scotland, Spain, Tonga, the United States, Wales and Zimbabwe. And that's just rep players, not even the thousands of good senior club players who have gone west. This hurts club and provincial rugby in this country. What's to be done?

In 2002, English clubs began targeting promising teenaged New Zealand players. This is a really sticky problem. What can the union do when English clubs are offering these youngsters full professional contracts, even though they have not reached Super 12 or even NPC level? The New Zealand union has offered some of these young players contracts of $400 a month, but, not surprisingly, this hardly acts as a lure when set against the big money available overseas.

These are some of the main challenges facing the New Zealand Rugby Union at the end of 2002. Things should never have got to this state. Rugby has squandered some of its advantages in New Zealand and many leading administrators have failed to do anything about it. They have betrayed New Zealand rugby.

Hopefully, on September 18, 2002, the first step was taken on the long road back. Jock Hobbs is a man of energy, commonsense and rugby knowledge. He is not ego-driven. He will make and oversee good decisions. But what a job he and his helpers have ahead of them. Or has the rot set in too deep already?